The Sexist Microphysics of Power

The Sexist Microphysics of Power

The Alcàsser Murders and the Construction of Sexual Terror

NEREA BARJOLA

TRANSLATED BY EMILY MACK

WITH A FOREWORD BY SILVIA FEDERICI

The Sexist Microphysics of Power:
The Alcàsser Murders and the Construction of Sexual Terror
Creative Commons license, CC BY-NC 4.0: 2024 Nerea Barjola
Translation © 2024 Emily Mack
This edition © 2024 AK Press (Chico / Edinburgh)

ISBN 978-1-84935-550-6
E-ISBN 978-1-84935-551-3
Library of Congress Control Number: 2023948368

AK Press   AK Press
370 Ryan Avenue #100   33 Tower Street
Chico, CA 95973   Edinburgh, EH6, 7BN
USA   Scotland
www.akpress.org   www.akuk.com
akpress@akpress.org   akuk@akpress.org

The addresses above would be delighted to provide you with the latest AK Press
catalog, featuring several thousand books, pamphlets, audio and video products, and
stylish apparel published and distributed by AK Press. Alternatively, visit our websites
for the complete catalog, latest news and updates, events, and secure ordering.

Cover design by Crisis
Cover collage by Carme Magem
Originally published as *Microfísica Sexista del Poder* by Virus Editorial (Barcelona) in
2019.

Printed in the United States of America on acid-free paper

Note to the English Edition

While the crime at the center of this study remains notorious and vividly remembered across Spain, this text purposefully does not narrate the specifics of these three girls' deaths or the discovery of their bodies, nor does it identify these girls or their families by name, except in quoted material. By resisting this expectation and its reproduction of violence, the text challenges us to ask why we feel entitled to public access to women's bodies and suffering.

CONTENTS

Foreword

The publication of Nerea Barjola's *Sexist Microphysics of Power* is a very timely event, at a time when thousands of women across the globe are mobilizing and denouncing, in different ways, the violence exercised against them. The book constitutes an important contribution to the task of unveiling some of the most insidious mechanisms that perpetuate this violence. This work examines the role that the media played in a case that became famous in Spain in the early 1990s, in which three young women were brutally murdered. Rarely has this phenomenon been analyzed with such clarity and understanding regarding its consequences and implications, although its conclusions denounce a situation that knows no borders.

In addition to living, since childhood, with the knowledge that our bodies will not be respected, that any man has the right to verbally abuse us when we are on the street, that we can expect the worst if we find ourselves alone and away from home at nightfall, this phenomenon assumes that once we have been sexually assaulted, we ourselves will be judged. As we already know, the questions about what dress we wore, whether we put up sufficient resistance against aggression, or inquiries regarding our sexual reputation—in the eyes of the police, for example, sex workers have no right to be protected from rape—are recurring questions when reporting a rape. As a consequence, most sexual violence against women ends up not being reported, as meetings with the police and court hearings are transformed into another form of aggression.

What *The Sexist Microphysics of Power* denounces is the close complicity of the media in this process, and specifically how, under the pretext of informing the public and even of helping in the investigation, the information transforms the violence committed against women into an accusation against their demands for greater autonomy. Faced with sexual assault, the media respond by praising family life and conservative sexual values, pointing out what our place is and what our appropriate behavior should be.

As the author strongly demonstrates, from the moment of the disappearance—a term that Barjola rejects, since it conceals the coercion that is involved, and that she redefines as forced disappearance—both newspaper and television journalists put the focus on the lives of young women, raising fear among listeners and viewers and insisting on the danger of suffering sexual assault. Again and again, they placed the source of the problem in excessive freedom and lack of parental authority.

The transformation of the Alcàsser crime into a blaming of young women, the terrorization and punishment of women who move away from the domestic environment, was exacerbated by the discovery and daily on-screen dissection of the bodies of the young women, in search of evidence of torture—regardless of the suffering this inflicted on the families and friends of the women. Meanwhile, the crime and what made it possible were rarely discussed, implicitly accepted as given, as a normal condition of women's lives. Even when the culprits were identified, the psychiatric examinations were charged with invalidating the questioning of the systemic factors responsible for it. Through the pathologization of the murders, the crime was blamed on the "abnormality" and cruelty of the murderers, instead of identifying and recognizing the social, economic, and political roots of violence, encouraging the public's response to be a call for the death penalty.

But how to explain the perverse inversion of the events that led to the death of three young Valencian women, on a night in which they were planning to have fun listening to some music? In search of frameworks to help make the distortion of events understandable, Barjola draws on the contributions of Michel Foucault, Judith Butler, and Giorgio Agamben, pointing to the behavior of the press as a textbook example of how the argument is constructed and how institutionality produces the truth. The author also applies Agamben's concept of a nonlife—that is, a life completely devoid of rights—to describe the position of the murdered young women in the treatment reserved for them by the media.

These conceptualizations must incorporate an analysis of the political economy whose defense—more or less conscious—determined the way of informing the public about the murders. There is no doubt that, after violence against women—from domestic abuse to rape and murder—there is a social and economic code that wants women locked up and tied to the home, engaged in caregiving work and readily accepting male control over their lives. In addition to doing long hours of unpaid domestic work, we are also currently asked to take a salary home, which complicates but does not alter the fundamental obligation, since the threat of violence guarantees that we comply with that order.

Recognition of the political economy that sustains violence against women—acknowledging that the fear of rape and other forms of sexual violence serves the exploitation of women's work—is essential if we wish to adequately confront the institutional investment in it. This happens especially in our time, given that with gentrification, industrial relocation, and the consequent disintegration of working-class communities, we increasingly depend on the media both to interpret and to gain knowledge about social events. The dismantling of that machine—through which reality is produced, the truth is hidden, and an artificial consensus is created—is an essential part of the liberation process.

This is the great contribution that *The Sexist Microphysics of Power* makes to the feminist struggle to counter not only violence against women but the complicity of the media with institutional sexism: the book is unique in its examination of the many tricks that journalists use in crime reporting to redirect attention toward the character of the victim, cruelly using women's fear and the suffering we see around us to denigrate our demands for freedom, and, finally, making the killers into monsters so as to continue ignoring the factors that make their crimes possible.

Barjola tells us that in 1992, when the murders happened, feminists failed to make their voices heard and to provide society with a counternarrative in the face of media manipulations. When feminists defended their views, they were understood as personal opinions and not as the expression of a political position.

However, I think this has changed somewhat over the past forty years. When, in October 2016, a young woman was raped and killed in Mar del Plata, Argentina—coinciding with the National Meeting of Women that brought together seventy thousand women in Rosario—the feminist response immediately reverberated around the globe. In the same way, attempts to blame the victim of a gang rape during the San Fermín festivities of 2016, in the context of the judicial process held in 2017, gave rise to a collective response under the slogan "Sister, I do believe you": this time they did bring feminist discourse to the forefront of sexual terror.

And the force of that echo has not waned, since we will not stop going to the streets to denounce, not only men individually, but a patriarchal capitalist system that produces violence on a daily basis, both against us and against everything they want to exploit. When this happens, we will do well to take *The Sexist Microphysics of Power* with us, as a reminder that we cannot depend on the media to represent our struggle, in the same way that we cannot trust them to show the damage inflicted on us every day. The media are not passive spectators but participants in a political project that is the equivalent of the witch hunts.

SILVIA FEDERICI

Introduction

*When one really wants to study the general, one need only look
around for a real exception.*

Giorgio Agamben, *Homo Sacer*

On November 13, 1992, Antonia Gómez, Desireé Hernández,
and Míriam García disappeared in the vicinity of Alcàsser, the
town in eastern Spain where they lived. The three teenagers
were planning on going to a party at a nightclub in the neigh-
boring town of Picassent, a few miles away. According to official
records, the girls hitched a ride in a car with at least two men
inside. Almost three months later, on January 27, 1993, their bodies were found in a place known as La Romana, near the Tous
reservoir. With the discovery of their bodies came evidence that
they had been subjected to sexual torture. Of those implicated in
the case, only Miguel Ricart—who is now free—was convicted;
Antonio Anglés's whereabouts remain unaccounted for.

Right from the start of this investigation, the use of the
word *disappeared* plagued me. I did not know why, but it got to
me. A bottled-up, age-old, towering rage at the violence and sexual torture enacted on women surfaced at every (antonymous)
"appearance" of this word in the texts. Without a doubt the
malaise I felt was a reaction sparked by the raising of a smoke
screen.

When it refers to crimes committed against women, there
is something in the word *disappearance* that implies a masking.
By definition, to say that the teenagers "disappeared" points to
an absence, a concealment. Metaphorically it injects a degree

of doubt, of neutralization that I have no intention of glossing over, either from a feminist perspective or in the semantic field.

I refuse to continue referring to the systematic disappearance of women in merely defining or descriptive terms. The equation is quite straightforward: women do not simply disappear; they are forced to disappear. Using the term *enforced disappearance* from the start of this introduction is a matter of feminist political positioning: in the framework of this work, this is part of a series of (re)conceptualizations that allow us to redefine the Alcàsser sex crimes.

Enforced or *involuntary disappearance* is a legal concept that has been used to designate those enforced disappearances enacted under authoritarian regimes. By extrapolation, in my view, this term may effectively be used to describe the abduction, murder, and torture that women systematically suffer. Defining the disappearance of women as *enforced* disappearances offers the opportunity to give the term a new use, and, thus, to appropriate the analytical and declaratory benefits of its legal definition.

The concept of enforced disappearance is far from neutral. It enables the murders and sexual torture to be situated within more accurate parameters: it redefines the space of disappearance as a political place and system.

The origin of involuntary disappearance as a classification lay in the need to fill a gap in legislation so as to be able to identify and recognize them. In February 1993, the UN General Assembly drafted the *Declaration on the Protection of All Persons from Enforced Disappearance*, stating that they were "deeply concerned that in many countries, often in a persistent manner, enforced disappearances occur." Enforced disappearance is understood in the sense that

> persons are arrested, detained or abducted against their will or otherwise deprived of their liberty by officials of different branches or levels of Government, or by organized groups or private individuals acting on behalf of, or

with the support, direct or indirect, consent or acquiescence of the Government.[1]

Based on this definition, the Alcàsser crimes and the analysis of them—and of sex crimes in general—can be situated within the framework and under the protection of a system in which women are *forced* to disappear by organized groups or by individuals who act, directly or indirectly, in the name of a sexist political regime. A regime is a system, a structure that enables the establishment of criteria and the regulation of operations; the political aspect of such a regime would be linked to the ideological management in which it is framed. A system that permits the enforced disappearance of women and sexual torture is a clearly defined sexist political regime. In other words, the sexual torture, murder, and disappearance of women is not a matter of bad luck; they are not things that "just happen." They are, rather, part of a political notion that constitutes the backbone, the very structure of our social system. Alcàsser is not a "case" or an "incident"; it is itself a political regime. The disappearance of the Alcàsser teenagers is a political consequence, a reaction, a punishment for their transgression.

This approach proposes a perspective shift: namely, to submit the Alcàsser sex crimes for review, with an eye to the atrocities committed during a little-investigated, unfinished chapter of a sexist regime.

In this sense, the Alcàsser crimes are a political system of representation concerning sexual danger that has yet to be unraveled.

Therefore, the meaning of the term *disappearance* forces me to establish, first, that *no*: They did not disappear. They were forced to disappear. And to ask: What are you hiding?

---

1. UN General Assembly, *Declaration on the Protection of All Persons from Enforced Disappearances*, February 12, 1993, A/RES/47/133, available at: https://www.ohchr.org/en/instruments-mechanisms/instruments/declaration-protection-all-persons-enforced-disappearance.

Disappearance is the key to an entire encrypted code: the use of the term *enforced disappearance* enables me to analyze the web of meanings, discourses, and information contained in what I have defined as the *sexual danger* narrative of the 1990s. Both concepts—enforced disappearance and the sexual danger narrative—lay the groundwork for the political redefinition of sex crimes.

A sexual danger narrative is a complex system of communication, and it is for this reason that I am interested in decrypting the Alcàsser story: doing so means gaining access to an entire system of social communication. The text that has emerged from this investigation is an attempt to pave the way for a feminist reinterpretation of the Alcàsser crimes. It also aims to serve as an effective tool or framework for the reassignment of the numerous sexual danger narratives that influence the everyday lives of women. What I want to do is to propose a maneuver that redesigns the narrative from its very inception—from its naming.

My starting point is the idea that the sexual danger narrative is an instrument that societal sexism constructed to counteract progress made by the feminist movement and, thus, to halt the advance of radical change for women. My objective is to deploy this narrative, including all the parts that were left out by omission. Converting "the Alcàsser case" into a sexual danger narrative inevitably entails a political-feminist rewriting of that sexual terror landmark from the 1990s.

Broadly speaking, when I set out to analyze the Alcàsser crimes, I had one conviction and two objectives in mind. I knew that narratives, meanings, and discourses on sexual danger function as a political project. Based on this notion, my objectives were clear: first, to analyze the influence that representations of sexual danger have on the everyday life and practices of women and, second, to explore how these are embodied by women themselves as a result of these narratives.

Representations are notions, knowledge, attitudes, images, and values that guide action. They are imbued with meanings that shape and constitute behaviors. Their capacity to challenge individual subjectivity and to impact and influence people's practices will depend to a considerable extent on prevailing discourses. In the same vein, as Miguel Ángel Cabrera notes, a discourse is a specific structure of

> sentences, terms, and categories, which are historically, socially, and institutionally established . . . through which meanings are constructed and cultural practices organized and through which, consequently, people represent and understand their world, including who they are and how they relate to others.[2]

In other words, as historian Judith Walkowitz writes, and more in line with our object of study:

> Women do not simply experience sexual passion and "naturally" find the words to express those feelings, nor do they experience sexual danger and naturally find the words to express the threat. In the simplest sense, women of different classes and races all have to rely on cultural constructs to tell their "truths."[3]

In this sense, the representations, meanings, and discourses that make up the Alcàsser narrative constitute a source that reveals the societal structure in its entirety. Therefore, a study of the discourses through which that narrative was constructed sheds light on the structure—regime—through which society

---

2. Miguel Ángel Cabrera, *Historia, lenguaje y teoría de la sociedad* (Madrid: Cátedra, 2001), 52. Translated for the present volume from the Spanish. Except where otherwise noted, all subsequent quotations from Spanish-language sources were translated for the purpose of this publication.

3. Judith Walkowitz, *City of Dreadful Delight: Narratives of Sexual Danger in Late-Victorian London* (Chicago: University of Chicago Press, 1992), 9.

at large made possible the creation of an episode of sexual terror. In order to approach the analysis and interpretation of the newspaper archive on the Alcàsser case, and the large volume of meanings and discourses that fed into that narrative, I make use of notions that have been of special interest to me. I begin with one from the French philosopher Michel Foucault:

> There can be no possible exercise of power without a certain economy of discourses of truth which operates through and on the basis of this association. We are subjected to the production of truth through power and we cannot exercise power except through the production of truth.[4]

Based on this argument, I understand that the narrative about the Alcàsser crimes may be observed as a systematic production of meanings and discourses that produce truth through power, and power through the production of truth. Moreover, this perspective also offers clarity in relation to the sexual danger narrative and configures it as a conspicuous social maneuver.

For Foucault, power has two main functions: exclusion and production. When power excludes, it is characterized by prohibition, denial, and concealment. On the contrary, when it produces, it generates truth and reproduces knowledge. The whole Alcàsser narrative is built on a profoundly sexist foundation of knowledge and truth production. And this is only achieved through the exclusion, by omission, of all those elements that could have offered an alternative perspective on the crimes.

The Alcàsser narrative is the best source of information to spot these prevailing power dynamics and the way they are exercised. They constitute strategies that are present and operative,

---

4. Michel Foucault, *Power/Knowledge: Selected Interviews and Other Writings, 1972–1977* (London: Vintage, 1980), 93.

with their own hidden structures and flexibility. Foucault writes, "The history of this struggle for power and the manner in which power is exercised and maintained remain totally obscured. Knowledge keeps its distance: this should not be known!"[5] This knowledge production, in which knowledge itself plays no part, is precisely the process that has prevented the Alcàsser sex crimes from being reconsidered and has thus kept the case's meanings masked. Through this narrative, sexist knowledge and truth are produced, thereby reproducing sexual violence. It is for the same reason that "the truth" about the Alcàsser case is so constantly produced: there is a continual restoration of sexual violence as meaning.

In the same vein, I would like to bring in some ideas, prompted by reading feminist scholar and activist Silvia Federici's *Caliban and the Witch*, that I find useful in demonstrating the significance of representations of sexual danger. Federici states that women could not have been devalued as workers and deprived of all autonomy with respect to men "without being subjected to an intense process of social degradation."[6] Thus the literary degradation of women was to be rapidly articulated: "The punishment of female insubordination to patriarchal authority was called for and celebrated in countless misogynous plays and tracts. English literature of the Elizabethan and Jacobean period feasted on such themes."[7] This depreciation was accompanied by the introduction of new laws:

> New laws and new forms of torture were introduced to control women's behavior in and out of the home, confirming that the literary denigration of women expressed a

---

5. Michel Foucault, *Language, Counter-Memory, Practice: Selected Essays and Interviews*, ed. Donald F. Bouchard, trans. Donald F. Bouchard and Sherry Simon (Ithaca, NY: Cornell University Press, 1996 [1971]), 219.

6. Silvia Federici, *Caliban and the Witch: Women, the Body, and Primitive Accumulation* (New York: Autonomedia, 2004), 100.

7. Federici, *Caliban and the Witch*, 101.

precise political project aiming to strip them of any autonomy and social power.[8]

It is precisely this idea of literary denigration that interests me most with respect to sexual danger narratives. These narratives, and specifically the narrative constructed around the Alcàsser crimes, are an accumulation of meanings that denigrate and blame women. And, in this sense, I would like to give myself license—literary license, perhaps—to declare that sexual danger narratives are the continuous—because it does not stop happening—return of the witch hunt. These narratives function as a witch hunt insofar as they caution, monitor, and punish women's conduct. Every generation holds its own witch hunt: a social inquisition that produces and reproduces violence and sexual torture on women's bodies and lives.

The Alcàsser narrative is, in short, a socio-literary production that creates and disseminates sexist truth and knowledge that blames and denigrates women.

Sexual danger narratives are not exceptional incidents, nor are they one-off news items with fleeting meanings; they are a well-defined system of communication. In the words of theorist Rita Laura Segato, "Violence, constituted and crystallized within a communication system, is transformed into a stable language and comes to behave in the nearly automatic fashion of any language."[9] In other words, narratives and representations of sexual danger form a system that uses violence against women and sexual torture as a highly specialized language for social communication. Hence the importance of analyzing the narratives in depth. Every instance involving the murder, torture, and enforced disappearance of women constitutes a communication system that speaks to us, interrogates us, and cautions us. My

---

8. Federici, *Caliban and the Witch*, 101.

9. Rita Laura Segato, "Territory, Sovereignty, and Crimes of the Second State," in *Terrorizing Women*, ed. Rosa-Linda Fregoso and Cynthia Bejarano (Durham, NC: Duke University Press, 2010), 81.

intention is to interfere as much as possible with the automatization of the language that sustains sexual torture as a fundamental social pillar—to unmask the sexual danger narrative. To do so, I will use what Foucault calls "prescriptive texts."

For Foucault, prescriptive texts are those "whose main object, whatever their form (speech, dialogue, treatise, collection of precepts, etc.) is to suggest the rules of conduct."[10] This analytical instrument complements the study of discourse; it serves as a radar to be configured with defined search parameters. The Alcàsser crimes thus acquire a new dimension in that the narrative may be understood as a compilation of meanings and discourses that aim to lay down "rules, opinions, and advice on how to behave as one should."[11] Deciphering prescriptive texts places us face to face with that which is hidden, stripping away the layers of that which should not be known.

One of the main characteristics of the Alcàsser crimes is that their narration in-corporates sexual terror: it manages to transfer the abuse suffered by the teenagers to the body, down to the smallest detail. The staging of the torture by the media, so visually, so directly, makes an impact without leaving room for comprehension, and this is what enables boundary in-corporation. Its strategy is clear and forceful: it "makes all things visible by becoming itself invisible."[12] Foucault's concept inspired my approach to the narrative analysis. It opened up the possibility of seeing the construction of the Alcàsser sexual danger narrative as a strategy. For critical analysis allows us to look at that which terrifies, to go beyond what the narrative shows— the horror, the visible—to approach the narrative structure, that which is invisible, what the story hides or omits: the strategy.

Suspicion situates the Alcàsser crimes as a political narrative rather than a horror story: a transcendental occurrence

---

10. Michel Foucault, *The History of Sexuality*, vol. 2, *The Use of Pleasure* (New York: Vintage, 2012), 12.

11. Foucault, *History of Sexuality*, 12.

12. Foucault, *Power/Knowledge*, 71.

in women's lives and on their bodies. But it is precisely this prolonged exposure to the terror of the crimes that masks the opportunity to truly understand the Alcàsser case in political terms. The perspective shift I propose involves a dissection of the *social body* rather than of the bodies of women. While the Alcàsser narrative dissects women's bodies, exposes them, invades them, and remakes them accordingly, a dissection of the social body, in contrast, assigns responsibility for sexual violence not to women but to society.

An important part of my investigation involved conducting life-history interviews. Alcàsser is, above all, a bodily narrative and, in this sense, I understand the sexual danger narrative as a device that is inscribed *on bodies.* The silence imprinted on the bodies of a generation of women was to complete the exercise of resignification of the Alcàsser crimes. The aim here is to put words to a silenced violence.

A Feminist (Re)Appropriation of Concepts

This short chapter is dedicated to the feminist (re)appropriation and expropriation of concepts. My objective here is twofold: to employ terms that have been used to define, name, or describe other phenomena; and to(gether) reappropriate these concepts from a feminist perspective, so as to apply them to the study of sexual violence. In what follows, therefore, I begin with insights gleaned from the nexus between my own vantage point and those of the writers who have served as a frame of reference for this work.

The Discipline of Sexual Terror

Not only do representations of sexual danger form the structure that supports sexual violence, but they themselves *are* sexual violence. In this chapter I trace the origins of the concept of *discipline* and how I came to associate it with sexual terror. I then break down the terms I use to establish spatial metaphors and the materialization of sexual violence.

In its essence, the Alcàsser sexual danger narrative is a cautionary tale that crudely punishes women's conduct. As Michel Foucault claims, "In our societies the systems of punishment are to be situated in a certain 'political economy' of the body."[1] In the Alcàsser case, it was the punitive systems of the social body that was to implement what Foucault calls disciplines.

---

1. Michel Foucault, *Discipline and Punish: The Birth of the Prison*, trans. Alan Sheridan (New York: Vintage, 1995), 25.

Foucault reflects on and analyzes the evolution of forms of punishment in the transition to modernity. In his study, under the descriptor *disciplines*, he points to the emergence of a new form of inflicting violence-punishment on bodies, and a new mechanics of power: "These methods, which made possible the meticulous control of the operations of the body, which assured the constant subjection of its forces and imposed upon them a relation of docility-utility, might be called 'disciplines.'"[2] According to Foucault, a whole series of pre-established, explicit instructions were to make bodies into useful machines. Disciplines would thus consist of general formulas of domination through which the more useful the body is, the more obedient it is rendered. Conversely, these operations also guaranteed the constant subjection of the body's strength. Foucault's concept of discipline can readily be extrapolated to sexual terror. In this investigation, *discipline* goes from a general notion to a more concrete one in the *discipline of sexual terror*: a sexist political bodily technology. The discipline of sexual terror is a punitive measure that society was to implement through narratives of sexual danger.

For Foucault, the transition from the ancien régime to modernity was defined by the appearance of a new practice in the power to punish, a new era in criminal justice with an important modification: the disappearance, at the beginning of the nineteenth century, of torture and its public representation. According to him, "[a] few decades saw the disappearance of the tortured, dismembered, amputated body, symbolically branded on face or shoulder, exposed alive or dead to public view.[3] In this way, less-physical punishments emerged, inflicting more discreet pain, "a combination of more subtle, more subdued sufferings, deprived of their visible display."[4] The public execution

---

2. Foucault, *Discipline and Punish*, 137.

3. Foucault, *Discipline and Punish*, 8.

4. Foucault, *Discipline and Punish*, 8.

came to be perceived as a focal point that fanned the flames of violence; and from that moment onward, punishment tended to be hidden in penal processes: "It leaves the domain of more or less everyday perception and enters that of abstract consciousness."[5] With the disappearance of torture comes a redefinition of the practice of punishment as a corrective measure. Although Foucault refers to punitive legal systems, there is no denying the connection between this idea of *correction* and representations of sexual danger. This is the part of Foucault's theory that interests me. The Alcàsser narrative is a punishment, a correctional tale imprinted on the bodies it speaks to.

For Foucault, with the disappearance of physical corporal punishment, the body was not displaced from its central position in the application of punishment. In modern penal systems, the body is caught up in a system of coercion and deprivation, of obligations and prohibitions. According to Foucault, "From being an art of unbearable sensations punishment has become an economy of suspended rights."[6] The executioner, the immediate representative of physical suffering, is replaced by the new sciences; doctors, psychiatrists, psychologists, educators, chaplains, and guards were to be the ones charged with ensuring that the body and pain were not the objectives of justice. It was to be "a utopia of judicial reticence: take away life, but prevent the patient from feeling it; deprive the prisoner of all rights, but do not inflict pain; impose penalties free of all pain."[7]

The legal power to punish was to be divided out between the different branches of scientific knowledge. Direct corporal punishment was transformed into more sophisticated punishment in which passions, instincts, anomalies, ailments, dysfunctions, and maladjustments were judged and monitored. The will of the subject was implicated in the crime: "[The soul] too, as well

---

5. Foucault, *Discipline and Punish*, 9.
6. Foucault, *Discipline and Punish*, 11.
7. Foucault, *Discipline and Punish*, 11.

as the crime itself, is to be judged."[8] This new technology of punishment and the soul's appearance on the scene necessitated new discourses and forms of scientific knowledge. Psychiatric examination, criminal anthropology, and criminology, among others, provided the mechanisms of legal punishment with justifiable pretexts.

The real aim of reform, rather than to introduce more equitable rights, was to imbue the power to punish with a newfound economy. In other words, the point was not to punish *less* but to punish *better*, to push the power to punish deeper into the social body. The disappearance of torture and the arrival of new forms of punishment that act on the soul and punish behavior mask the trap inherent to the new technology of the power to punish. The body as the main target of penal repression does not disappear but, rather, takes on a new form. When Foucault states that the punitive systems of our societies must be situated in a political economy of the body, he is expressly referring to the fact that, even when not resorting to violent or bloody punishments, even when lenient or subtle methods are used "involving confinement or correction, it is always the body that is at issue—the body and its forces, their utility and their docility, their distribution and their submission."[9] The body is immersed in a political field where the relations of power operate on it, encircle it, mark it, teach it, force it to do certain jobs, to behave in certain ways, to perform certain rites—in short, subjecting it to torture. For Foucault, the *docile body* is the body that can be subdued, manipulated, and perfected: "The body that is manipulated, shaped, trained, which obeys, responds, becomes skillful."[10]

Punishment does not have to use the body. It can rely on representation, on the submission of bodies through control over ideas, and, through them, the introduction of self-restraint

---

8. Foucault, *Discipline and Punish*, 18.

9. Foucault, *Discipline and Punish*, 25.

10. Foucault, *Discipline and Punish*, 136.

or self-domination. The knowledge that subjugates the body is confined to the body. This technology of power over the body, says Foucault,

> is exercised on those punished—and, in a more general way, on those one supervises, trains and corrects, over madmen, children at home and at school, the colonized, over those who are stuck at a machine and supervised for the rest of their lives.[11]

These concepts from Foucault's work are particularly valuable for my analysis for two main reasons: first, because the representations of sexual danger contained in the narratives are forms of punishment that seek to caution, correct, and coerce women; and, second, insofar as established patterns of social surveillance over what women can and cannot do seek to indoctrinate women's bodies, disregarding their capacity to make decisions in an attempt to subject them to continuous self-control and self-restraint. I also set out to apply this reasoning to the corpus of stories about the Alcàsser crimes in the form of an analytical tool: as I see it, these narratives are used on women's bodies as the instrument of a technology of power.

Foucault's theories allow me to establish sexual terror and its narratives as a disciplinary technology. However, I dispute his claims in relation to two aspects that I consider fundamental when it comes to violence against women. First, Foucault argues that in the transition from the ancien régime to modernity, torture and its public representation disappeared. To leave this supposition unchallenged would be tantamount to a negation of feminicide. When Foucault proclaims the emergence of a new form of punishment over bodies, to the detriment of public torture, he clearly obscures the systematic sexual torture suffered by women. In the case of women, there has been

---

11. Foucault, *Discipline and Punish*, 29.

no such disappearance of tortured, dismembered, amputated bodies, of bodies with marked faces, exposed dead or alive. Evidently, their public exposure has not disappeared either. On the contrary, the ancien régime and modernity are united when it comes to violence against women. Women's bodies are still publicly exposed, marked, and amputated, dead or alive. In fact, the case of the Alcàsser crimes illustrates this aspect of the public exposure of the teenager's bodies like no other. Second, I take issue with Foucault's idea that disciplines are *new* ways of exercising punishment on bodies. Presumably, the subjects to which Foucault was referring are men. Otherwise, he would not have been able to claim a new form of punishment had appeared. Representations of sexual danger are ancestral formulas for inflicting punishment on women's bodies. And, in this sense, it is clear that these disciplines are far from constituting "new" ways of inflicting punishment on women.

I would like to point to representations of sexual violence that were present within that very transition from the ancien régime to modernity in which, according to Foucault, the art of punishment evolved. These are notions that, in the form of stereotype or myth, are maintained in today's narratives. They merit a brief explanation as they have reemerged in different contexts in the course of this investigation. The myths that usually accompany these meanings construct a pattern of social surveillance—that is, a punitive social system—by which women correct their behavior, mold their bodies, deny themselves space, control their schedules, and restrict their movements and gestures: this is the *discipline of sexual terror* permeating each era.

One traditional conception of rape holds that women either seduce their attackers or do not resist sufficiently. This idea is based on the assumption of the difficulty of establishing the difference between consent and nonconsent, and it also provides the basis for justifying perpetrators' actions and blaming women for being assaulted. The jurists of the ancien régime, as historian Georges Vigarello recounts, considered assumed consent to be practically fact: "Rape attempted by one man alone on a determined woman was impossible on simple physical grounds: women were strong enough to defend themselves; they were always in possession of sufficient 'means.'"[12] The assumptions underpinning this idea can be found in the wording of different penal codes in which the crime is classified under these two categories: *abduction by seduction* and *abduction with violence*. Although Vigarello focuses his study on sixteenth- to twentieth-century France, the term *abduction* is not unheard of in the Spanish penal code. In fact, in the Alcàsser crimes, the press of the time used the word *abduction*. *Abduction with violence* is that which involved physical violence, coercion, and blood, in addition to sexual violence. *Abduction by seduction*, as the word *seduction* itself indicates, takes on various meanings in which acts of freedom and coercion are intertwined. It thus constitutes a kind of consent extracted by coercion. The absence of violence in an aggression led to the assumption that what had actually occurred was consensual. This meant that proving what had happened relied on physical evidence of violence; without this, the conclusion was that no attempt at resistance had been made. These claims were further reinforced by the "intellectuals" of the time, including the Genevan philosopher Jean-Jacques Rousseau, for whom "nature has given the weaker party strength enough to resist if she chooses."[13] He writes, "Is it weakness that yields to force or is it voluntary self-surrender? This uncertainty constitutes the chief delight of the man's victory, and the woman is usually cunning enough to leave him in doubt."[14] Here, the word *abduction* implies that the woman must have been taken away from someone by force, be it her father, husband, or guardian. Undoubtedly, this concept is of a kind with the *delitos contra*

---

12. Georges Vigarello, *A History of Rape: Sexual Violence in France from the Sixteenth to the Twentieth Century*, trans. Jean Birrell (Oxford: Polity, 2001), 42.

13. Jean-Jacques Rousseau, in Vigarello, *History of Rape*, 43.

14. Rousseau, in Vigarello, *History of Rape*, 43–44.

la honestidad ("crimes against decency") in force in the pre-1989 Spanish penal code.

Moreover, with the onset of modernity, and in parallel to the emergence of "new forms of punishment," there was a deployment of a whole body of scientific knowledge that began to look for evidence of crimes in women's bodies, through signs of violence, resistance, and proof of virginity. In reality, this scientific knowledge was to be configured as a readaptation of the old pattern of blaming women for being sexually assaulted.

In stark contrast, that same modernity was to be synonymous with rationality and civilization. A shift took place whereby rape was understood as a symptom of nonadvanced states, as Vigarello points out: "Rape is not common in the large towns, where prostitution is regarded as a necessary evil."[15] In modern society, the belief that civilization was incompatible with rape was to emerge. Rape took place in places far removed from the cities, where rationality was seen to triumph over bestiality. Nevertheless, the overcrowding and poor living conditions of urban centers were to subsequently serve as a justification for why rape also took place in civilized society. This set of beliefs, according to which rapists are referred to as savages, illiterates, or beasts of the woods, is still firmly in place. Indeed, as I discuss below, I find this same imaginary portrayed in the written press in the Alcàsser case, as does Judith Walkowitz in the crimes of Jack the Ripper in the late Victorian period.

Thus, to restate my counterargument to Foucault: for women, no new form of bodily punishment emerged, and neither torture nor the public exposure of the tortured body ceased. Sexual danger narratives have the particularity of both cautioning and punishing, while at the same time exposing the tortured body.

In addition, at the heart of the Alcàsser narrative lies a metaphor that can be interpreted using concepts from the philosopher Giorgio Agamben. Far from inoffensive, this metaphor

---

15. *Gazette des Tribunaux*, in Vigarello, *History of Rape*, 66.

is capable of organizing space or territory and endowing it with political content. Here, I am primarily interested in Agamben's concepts of *exception, bare life,* and *state of exception.* I apply the first term to the Alcàsser case as a whole. For Agamben, those situations that are understood, managed, or constructed as exceptional reveal the very essence of the norm. Starting from this idea—that it is the exceptional case that shows us, like no other, that which is commonplace—I situate the Alcàsser crimes as representative of a quotidian social situation. Agamben's approach allows me to detach the Alcàsser crimes— and any crime of sexual violence—from their consideration as "horrific" or "incidental" and to confer them with political import. Thus, the Alcàsser crimes allow us to decipher the political-cultural codes of sexual violence that governed society at the time.

Both Agamben's *state of exception* and *bare life* help (re)think and (re)signify the Alcàsser crimes. A brief exploration of these terms in the context of the author's work is imperative at this point to foster a better understanding of their meaning.[16] In his best-known book, *Homo Sacer,* Agamben covers concepts that, from a historical and philosophical point of view, shaped the intervention of power in the management of human life. At the beginning of this book, Agamben explains how the Greeks had two different terms for *life*: "*zoé,* which expressed the simple fact of living common to all living beings (animals, men, or gods), and *bios,* which indicated the form or way of living proper to an individual or a group."[17]

Thus, Agamben's starting point is the *biopolitical.* As defined by Foucault, this is the political management of life, that is, the

---

16. Giorgio Agamben published *Homo Sacer* in three volumes. First, *Homo Sacer: Sovereign Power and Bare Life* (Stanford: Stanford University Press, 1998); second, *State of Exception* (Chicago: University of Chicago Press, 2005); and third, *Remnants of Auschwitz: The Witness and the Archive* (New York: Zone Books, 1999).

17. Agamben, *Sovereign Power,* 1.

intervention of power in human life. In parallel, Agamben rescues a legal figure from ancient Roman law, *homo sacer* (Latin for "the sacred man" or "the accursed man"), and associates it with the concept of biopolitics. He thus aims to show that the legal history of the West is an attempt to manage human life by subjecting it to *bare life*—a term by which the author refers to life that is not qualified, the simple fact of living that is, therefore, devoid of any transcendence whatsoever. In the Roman world, according to Agamben, the *homo sacer* was the condemned person who could be killed without the commission of homicide. The *homo sacer* is devoid of all rights; they have an animal life whose essence is the mere fact of living, which is why they can be killed without the commission of homicide. The *homo sacer* is useless: they are not a valid person but a non-human being. This figure from archaic Roman law was applied to those subjects whose life, after having committed a crime, was exposed to sovereign power. In Agamben's words: "He is a living dead man."[18] In other words, their life, and therefore their body, belonged to the sovereign, and it was the sovereign, in the last instance, who had the power to manage what was no longer life but simply existence.

Subsequently, the philosopher establishes links between ancient Roman law and modern states in which life is managed through biopolitics: "Placing biological life at the center of its calculations," he writes, "the modern State therefore does nothing other than bring to light the secret tie uniting power and bare life."[19] Bare life is life stripped of all meaning, life that anyone can kill "insofar as it operates in an inclusive exclusion as the referent of the sovereign decision. Life is sacred only insofar as it is taken into the sovereign exception."[20] Life is therefore included in the legal order in the form of its exclusion, that is,

---

18. Agamben, *Sovereign Power*, 99.
19. Agamben, *Sovereign Power*, 6.
20. Agamben, *Sovereign Power*, 85.

"the absolute capacity of the subject's body to be killed."[21] From this perspective, the political management of life decides on the humanity of the living being, stripping it of all significance. Life in modernity is therefore no different from *homo sacer* insofar as both depend on the will of sovereign power. It is for this reason that he understands bare life, or sacred life, to be the original political element.[22] Agamben thus situates sovereign power at the center of the legal order of modern states, and the concept of bare life as part of it, on the basis of its exclusion. The consequence of this is that anyone can remove such life from any political, social, and cultural context and eliminate it, without the slightest effect on the configuration of the system itself. To explain this, Agamben uses the term *state of exception*. For the author, the state of exception is that part of the law in which the law itself is suspended in order to guarantee its continuity, even its very existence. In a state of exception, the prevailing legal order is suspended, which allows human life to be treated as bare life—as simultaneously within the legal sphere and outside it.[23]

Agamben suggests that the state of exception can become a permanent, paradigmatic form of government, in such a way that, under the suspension of the law and under the protection of what he calls the *zone of indifference*, bare life is included

---

21. Agamben, *Sovereign Power*, 125.

22. "The sacredness of life, which is invoked today as an absolutely fundamental right in opposition to sovereign power, in fact originally expresses precisely both life's subjection to a power over death and life's irreparable exposure in the relation of abandonment." Agamben, *Sovereign Power*, 83.

23. "In truth, the state of exception is neither external nor internal to the juridical order, and the problem of defining it precisely concerns a threshold, or a zone of indifference, where inside and outside do not exclude each other but rather blur with each other. The suspension of the norm does not mean its abolition, and the zone of anomie that it establishes is not (or at least claims not to be) unrelated to the juridical order." Agamben, *State of Exception*, 23.

in the legal order through its *inclusive exclusion*. In his words: "The exception is, as we saw, an inclusive exclusion (which thus serves to include what is excluded)."[24]

In the third volume of *Homo Sacer*, Agamben draws on the concentration camp (Auschwitz) to explain how the state of exception can guarantee the continuity or existence of suspended rights. For him,

> in its archetypal form, the state of exception is therefore the principle of every juridical localization, since only the state of exception opens the space in which the determination of a certain juridical order and a particular territory first becomes possible.[25]

Agamben reveals the existence of the figure of the "Muselmann" within the concentration camp as a metaphor for how bare life is included within the legal order. The Muselmann represents those camp prisoners who have lost all human dignity. Dead in life, malnourished, they have lost all will and conscience. For Agamben, the ultimate threshold between life and death, between the human and the nonhuman, that the Muselmann inhabits has a political significance that in fact demonstrates the existence of the state of exception as a strategy to include bare life:

> [It] is not so much that their life is no longer life (this kind of degradation holds in a certain sense for all camp inhabitants and is not an entirely new experience) but, rather, that their death is not death. This—that the death of a human being can no longer be called death (not simply that it does not have importance, which is not new, but that it cannot be called by the name "death")—is the

---

24. Agamben, *Sovereign Power*, 21.

25. Agamben, *Sovereign Power*, 19.

particular horror that the *Muselmann* brings to the camp and that the camp brings to the world.[26]

The author explains how the bare life to which the person has been reduced to "neither demands nor conforms to anything. It itself is the only norm; it is absolutely immanent. And 'the ultimate sentiment of belonging to the species' cannot in any sense be a kind of dignity."[27]

To my mind, the terms and concepts of Agamben's philosophical thought open up the possibility of resignifying the Alcàsser case. With Alcàsser as my starting point, after outlining the corresponding narrative, I develop a theoretical approach to what I term the *metaphor of the Alcàsser sex crimes*. Thus, the state of exception materialized in the Alcàsser sex crimes represents those places, those intersections in which women's bodies and men's rights over them are being resignified. The zone of indifference, in which all rights are suspended, was in fact shaping a new configuration that was to be conveyed to women in the form of discipline. Moreover, the invocation of the threshold at which life is no longer life and death is no longer death enables sexual violence to be placed at the heart of the social norm and, consequently, frees bare life from its exclusion. It also makes it possible to hold responsible society as a whole. The suspension of the norm (within the norm) in the Alcàsser crimes opened an intersection in which the teenagers became bare life. Bare life, the bare fact of living, stripped of all human dignity, culminates in the house of La Romana—the place where the teenagers were tortured. From a biopolitical point of view, the violence and sexual torture committed there bring the constant threat of death and sexual danger to bear on women's bodies. In a state of exception, the norm is applied precisely through its cessation. The house in La Romana managed to readapt, reacquire, and

---

26. Agamben, *Remnants of Auschwitz*, 70.

27. Agamben, *Remnants of Auschwitz*, 69.

resignify disciplinary forms that were to ensure the bare life of all women.

The potential to reduce a person to a mere animal existence, to *bare life*—albeit fleetingly—also confers the privilege of remaining on the threshold, the point at which that person can be killed without the commission of homicide. The state of exception of the Alcàsser crimes is a space of negotiation; it is a place that the system itself allows and to which it consents. In this (regulatory) vacuum, the border that was crossed is recycled, and the boundaries the women were not supposed to cross are resituated. Consequently, a new biopolitical paradigm was established in the wake of the Alcàsser crimes: women of that generation became aware of bare life, of their belonging to it, and of the spaces, boundaries, and territories in which they played an active role in the danger. I intend to apply and adapt Agamben's ideas to the Alcàsser crimes in order to show that sex crimes are not exceptional or isolated, but rather that they constitute the norm, produce the norm, and safeguard social normativity. In other words, sexual danger narratives constitute a new way of trying to secure bare life in women. Furthermore, I aim to name all those spaces that lie within that zone of indifference that sustains and condones sexual violence and that women navigate on a daily basis throughout their lives.

When I allude to the effect the Alcàsser sexual danger narrative had on a whole generation of women, I am referring to the aspects derived from the biopolitical paradigm that the house of La Romana, directly and indirectly, brought upon the body. The La Romana house introduces not only a whole series of disciplinary measures but also a new system. This brings me to a quote from *Caliban and the Witch* where Federici states, with regard to the burning of witches:

> Here [on the stakes] those irrationalities were eliminated that stood in the way of the transformation of the individual and social body into a set of predictable and controllable mechanisms. And it was here again that the scientific

use of torture was born, for blood and torture were necessary to "breed an animal" capable of regular, homogeneous, and uniform behavior, indelibly marked with the memory of the new rules.[28]

The burning of witches—dating back to well before Auschwitz—was also an exercise in enabling the state of exception. And the biopolitics of the modern state (that is, Foucault's) would fall back onto a timeless—pre-existing—framework when there was once again need for Agamben's state of exception, when it was women's bodies and lives that were at stake. Thus, the state of exception has historically been the legal-philosophical figure that protected the social body and permitted the use of sexual torture and the systematic murder of women.

I understand La Romana as the symbolic place where the state of exception and bare life reinstate the border and corporealize boundaries, marking the new rules for women through sexual torture. For it is in the house in La Romana that the space opens up "in which the determination of a certain juridical order and a particular territory first becomes possible."[29]

Lastly, I draw on Judith Butler's work to explore the production of bodily materiality in the question of sexual violence. In this sense, Butler allows me to show the relationship between representations and the body, and how both materialize. First, I link Butler's thought to Agamben's concept of bare life. For Butler,

specific lives cannot be apprehended as injured or lost if they are not first apprehended as living. If certain lives do not qualify as lives or are, from the start, not conceivable

28. Silvia Federici, *Caliban and the Witch: Women, the Body, and Primitive Accumulation* (New York: Autonomedia, 2004), 144.

29. Agamben, *Sovereign Power*, 19.

as lives within certain epistemological frames, then these lives are never lived nor lost in the full sense.[30]

What Butler means by *life*, then, is not that which is attributed ontogenetically but that which comes from social ontology. The meanings, the discourses that construct social reality, and the way in which people understand their lives and experiences, in turn, produce discourses and meanings about what life is. Similarly, sexual violence is contextual, discursive, and corporal.

To think about bodies, says anthropologist Mari Luz Esteban,

> is to think about concrete representations and conceptions, in relation to specific ways of understanding the subject and gender. There is also an intimate connection between bodies and the historical and geographical contexts in which these bodies are configured and lived.[31]

Representations of sexual danger get women to in-corporate torture and sexual violence. Discourses, in Butler's words, inhabit bodies. In this sense, the discourses contained in the narratives of sexual danger are a constitutive and constituting part of women's bodies. On the other hand, they state, "language and materiality are never fully identical nor fully different."[32] With this idea, Butler opens up the vanishing point, the place from which the norm can be reversed, transgressed. Text and meanings produce the body; in the same way, the body can produce meanings.

---

30. Judith Butler, *Frames of War: When Is Life Grievable?* (London: Verso, 2009), 1.

31. Mari Luz Esteban, "Cuerpos y políticas feministas," lecture presented at Jornadas Estatales Feministas, Granada (December 5–7, 2009), on the panel "Cuerpos, sexualidades y políticas feministas," in *Granada, treinta años después: Aquí y ahora* (Granada: Coordinadora Estatal de Organizaciones Feministas, 2010), 391–96.

32. Judith Butler, *Bodies That Matter: On the Discursive Limits of "Sex"* (London: Routledge, 1993), 69.

Thus, my starting point is an idea of the body as a place in which women's boundaries are imprinted, their behavior resignified. In Butler's words, "To be a body is to be exposed to social crafting and form, and that is what makes the ontology of the body a social ontology."[33] The inscribed boundaries are therefore associated with social terrain through meanings. The discipline of sexual terror follows a gradual, repetitive process that constructs—or attempts to construct—docile bodies and materializes the sexual violence that is itself apprehended. What bodies apprehend is facilitated by the norms of recognition. To apprehend sexual violence is, for women, to be in the realm of imprecise terms. As Butler explains, apprehension is a less than precise concept that can involve marking, registering, or acknowledging without full cognition. It is a form of knowledge that is not conceptual but is associated with feeling or perceiving.

An apprehended violence is there, generating consequences and effects, but, at the same time, it is not there. It exists as a possibility, because it is in-corporated and, from a discursive point of view, naturalized. This construction, Butler says, in reference to sex,

> is neither a single act nor a causal process initiated by a subject and culminating in a set of fixed effects. Construction not only takes place in time but is itself a temporal process which operates through the reiteration of norms; sex is both produced and destabilized in the course of this reiteration.[34]

In other words, the systematic reiteration of norms of sexual danger stabilizes sexual violence on women's bodies, producing and reproducing bodies that are materialized in sexual violence.

---

33. Butler, *Frames of War*, 3.
34. Butler, *Bodies That Matter*, 10.

It is this materiality that gives rape its political circumstance: an act directed against and at women. Butler describes the body as an intentionally organized materiality; the body is, according to them, a historical stage that involves predisposition to a way of representing, dramatizing, and reproducing historical situations. The body adapts to a specific historical script that, through repetition, materializes, renews itself, persists, and resists. This way of defining the body helps to both home in on the fact that sexual violence is materialized in women's bodies and to situate the transmission of sexual violence as fully discursive and entirely of the body. The body is no mere writing system; it is a writing system with memory.

From Jack the Ripper to the Alcàsser Crimes

*Here suffice it to say that, in response to the new female indepen-
dence, we see the beginning of a misogynous backlash.*

Silvia Federici, *Caliban and the Witch*

To understand the rationale behind sexual danger narratives, we
must situate these accounts in context.

A century before the Alcàsser case, something similar happened in London. Judith Walkowitz's study of it, *City of Dreadful
Delight*, has served as inspiration for the present investigation.
Walkowitz examines the cultural dynamics and social struggles in the Victorian period that led, in 1888, to the creation of
the persona of Jack the Ripper. From her perspective, rather
than being merely a legend or a horror story, Jack the Ripper
embodies the sexual danger myth of the late nineteenth-century
Victorian period. Thus, rather than focusing on the murderer
or the macabre nature of his acts, she focuses on the social
motifs and characteristics that set up the ideal context for the
creation of the myth. The author situates this story "as part of
a formative moment in the production of feminist sexual politics and of popular narratives of sexual danger."[1] In this case,
she emphasizes the importance of the historical context and
the social circumstances that came with it. Had it happened at
a different time, a character like the Ripper might have gone

---

1. Judith Walkowitz, *City of Dreadful Delight: Narratives of Sexual
Danger in Late-Victorian London* (Chicago: University of Chicago Press,
1992), 2.

unnoticed in the accident and crime pages of any newspaper. However, Walkowitz explains, "a conjunction of shifting sexual practices, sexual scandals, and political mobilizations provided the historic conditions in the late Victorian period for the elaboration of such narratives."[2]

The last decades of the nineteenth century saw London at a historic turning point in relation to women's sexuality. Middle-class women began to speak publicly about sexual danger and passion—an undeniably subversive act in a society characterized by decorum, good manners, and sexual repression.[3] In a redefined public arena, the Ripper moved through the city committing his crimes freely, "exposing the private parts of 'public women' to open view."[4] No one saw him, no one knew what his face looked like, he left no trace, and just as he appeared, he was gone: "the myth of an 'eternal' Ripper, 'the never named, could-be-anyone killer,' unifying past and present terror."[5]

Various tales were concocted about the identity of the killer and the meaning of his crimes. In the absence of a coherent account, the blend of impressions rendered the murders "a cautionary tale for women, a warning that the city was a dangerous place when they transgressed the narrow boundary of home and hearth to enter public space."[6]

Considering that the Ripper only murdered "public women," the curfew goes hand in hand with the metaphor. The crimes against sex workers alluded, with significant symbolic charge, to

---

2. Walkowitz, *City of Dreadful Delight*, 5.

3. "Through the feminist politics of prostitution, middle-class women inserted themselves into the public discussion of sex to an unprecedented extent, using access to new public spaces and to new journalistic practices to speak out against men's double lives, their sexual diseases, and their complicity in a system of vices that flourished in the undergrowth of respectable society." Walkowitz, *City of Dreadful Delight*, 5.

4. Walkowitz, *City of Dreadful Delight*, 3.

5. Walkowitz, *City of Dreadful Delight*, 4.

6. Walkowitz, *City of Dreadful Delight*, 3.

what could happen to women if they went beyond the private sphere—because outside, they were all public women. Threats, rape, and murder were the price to pay for occupying terrain in which men alone could move. Walkowitz maps the cultural framework for and representations of sexual danger circulating in late nineteenth-century London: from the sex-crime narratives of urban extraction to the stories of sex and sexuality resulting from journalistic scandal. In this way, she lays out the context and the environment that produced the figure of Jack the Ripper, who became a myth of sexual terror at the end of the Victorian period. This idea is worth extrapolating to the Alcàsser case, not only because of the shared historical context in which new freedoms were being opened up for women but also due to the ghastliness of the crimes, which involved physical punishment and torture. Still further parallels can be drawn in the degree of entrenchment in collective memory and the fact of the unknown whereabouts of the perpetrator, which fed into the legend and forestalled its closure.

In analyzing the Alcàsser tale, I have identified similarities, in the form of patterns and categories, to the case Walkowitz explores. Thus, her investigation's governing model may also be valid for deciphering the Alcàsser crimes and conceptualizing them as a sexual danger narrative.

Here, it is worth reflecting on concepts and meanings that, despite the difference in context, coincide in both narratives and are related to the myths, beliefs, and categories through which sexual violence is understood and transmitted. Largely, I have chosen to focus on elements that appear, either explicitly or subtlety, in the story of the Alcàsser crimes. For example, Walkowitz offers a detailed depiction of what I call *the figure of the public woman*. As she delves into the City of London, describing its spaces and its protagonists, she locates one character to whom she attributes particular relevance:

> No figure was more equivocal, yet more crucial to the structured public landscape of the male flaneur, than the

woman in public. In public, women were presumed to be both endangered and a source of danger to those men who congregated in the streets.[7]

In this way, the author draws our attention to the uncomfortable presence of women in a space explicitly assigned to men. The presence of women on the streets posed a danger to themselves, but also to the existing sexual status quo.

After the murders, Walkowitz adds, "Champions of female independence had to confront the popular prejudice that when a woman met with a 'certain order of disagreeableness,' she 'brought it on herself—if only by leaving home.'"[8] In other words, the author depicts a context in which the presence of women in public space was already understood to be problematic even before the Whitechapel murders. This means that, in the social atmosphere in which Jack the Ripper emerged, the groundwork had already been laid for the sexual danger narrative that the murders would merely serve to sanction. Walkowitz brings us into contact with one form of masculine rationale from the period that justified habits like following or targeting respectable women:

> A woman who goes about the "haunts of men" in a "tailor-made dress" (whose tight fit, according to one private letter circulated at the time, simply accentuated the "false bottoms and stays—and other erotic adornments," that women wore to "excite the male sex") should not feel "insulted" if approached by a stranger.[9]

This way of thinking, which lurks behind the idea of a woman in public space, is practically identical—as we shall see—to those

---

7. Walkowitz, *City of Dreadful Delight*, 21.
8. Walkowitz, *City of Dreadful Delight*, 52.
9. Walkowitz, *City of Dreadful Delight*, 129.

meanings that, after the Alcàsser crimes, gained momentum in the press of the time. Like in the London of 1888, after the Alcàsser crimes there was a tendency to push women back into their homes, back under male protection. Likewise, they were urged to proceed with more caution to avoid putting themselves in danger.

Walkowitz's way of situating women in public space was what encouraged me to think of the public woman as a concept. This representation has inspired me throughout my investigation; it is a political category that has helped structure the resignification of the Alcàsser narrative. I use the category of *public woman* as a metaphor that allows me to enable an in-between space, a no-man's-land that, in the framework of the present study, comes to refer to all those spaces enabled by the system within which women belong to no one. That is to say, in the absence of male company and protection, women in no-man's-land belong to anyone, to everyone.

In examples provided by Walkowitz, the risk management practiced by women of the time is plain to see:

> Women adopted a series of strategies to deal with this situation, assisted by the prudential advice of parents and magazines. Early in her adolescence, a girl had to learn to free herself of unwanted admirers. In her gestures, movements, and pace (always dignified and purposeful), she had to demonstrate that she was not available prey.[10]

This clear example of how the discipline of sexual terror, which the women of Jack the Ripper's time began to experience, hung over each and every activity, every space they occupied: "Some women devised personal maps and proscribed zones to organize their walks around the West End."[11]

---

10. Walkowitz, *City of Dreadful Delight*, 51.
11. Walkowitz, *City of Dreadful Delight*, 51.

Another important similarity in both cases is the fact that the press of the time played an extremely significant role in the dissemination of sexual terror. As in Alcàsser, in London, stories of sexual violence not only spread fear among women but also provoked fascination and "addiction" to news relating to sexual terror. It should be noted that the precontext of violence in which the public had been instructed prior to the Ripper murders made it possible for the emergence of "Jack" to constitute a turning point. As Walkowitz explains, all such myths of the time were unified in a serial called "The Maiden Tribute." The story

> documented in lurid detail how poor "daughters of the people" were "snared, trapped, and outraged, either when under the influence of drugs or after a prolonged struggle in a locked room." The series had an electrifying effect: by the third installment, mobs of "gaunt and hollow-faced men and women with trailing dress and ragged coats" were rioting at the *Pall Mall Gazette* offices, in an attempt to obtain copies of the paper.[12]

The similarities with the Alcàsser crimes are evident. However, the important thing is not so much to discern whether or not the similarities exist, but rather to comprehend the fact that they come from significatory structures that produce and reproduce concepts and categories about sexual danger and, therefore, about the way in which societies understand and manage sexual violence. In the words of Walkowitz, "Disciplining as well as inciting, fictions of sexual danger significantly shaped the way men and women of all classes made sense of themselves and their urban environment."[13]

One element that characterizes both narratives is to be found in the character of Jack the Ripper himself. Legends about

---

12. Walkowitz, *City of Dreadful Delight*, 81.

13. Walkowitz, *City of Dreadful Delight*, 80.

his person and whereabouts plagued the collective imagination. As in Alcàsser, all kinds of arguments were used to displace the offender from space or territory. In the case of the Ripper, "it was repeatedly asserted that no Englishman could have perpetrated such a horrible crime."[14] Stories about the character of Antonio Anglés, in particular—about who he was or was not—were among the most recurrent in the reconstruction of the crimes.

In terms of the importance of the media, focusing on Alcàsser specifically, the transcendental role played by both print and broadcast coverage in the construction of the narrative cannot be ignored. In fact, this was what set in motion a whole mechanism of terror production and where the most lurid details of the crimes were displayed. For the first time, cameras portrayed moments of pain, introduced us to the victims, showed us their houses, their rooms, what they were doing, what they were saying, what kind of people they were. They showed the scenes of the crimes, the areas that had been traversed, and the place where the abuse and murders were committed. Broadcast on TV, the new spectacle of the town square found unprecedented reach, and the images become a kind of contemporary executioner. In the words of historian Georges Vigarello: "Written accounts replaced the old spectacle of the Gibbet."[15] And it is precisely along these lines that the representations contained in the Alcàsser narrative constitute "a politics of bodies that was much more effective than the ritual anatomy of torture."[16] It is on the basis of this idea that I bring together the whole argument relating to the (in)corporation of sexual violence through the discipline of sexual terror.

---

14. Walkowitz, *City of Dreadful Delight*, 203.

15. Georges Vigarello, *A History of Rape: Sexual Violence in France from the Sixteenth to the Twentieth Century*, trans. Jean Birrell (Oxford: Polity, 2001), 109.

16. Michel Foucault, *Discipline and Punish: The Birth of the Prison*, trans. Alan Sheridan (New York: Vintage, 1995), 102.

The Alcàsser crimes, like the murders committed in Whi-techapel, occurred in a changing society amid shifting cultural dynamics. To understand the achievements and demands of the feminist movement during the transition to democracy and the 1980s and '90s, it is imperative that we first outline the political, social, and cultural context in which those demands began to take shape.

The progress toward sexual liberation finds precedent in an international framework that situates the birth of the women's liberation movement, from the 1960s onward, in the United States, amid the heat of the so-called sexual revolution. As sociologist Raquel Osborne explains, "It was no coincidence that the original focus of early feminists was on knowledge of one's own body, on the need for autonomy in all areas, and on the search for sexual satisfaction."[17] This new forum, in which women began to talk about their practices and experiences, brought the concerns about and fear of assault that the vast majority experienced to the surface: "The pursuit and need for greater sexual freedom itself led to sexual violence being highlighted as one of the ways in which this freedom was restricted."[18] The sexual revolution opened new avenues for speaking out against sexual violence as hindering the development and enjoyment of free, autonomous sexuality for women. In this way, it also highlighted the reality of a revolution that was liberating men's sexuality, but not women's. The British scholar and activist Jeffrey Weeks explains, "The 'sexual revolution' that supposedly took place in the 1960s is therefore, by definition, a male-oriented one which subordinated women ever more tightly to the heterosexist norm."[19] Weeks

---

17. Raquel Osborne, *La violencia contra las mujeres: Realidad social y políticas públicas* (Madrid: UNED, 2001), 19.

18. Osborne, *La violencia contra las mujeres*, 20.

19. Jeffrey Weeks, *Sexuality and Its Discontents: Meanings, Myths, and Modern Sexualities* (London: Routledge, 2002), 19.

establishes the 1980s as the time at which sexuality came closest to provoking public debate by producing "a crisis over sexuality: a crisis in the relations of sex, especially in the relations between men and women, but also, perhaps more fundamentally, a crisis around the meaning of sexuality in our society."[20] In Weeks's view, in the aftermath of the sexual revolution, sex was situated at the center of a powerful political controversy: "[It] has long been a transmission belt for wider social anxieties, and a focus of struggles over power, one of the prime sites in truth where domination and subordination are defined and expressed."[21] Reflection on sexuality led to an awareness of the threats and sexual aggressions faced by women and, inevitably, changes that destabilized and challenged social norms began to take place.

Discussions around female sexuality enabled the visualization of the close relationship between women's sexual autonomy, their right to pleasure, and the danger that this freedom could pose to their physical and sexual integrity. Feminists placed this threat in the context of a form of patriarchy that used sexual violence as a means of limiting and restricting their fundamental rights. Anthropologist Carole Vance explains, "Beyond the actual physical or psychological harm done to victims of sexual violence, the threat of sexual attack served as a powerful reminder of male privilege, constraining women's movement and behavior."[22] As experiences were shared, sexual aggression began to be understood as part of everyday life. Its ubiquity also shed light on the impact that fear of sexual aggression was having on women's lives. In the same vein, Susan Brownmiller, a journalist and feminist activist, has stated that rape is "a conscious process of intimidation by which all men keep all women

20. Weeks, *Sexuality and Its Discontents*, 16.

21. Weeks, *Sexuality and Its Discontents*, 16.

22. Carole S. Vance, "Pleasure and Danger: Toward a Politics of Sexuality," in *Pleasure and Danger: Exploring Female Sexuality*, ed. Carole S. Vance (London: Routledge, 1984), 3.

From Jack the Ripper to the Alcàsser Crimes

41

in a state of fear."[23] Raquel Osborne develops this idea further, situating rape as an element of coercion and fear that curtails women's freedom:

> When it is argued that rape constitutes an attack on women's individual and collective freedom, the aim is to highlight the way in which not only rape itself, but the fear of being raped, represents a palpable confirmation of the devaluation, objectification, and lack of autonomy of women, which acts as a mechanism of dependence and subjection to male control.[24]

Another major challenge faced by feminists of the time (which persists to this day) was the struggle to destabilize a whole structure of meanings that reinforced the fear of sexual danger and held women responsible for being assaulted. In this way, sexual violence succeeded in restricting the public expression of female sexual desire while, at the same time, blaming women themselves for sexual aggressions. Consequently, Vance argues, "if female sexual desire triggers male attack, it cannot be freely or spontaneously shown, either in public or in private." For Vance, this method of control forced women to return to the protection and shelter provided by the political-cultural system: "Female desire should be restricted to zones protected and privileged in the culture: traditional marriage and the nuclear family."[25] This kind of reasoning, which feminism began to elucidate, clearly exposes the existence of a separation of spaces: the boundaries in which women can move with peace of mind and those in which they are automatically at risk. Consequently, "better safe than sorry," Vance explains, remained a widespread warning. For

23. Susan Brownmiller, *Against Our Will: Men, Women, and Rape* (New York: Fawcett Columbine, 1975), 15.

24. Raquel Osborne, *Apuntes sobre violencia de género* (Barcelona: Ediciones Bellaterra, 2009), 59.

25. Vance, "Pleasure and Danger," 3.

Vance, "Women inherit a substantial task: the management of their own sexual desire and its public expression. Self-control and watchfulness become major and necessary female virtues."[26] The sexual revolution, therefore, had to be contextualized.

According to Osborne, from the 1960s onward and in the wake of the feminist movement, there was a change in the way sexual aggression was defined:

> no longer as the loss of female honor by which the pact between men was broken because it sullied the honor of the family—between the men responsible for settling the conflict—but as an act of violence that one man or more exercised over one woman or more. Moreover, such violence was interpreted as an act of coercion against all women who could be assaulted or threatened with sexual aggression.[27]

Sexual aggression thus began to be conceived as an act of abuse and domination against women. This disentangled a whole web of arguments that did nothing more than justify and condone the use of violence against women. For Osborne,

> The essence of rape was thus laid bare. It was not the inevitable result of the male's great sexual potency, nor was it the result of some mental disorder. Rather, it was an extreme form of a socially sanctioned pattern of behavior whereby men are supposed to dominate women, to make it clear who is in charge.[28]

This direct association between the seizure of public space, sexual freedom, and the danger of living one's sexuality freely

---

26. Vance, "Pleasure and Danger," 4.

27. Osborne, *La violencia contra las mujeres*, 20.

28. Osborne, *La violencia contra las mujeres*, 12.

forced the feminist movement to organize its efforts on several fronts. Thus, not only would they speak out against sexual aggression and danger, but they would also work to promote sexual practice, desire, and pleasure for women. Denunciation of sexual aggression could not be reduced to mere campaign work that would end up restricting women's practices anyway; danger and the struggle for sexual freedom were now inseparable. Feminists provided the movement with theoretical tools through which to articulate the everyday problems women faced. Speaking out against sexual aggression became a priority for a feminist movement that was bringing to light that which had previously been kept in the private sphere.

The Feminist Movement on the Rise:
Women's New Corporal-Political Arena

> *Let's not kid ourselves, the law on private television is like women: it was made to be violated.*
>
> **Luis Ángel de la Viuda, on "Aquí te espero," aired April 9, 1988, Radio Nacional de España**

Situating and mapping out social struggles prior to the murder of the three teenage girls is an essential step in understanding the creation of the Alcàsser sexual terror narrative. This exercise in contextualization is important insofar as the popular account is a violent response to the freedom that was being consolidated for women through and by feminism. The dominant narrative sought to protect and restore each and every one of the axes of domination that the feminist movement had flagged and spoken out against. One fundamental aspect masked in the Alcàsser narrative is the feminist context in which it originates. It is through studying the feminist movement's struggles that the reasons behind the creation of the sexual danger narrative will become clear. Just as the sexual status quo began to undergo upheaval, Alcàsser was the mechanism through which attempts to introduce immobilist elements were made.

The end of the 1970s and the beginning of the 1980s, saw extensive feminist political activity. Charting feminist demands from that time will help situate us in the society immediately prior to the triple crime and provide us with a more global overview of the changes underway.

I want to (de)situate this period, known as La Transición, the Transition to democracy in Spain, from its particular historical-political framework to explore it in political-corporal terms. What I am interested in studying is not so much the regime that was established but the political-feminist struggle that made a bodily transition possible for women—a corporal transition that cannot be dissociated from the Alcàsser sex crimes. The space for renegotiation made possible by the transition process involved demands for a redefinition of women's individual and social rights. Feminism during this period sought to publicly challenge the relations of domination that women had to endure at the hands of their husbands, fathers, and sons—to take the streets, making these relations a political, rather than a private, matter.

However, feminist demands encountered numerous obstacles and resistance to their struggle. The first of these was the consolidation of the new regime itself, from which many feminist demands were ultimately excluded. The second was the effect of the Alcàsser crimes, which served as a blockade against women's sexual freedom. What lay ahead for the feminist movement was, for starters, to demand the repeal of an entire legislative framework that restricted women's fundamental rights. The main premise was to bring about a comprehensive shift in the meaning ascribed to the power relations that regulated society. The ideological stance of the feminist movement focused much of its discourse on the firm belief that the political change to which they aspired did not lie exclusively within legal frameworks. As the Spanish feminist activist Justa Montero explains, "It was not just a question of achieving concrete legislative and welfare changes, but of doing so by formulating new rights: the right to your own body, to experience sexuality and motherhood with the freedom to choose."[29] Feminist proposals were not confined to official spheres but sought to filter through to every nook and cranny, impacting every aspect of society. The activity of the feminist movement in the late 1970s and early '80s thus ran parallel to the political processes involved in the change of regime.

Hopes of change were overshadowed by resistance to adopting and incorporating feminist principles from the new 1977 Cortes Constituyentes (Constituent Courts), and even from militant comrades.[30] The new political scenario placed women back in the bosom of the family, including those who had been comrades in struggle during the dictatorship of Francisco Franco. As "democracy" was established, most feminist demands were excluded from the process and from the constitution itself. Subtly, the political parties sent an abysmally clear message: once you vote, it is time to go home.

Despite these obstacles, feminist political work did not slacken. The movement pressed on with its demands, pursuing a struggle articulated around rights and freedoms that, from a political and legislative point of view, would place women on an equal footing with men.

The 1980s were a period of intense feminist political activity in Spain: among the movement's striking achievements were the partial decriminalization of abortion, the legalization of divorce, and the reform of the penal code in sexual matters. These new openings constituted, in the context of the time, a significant blow to the major structural axes of patriarchy: the institution of

---

29. Justa Montero, "Las aspiraciones del movimiento feminista y la transición política," in *El movimiento feminista en España*, ed. Carmen Martínez Ten, Purificación Gutiérrez López, and Pilar González Ruiz (Madrid: Cátedra, 2009), 284.

30. This was essentially an interim government to oversee the first elections after Franco's death and the drafting of a new constitution that would be put to a referendum—Trans.

the family, domination over women's bodies and sexuality, and the sexual division between public and private space.

Feminists understood the institution of the family as one of the economic and political structures that oppressed women. For Inés Alberdi, a sociologist and former director of the UN Development Fund for Women, those years, and the ideological debates that took place therein, reflected a radical critique of the family "as a key institution of patriarchy."[31] While the anti-authoritarian movements focused all their arguments against the Franco regime, feminism pointed out the two-fold repression experienced by women: that of the dictatorial regime and that of the patriarchal regime centered in the family.

Throughout the process, the emancipation of women from the nuclear family encountered clear opposition from conservative groups, including the Catholic church. Mónica Moreno has emphasized that, although the Episcopal Conference was led by moderate bishops during the transition, they nevertheless "advocated for very traditional moral principles in defense of the family and of ways of life, which, in their opinion, should be taken up by the State."[32]

All this demonstrates the importance of the institution of the family for the perpetuation of the patriarchal regime and the fear and anxiety that change was producing in social, political, and religious structures.

The institution of the family includes a number of elements that work in a disjointed but coordinated manner. For this reason, it cannot be separated from the protection or safeguarding of women in the shelter of the home. Therefore, when the

---

31. Inés Alberdi, "El feminismo y la transición democrática," *Leviatán: Revista de hechos e ideas* 65 (1996): 90.

32. Mónica Moreno, "Feminismo, antifeminismo, catolicismo y anticlericalismo en la transición política a la democracia," in *Feminismos y antifeminismos: Culturas políticas e identidades de género en la España del siglo XX*, ed. Ana Aguado and Teresa Ortega (Valencia: Universidad de Valencia, 2011), 326.

feminist movement made the family a high-priority target, the movement was not only condemning the sexual division of labor and how women's bodies were essentialized and determined by motherhood but was also demanding that public space be a place where women have rights.

Among the first goals came the decriminalization of contraceptives and the legalization of abortion and divorce. The social significance of these demands was twofold: the decriminalization of contraceptives and abortion was associated with women's sexual freedom, while the legalization of divorce would significantly hinder the stability of the institution of the family. The law decriminalizing contraceptives was passed in 1978—the same year as Spain's new constitution—without much resistance. However, the legalization of abortion and divorce was met with strong opposition, especially in more conservative sectors. For feminists, the divorce law was a coup, hitting the institution of the family head on. Similarly, women's access to the world of work implied their incorporation into spaces that had largely been occupied by men. The economic independence that paid work would bring to women would also facilitate their personal independence. The potential of both of these changes challenged male authority and weakened the institution of the family. The campaign of the state-wide feminist organization the Coordinadora Estatal de Organizaciones Feministas in favor of the divorce law brought with it, as Justa Montero explains, "the harsh criticism of the family institution as a bastion of women's oppression, and the defense of other forms of organizing social relations."[33] The church's opposition to the divorce law, notes Pilar Tobo, "led several women from the platform to chain themselves to the bars on the ecclesiastical courts' windows in September 1979, an action that concluded with the arrest of a number of them."[34] Finally, in

33. Montero, "Las aspiraciones del movimiento feminista," 281.

34. Pilar Toboso, "Las mujeres en la Transición: Una perspectiva histórica," in Ten et al., *El movimiento feminista en España*, 93.

1981, these actions and the constant demands culminated in the passage of the divorce law, which included some of the points proposed by the feminist movement.

Negotiations for the decriminalization of abortion followed a similar pattern. The first legislation on the subject was passed in 1983, which proposed a partial decriminalization. However, this law did not come into force until 1985, due to the opposition of the Coalición Popular parliamentary group, which lodged an appeal of unconstitutionality. The decriminalization of abortion meant women were granted legal autonomy over their bodies. This issue was the basis for ongoing social and political resistance, as shown by the trials held in Basauri, in the Basque Country, against eleven women accused of having abortions. Beginning in 1976, these trials did not end until almost a decade later, in 1985, with an unfavorable sentence for the defendants. The Basauri trials, a milestone in the feminist movement's struggle for the decriminalization of abortion, managed to unite a large number of women under the same banner.

The feminist sexual revolution was beginning to open up spaces for women. This shift entailed a redefinition of women's bodies and of men's rights over them—exactly what the Alcàsser sexual danger narrative would attempt to reestablish.

Experiencing Sexual Violence in 1970s and '80s Spain

When we examine the fabric of society prior to Alcàsser, we see a forceful feminist movement that called sexual violence by name, framing it in the context of the domination of women in the face of the unquestionable authority of men. In this respect, the 1980s saw fierce campaigns calling for the condemnation of rape, abusive behavior, paternal abuse, and harassment at work. The rights of single and divorced mothers were also defended, sexual freedom was made more accessible, and there were soon emphatic calls for lesbian visibility that had been long overdue. The expression of control over women's sexuality found its culmination in sexual violence. Under Franco's dictatorship, Article 28 of the penal code was an accurate illustration of this statement. According to this section, a father or husband was allowed to kill a woman and her lover if they were found lying together. This regulation was in force until the decree of March 21, 1963, which abolished it. Article 28 not only illustrates the power men had over women's bodies, but it also depicts killing women as an act that is not punishable and therefore totally licit. This article is a legal representation or depiction that, despite its elimination, synthesizes the idea of power and privilege that men hold over women's bodies.

As was the case in the international context, debates about sexual practices between men and women opened an avenue for women to analyze sexual violence. At the time, feminist activity was immersed in an active campaign against sexual aggression, and exposing and condemning these acts was a top priority for what feminists understood should be identified as a social issue. In 1983, the First Conference against Sexual Violence was organized in Navarra. and positions on how to frame future actions were put forward and debated:

> We have to take a clear stance that not a single rape may go unchallenged. That no instance of rape can remain shrouded in anonymity. We must start by speaking out publicly, first, in order to get rape recognized as a crime, and second, as a way of fighting the burden of guilt laid on women who have been raped. Speaking out shows that there is no doubt about who is the victim and who is the perpetrator. Speaking out raises awareness that these crimes happen all too often, lets these women know they are not the only ones, and builds solidarity that leads to social pressure in the face of oppressive chauvinism.[35]

---

35. Dossier violaciones, Coordinadora Feminista de Navarra, 1982–1984, Centro de Documentación de Mujeres Maite Álbiz, Bilbao, 109.

At the 1988 state conference against sexist violence, the Jornadas Contra la Violencia Machista, held in the Galician capital of Santiago de Compostela, the consequences of sexual violence on women's daily lives were front and center:

> Through violence we are told that we cannot go out alone at three o'clock in the morning; or that those tights we like so much are a provocation. Through violence, in the cruelest of ways, as young women we are told to be afraid, to feel unsafe, to seek protection from a man, or to stay at home.[36]

Feminists were documenting an everyday reality that was an integral part of society. The risk or threat of rape was articulated as a political concept, creating debate around issues relating to various freedoms and the "natural" submission of women.

> That this risk [of rape] is established and calibrated is not accidental; it is part of the set of rewards and punishments that serve to control women socially and keep them in their place, within the patriarchal order. This order divides women into those who accept the rules of the game, whom society will protect, and those who can be raped. She who goes out at night, who lives alone, who dares to go to the cinema unaccompanied, who dares to enter cafés and bars or to hitchhike risks catcalls, or being pestered, groped, felt up, or raped.[37]

One of the most difficult tasks facing feminists was to dismantle the stereotypes that established a series of meanings

---

36. "Desobediencia: Ponencia mujeres jóvenes de Valencia," Jornadas Feministas contra la Violencia Machista, 1988, Centro de Documentación de Mujeres Maite Álbiz, Bilbao, 56.

37. *Agresiones* vii/7, "La violación" (Bilbao: Centro de Documentación de Mujeres Maite Álbiz, n.d.), 3.

about rape and shaped thinking about what was and was not understood as an aggression in the society of the time. The idea that rapists were psychopaths who had been cast out by society and who had sexual and social problems had to be dismantled early on:

> Men do not rape because they want to have sex—many, so many of them, have fairly "normal" sex lives; they have wives, girlfriends, friends. Men who rape do it because that is what they want: to have violent sex against the will of the women.[38]

In an article published in the regional newspaper *Diario de Navarra*, a psychiatrist outlined the following profile of women who are sexually assaulted: "Most women who are raped are single, separated, or divorced. Married women generally avoid any man's approach and shy away from any relationship. This makes them less vulnerable to rape."[39] Such claims blamed single or divorced women for being assaulted, and the response of the Coordinadora Feminista de Navarra (Navarra Feminist Coordinating Committee) was not long in coming.

> The message is clear; woman, if you don't want to be raped, get married and don't even think about splitting up with your husband. If you don't want to be raped you must have an owner, because a woman without an owner belongs to everyone.[40]

Responses of this kind from the feminist movement were of fundamental importance because, gradually, they began chipping

---

38. *Antiagresiones* vi/50, "Ante la violación" (Bilbao: Centro de Documentación de Mujeres Maite Álbiz, n.d.), 11.

39. *Diario de Navarra*, February 13, 1983, in "Coordinadora" (Bilbao: Centro de Documentación de Mujeres Maite Álbiz, n.d.), 37.

40. *Diario de Navarra*, February 13, 1983, in "Coordinadora," 37.

away at the idea that only a few men raped, and only certain women were raped.

One of the projects that was set up at that time, and which would later be taken over by government institutions, was the shelters. Initially, clinics of a sort were set up, staffed by feminists and organized by neighborhood, where women who had been assaulted could go and be assisted, informed, and accompanied through the lengthy process involved in reporting rape. That process, after suffering an aggression was too long and painful for survivors to be left alone in the hands of police officers who made statements such as, "Of all the cases where the woman reacted by screaming and scratching, rape was never successful; it is not easy to rape a woman if she resists."[41]

The legal procedure was another major obstacle to reporting aggressions. For many women, the reporting process meant experiencing more violence thanks to the actions of judges, the police, and forensic doctors:

> It is not enough just to report the act; the woman also has to prove that she was attacked against her will, that there was no consent, that she resisted with all her might, and that she did not provoke the perpetrator.[42]

Judges' interpretations of the facts and the application of the law were based on their own prejudices and revealed a sexist and misogynist judiciary. Most judgments placed special emphasis on the guilt of the woman. Above all, factors such as the time, the place, or the behavior of the woman, or her day-to-day life, could be deployed to justify rape. The way she was dressed on the day of the aggression was, for many judges, a key piece of evidence in determining whether she had resisted

41. *Agresiones* v/19, "I encuentro de Euskadi" (Bilbao: Centro de Documentación de Mujeres Maite Álbiz, n.d.), 1.

42. Dossier violaciones, Coordinadora Feminista de Navarra, 115.

or acted provocatively. In a 1989 trial for a sexual aggression committed the previous year, the president of the Lérida Court of Appeal "asked the young woman whether she had been wearing knickers when she was raped, arguing that, in view of contradictions as to the type of clothing, this was necessary to assess whether the victim resisted."[43] Judge Josep Gual justified his question by stating that it was necessary because "he wanted use this question to gauge whether the young woman resisted."[44] Ultimately, the judge sentenced the offender to twelve years in prison.

Most sentences cast doubt on the testimony or credibility of those assaulted. Conversely, the attitudes and practices of the perpetrator or perpetrators were usually not reexamined. In cases in which they were, such reexaminations served to confirm the improbability of such a man (a man who was a father, for example) committing a sexual aggression. In 1989, the newspaper *El País* reported on a triple rape committed two years earlier: "three rapists sentenced to forty-two years in prison because they had false alibis."[45] Apparently, according to the newspaper, the accused were "atypical rapists" because "the three convicted men, who had no criminal record, two of whom were fathers, did not fit the typical image of rapists, and the court's findings were therefore remarkable."[46]

For men, lifestyle could function as an asset in proving allegations to be false. Parenthood was apparently incompatible with being a rapist. Two rulings from the 1980s further illustrate this point. These sentences triggered the indignation of not only the feminist movement but society at large: one, now infamous, concerns the victim's miniskirt; the other is the acquittal of two young men for the crime of rape due to the alleged

---

43. *El Correo*, June 30, 1989.
44. *El País*, June 30, 1989.
45. *El País*, December 16, 1989.
46. *El País*, December 16, 1989.

"licentious and disorderly life of the victim"[47] in Pontevedra. Both sentences evince the profoundly misogynist leanings of certain judges.

The miniskirt ruling from the Court of Lérida—the same court that asked a woman whether she had been wearing knickers at the time of the aggression—justified the sexual assault of a seventeen-year-old employee on the basis that her miniskirt "provoked" her boss's baser instincts. According to the sentence,

> When she appeared there in a miniskirt that made her look particularly attractive, or at least that is how it seemed to her employer, who was visibly impressed, he indicated that if she agreed to his lustful desires, he would extend her contract and offer her special protection.[48]

The accused groped the girl several times, as acknowledged in the sentence, and took advantage of his position of power to sexually abuse the woman, "though she, with her distinctive attire, in a certain way, perhaps innocently, provoked this reaction in the businessman, who could not contain himself."[49]

The miniskirt ruling outraged not only the feminist movement but also society and the judicial community, which openly criticized it. The two judges who signed the sentence received a light sanction. In celebrations of International Women's Day on March 8 of the same year, many protestors wore miniskirts.

Another controversial judgment was handed down by the Provincial Court of Pontevedra. In its ruling, it acquitted two men of the crime of rape because of the alleged nonconforming lifestyle of the woman who had been assaulted. The judgment questioned how much resistance the woman would have put up, based on her personal circumstances. The fact that she had

---

47. *El Correo*, March 8, 1989.

48. *El País*, February 21, 1989.

49. *El País*, February 21, 1989.

gotten married and then separated implied to the judges that she was "sexually experienced," and that, in addition, "she led a licentious and disorderly life, as demonstrated by the fact that she had no fixed abode and was alone in a club in the early hours of the morning after having drunk alcohol."[50] The court decision went further, adding that the woman voluntarily agreed to travel in a van belonging to the defendants, "sitting in the front seat between the two men, thus putting herself, without the slightest opposition, in the position to be sexually used."[51]

The court's ruling shone a spotlight on the major axes underpinning the contemporary feminist struggle. Firstly, the fact that the woman was divorced, in the judge's opinion, denoted sexual experience, which, by implication, meant that there was no one with whom she would not willingly have sex. Furthermore, her being alone in the club late at night drinking alcohol with strangers reinforced the judge's decision. In short, the sentence was handed down on the basis of liberties that the woman had taken in a place that belonged to men. As a result of this ruling, feminists and legal advocates took action against the judge, and the judgment was referred to the disciplinary commission of the Consejo del Poder Judicial (General Council of Judicial Power) to consider potential sanctioning; however, in the end the case was dismissed on the grounds of judicial discretion.

The demands of the feminist movement were thus framed in an unfavorable environment: they faced a great many obstacles and much resistance to change. The cultural, political, legal, and social context was not just permissive of sexual violence; it was constitutive of it.

The feminist struggle against sexual aggressions saw the 1980s out with the passing of the reform of the penal code. The fronts opened by feminism put pressure on society at large, which put up resistance but could not prevent feminism's

---

50. *El Correo*, March 8, 1989.

51. *El Correo*, March 8, 1989.

advance. Myths were deconstructed, concepts were (re)constructed, and feminism armed itself with theoretical tools that allowed it to lay out solid arguments and put pressure on society and public authorities. After years of struggle, all these elements helped foment the conditions for the passage of the 1989 reform of the penal code on sexual violence. The objective was not just a shift in the application of sentencing; it was also about concepts. It was a question of how and under what title rape was classified.

Prior to this reform, the crime of rape was included in title IX of the penal code, "Crimes against Decency," which meant, as denounced by feminists,

> that the law does not consider rape as a crime against the person, but as a crime against public morals and decency, i.e., a crime against the honor of our fathers, brothers, and husbands, who are the ones who are understood to have been assaulted.[52]

Another article in the code contained what was called "indecent abuse"—that is, all other aggressions that were not considered rape. The offense of "indecent abuse" carried a lesser sentence and encompassed statutory rape. Statutory rape was defined as the abuse of authority over or trust of a female minor aged twelve to eighteen in order to have sexual intercourse; it was considered rape if the man was her father, brother, guardian, or relative. In addition, there was the figure of "the offended party's pardon," which allowed the option of forgiving the perpetrator. This meant that, in many cases involving minors, it was the father who, having previously reached an economic agreement, had the power to grant pardon. The transfer of a sum of money or "dowry" was also stipulated in the code: if the woman

---

52. *Agresiones* i/2, "Dossier violaciones" (Bilbao: Centro de Documentación de Mujeres Maite Álbiz: 1982–1984), 11.

was widowed or unmarried (i.e., not owned by a man), the rapist had to pay her a dowry in lieu of damages.

On June 25, 1983, a minimal reform took place with the elimination of "the offended party's pardon," but this applied only in cases of rape, and only for penis-in-vagina rape. For all other forms of abuse, the restricted framework of what was considered "indecent abuse" remained in force. The fact that a pardon continued to exist meant that if the victim granted the pardon before the sentence was passed, the crime disappeared, even if the perpetrator had acknowledged it. The dowry also disappeared and was replaced by compensation, regardless of the woman's marital status. That is as far as the 1983 reform of the penal code went. As for the other issues, the situation remained the same as in the penal code under Franco.

The feminist movement had to keep making demands and voicing dissent in relation to changes it considered insufficient. Demands for the reform of the penal code emphasized the "crimes against decency" title, attempting to decode that which was encrypted according to the following conceptualization:

> These are not crimes against dignity, against personal free-
> dom, against the sexual freedom of women, but against
> their decency, i.e., against modesty, chastity, purity, integ-
> rity, virtue, honor or propriety (normally of the husband
> or other male members of the family) and other meanings
> of decency.[53]

In this context, feminists called for changing "crimes against decency" to "crimes against sexual freedom." In addition, they demanded that the penal code recognize rape not only as forced vaginal penetration, but also as anal and oral penetra-tion, whether with a penis or with objects. They also called for the definitive elimination of

---

53. *Agresiones* vi/50, "Ante la violación," 11.

the offended party's pardon in relation to all sex crimes and for these crimes to become public crimes. For officials (police, prosecutors, and judges) who denigrate woman who have been assaulted in the investigation of these crimes to be penalized, and the investigation into the victim's private life prevented. Every woman has the right to say no at any time, and therefore the law must protect this right.[54]

Eventually, in 1989, the reform of the penal code in the area of sexual violence was achieved, going into force from July 21 of that year until May 26, 1996. The momentous change introduced by the reform was to define sexual aggressions as an attack against the sexual freedom of women, rather than as a crime against decency. In addition, the offended party's pardon disappeared once and for all. From a feminist perspective, the reform was still insufficient and left crucial gaps. But despite the fact that the reform did not meet all the demands made, it was still a victory for the feminist movement and a turning point for conceptualization of the crime of rape in Spain's penal code.

Legal discourses are an extension, a representation of how society understands and interprets sexual violence. The reform of the penal code was not, therefore, about to produce immediate social change. Explaining the way in which discourse on sexual violence evolved is so relevant here, precisely because of how important it is to consider the Alcàsser crimes' social, legal, and cultural context. Indeed, in 1992—at the time of the crimes—barely two years had passed since the new penal code had come into force. Clearly, this was not enough time for the promotion and production of significant cultural change in the society of the time.

With the advent of the 1990s, a new, unstable political, legal, and social atmosphere emerged. It was a period in which

---

54. *Agresiones* vi/50, "Ante la violación," 27–28.

institutions began to appropriate feminist rhetoric; the first "equality plans," were drawn up, and the problem of violence against women was recognized at an international scale. As the feminist activist and philosopher Sylvia Gil observes:

> In the 1990s, the world we had known was changing by leaps and bounds. There were changes in work and the forms of production, the family, the role played by women, public policies, relationships with consumption, modern technologies, lifestyles, neighborhoods, cities, the disappearance of the great social movements. Against this backdrop, the decade presents itself as the end of a century marked by uncertainty, a vacuum opens. A vacuum from which, however, new ways of working together were beginning to be explored, with greater or lesser degrees of success.[55]

The Alcàsser crimes erupted at a stage when feminist demands were largely beginning to be in-corporated, practiced, and taken on by women. With the uncertainty of the early 1990s, the primary objective of these new ways of organizing together was safeguarding against sexual violence. In the years immediately prior to the Alcàsser crimes, sexual aggression and murder were proliferating. The year 1992 was a particularly sensitive period in which society had been shaken by a succession of murders and sexual assaults against teenagers and girls. Leticia Lebrato, a seventeen-year-old, and Olga Sangrador, aged nine, in the Valladolid area, were victims in two considerably high-profile cases from that year.

Another case, which received only scarce attention, occurred seven months before the disappearance of the three teenagers from Alcàsser. On April 23, 1992, in Aguilar de Campoo (in the

---

55. Silvia L. Gil, *Nuevos feminismos, sentidos comunes en la dispersión* (Madrid: Traficantes de Sueños, 2011), 68.

province of Palencia), Virginia Guerrero and Manuela Torres, aged fifteen and sixteen respectively, disappeared. Both teenagers had been to a disco in Reinosa, a town in the northern autonomous community of Cantabria. After spending the day with their friends, at 9:00 p.m. they set off for home. According to the testimony of witnesses, they were last seen they were hitchhiking and may have gotten into a white car. Thirty-two years later, nothing is known of the teenagers' whereabouts.

The Aguilar de Campoo case did not receive the same media coverage as the Alcàsser crimes, despite conforming to practically the same pattern, characteristics, and context. It was the Alcàsser crimes, and how that narrative unfolded, that had the elements required for a rupture from all the avenues opened by the feminist movement. The story had to be of a magnitude sufficient to halt the advances, in terms of freedoms being won, that had been progressing since the 1980s. A narrative of lesser intensity would not have succeeded in curtailing a whole decade of social and political struggle and feminist theorizing.

The Construction of a Sexual Danger Narrative

The Alcàsser sexual danger narrative was not built based on the way events unfolded. Although certain meanings gained force after the bodies had been found, the truth is that even before the ending was known, those meanings had already appeared in the narrative. It was in the mistrust surrounding the teenagers' whereabouts and the disapproval regarding their conduct—were they just partying or playing a practical joke on society as a whole?—that the first traces of the narrative that was to assign responsibility to the girls' behavior began to emerge.

The (Dis)Appearance of the Account

I talk of the (dis)appearance of the account here because, just as the narrative starts to take shape, a process of erasure begins. News stories were to become a subtle means of transmitting violence against the teenagers and against young women in general.

The repercussions of the Alcàsser case in the media must be considered in light of the set of circumstances that preceded the unchecked media explosion following January 27, 1993, when the lifeless remains of the teenage girls were found. Much of what happened in the aftermath can be attributed to a series of factors that emerged beforehand—the most important being the speed with which that small Valencian town responded to the enforced disappearance of the teenagers. Indeed, this was what gave rise to such unprecedented social and media coverage.

The three young women were last seen on November 13, 1992, on the road linking Alcàsser—where they lived—and Picassent, where Coolor, the nightclub to which they were headed, was located. For the local population, finding them quickly became the top priority, as they gathered to start looking for the young women in the hours after they had vanished: "They disappeared one afternoon," recounted the teenagers' close friend Gemma Valero, "and that night, us friends got together and went looking for them."[1] Those closest to the families began a small-scale search and offered them their support. As another friend, Marta de la Fuente, wrote in her diary,

> We saw two friends, who asked us if we'd seen them, as they'd not yet returned home. It was two in the morning, and they still hadn't got word. We went to Toñi's house . . . and stayed at her door until really late.[2]

The following morning, a Saturday, the teenagers' relatives reported their disappearance to the Guardia Civil police force. However, the official search was not launched until the Sunday. José Manuel Alcaina, then deputy mayor of the town, recalled:

> Normally, if it's young people, teenagers, people always say they'll be back after the weekend. This was not the

---

1. Gemma Valero, interview, October 25, 2011. Gemma Valero was thirty-six at the time of the interview and has always lived in Alcàsser. At the time of the enforced disappearance of her friends, she played an active part in the search for them. When the bodies were found, she did not talk to the media. She remembers the media interference and the pain this caused her and her friends.

2. Marta de la Fuente was close to the three teenagers. As they belonged to the same generation, they shared leisure and nightlife spaces where they spent time together. This paragraph is an extract from the diary she wrote at the time, which was shared with the author as a documentary source for this investigation in the interview conducted on October 26, 2011.

case. In this case, there were certain circumstances indicating that it wasn't like that. I found myself that day at midday . . . I had a sense of what might've happened, I knew it wasn't voluntary, it wasn't some kind of childish running away. Not from those little ladies.[3]

Those closest to them were sure that the teenagers had not left voluntarily: "From the beginning, knowing them," Valero said, "I didn't think they'd run away from home. I think, all of us, all their friends, were quite sure of that."[4] The town square had become a space for meeting and social organization. Alcaina remembered that "by Saturday afternoon, no less than 200 to 300 people had lined up in front of the town hall."[5]

The initial organization soon evolved into a more effective operation: the first posters with photographs of the teenagers were printed, and the rapid mobilization of the population facilitated the deployment of a significant countywide search effort. As Diana Molina, another of the teenagers' friends, recalls:

In the afternoon we started to organize a search party, and we all met in the square. I went with my father in the car: with my father, a classmate from school, and another guy friend. We went to several nightclubs; it was Saturday night, and the clubs were open.[6]

---

3. José Manuel Alcaina, interview, October 28, 2011. At the time of the interview, José Manuel Alcaina had been a councilor on Valencia City Council for twenty-eight years. Alcaina was list leader for Alcàsser and held governing responsibility for two terms as deputy mayor. From his position as deputy mayor at the time of the events, he coordinated and managed the search efforts and was active in the media. Subsequently, he provided institutional and logistical support to the girls' families.

4. Valero, interview.

5. Alcaina, interview.

6. Diana Molina, a close friend of the teenagers', participated in the search efforts as did her other friends. Subsequently, she has kept away

Barely twenty-four hours had passed since the girls had failed to return home, and a considerable number of people were already out looking for them. The pooling of resources gave way to a truly specialized search, perfectly coordinated and organized, in which no detail was left to chance. As Alcaina explained:

> I personally coordinated nine or ten search teams. There were ten cars, with one youngish person driving, an older person, and another young person. So, dividing up the province of Valencia, we established ten or twelve plots and assigned each group an area in which to put up the photos of the three young ladies with telephone numbers in petrol stations, nightclubs, and pubs. The telephones that we set up for this were the town council's own lines.[7]

The two newspapers with the largest circulation in Valencia and the surrounding area, *Las Provincias* and *El Levante Valenciano*, published the news of the enforced disappearance of the girls on the morning of Sunday, November 15, on the back cover. The photo of the three teenagers was shown next to the headline, "The Strange Disappearance of Three Girls in Alcàsser Mobilizes Four Counties: Rescue Teams Search the Whole Area within a Radius of Thirty Miles."[8] The article stressed the involuntary nature of the disappearance: "the minors' hometown rules out any chance they left of their own free will."[9]

The people of Alcàsser managed to mount a huge search operation in record time that pushed the Guardia Civil to put their protocols into action, and by Sunday units were placed on all the roads. Andrés Domínguez, a boy from Alcàsser who was

---

from the media, who still contact her from time to time around the anniversary of the case.

7. Alcaina, interview.

8. *El Levante Valenciano*, November 15, 1992.

9. *El Levante Valenciano*, November 15, 1992.

a few years younger than the three teenagers, had a clear recollection of that first Sunday:

> The Guardia Civil police stopped us about twice on the
> journey from our country house to Alcàsser. They stopped
> us and searched our car. I remember that moment I
> have the image of them giving us the sheet of paper their
> photos were printed on, and that tension. And I remem-
> ber seeing, between the country house and Alcàsser, a
> lot of police patrols, the Guardia Civil, and people and
> neighbors from Alcàsser who were organized in groups
> looking for them.[10]

Arguments claiming the teenagers had probably just run
away, attempting to refute those who affirmed the contrary,
surfaced time and time again. The journalist in charge of the
Canal 9 news programs that Sunday told Alcaina the girls were
sure to return on Monday, implying that the search had been
somewhat premature and that the story was not yet newsworthy.
Alcaina recalls that he then took a very firm stance, forcefully
stating the reasons he thought the story should come out as
soon as possible:

> I tell her, "This is not normal. . . . I think this is a very seri-
> ous matter. Three little ladies are involved and that makes
> it more serious." And I tell her, either she pays the case
> the attention I think it deserves and does what she has
> to do to get the story on the Canal 9 news program . . . or
> she'd regret it. She wouldn't get past the first step of the

---

10. Andrés Domínguez, interview, December 17, 2010. Domínguez
was thirty-four at the time of the interview and had always lived in Alcàsser.
He remembers having an incredibly happy, carefree childhood. Andrés
experienced the entire process of the search for the teenagers firsthand as
well as the end of the search. He highlights the impression made on him
by the media deployment in the village.

three steps in the Alcàsser Town Hall. I wouldn't let her get through. In the unfortunate event that I was right and she was wrong, Canal 9 would be kept completely out of the loop.[11]

In the end, Valencian public TV broadcast the news that same day on the midday and evening news. Televisión Española (TVE) and the other channels followed suit, which meant that, Alcaina recalls, "by Sunday night, the whole of Spain was looking for them."[12]

Over the next few days, TV channels and the press began to create a sort of news continuum. By the end of the week, TVE's weekly news show, *Informe Semanal*, made its first report. The program presented Alcàsser as a quiet town, stricken by tragedy—"The disappearance of three teenagers dealt its inhabitants a harsh blow"—and highlighted locals' high degree of involvement: "The search has become an unprecedented show of solidarity, with drives all day and night. They are combing ditches, gutters, and ravines."[13]

Political leaders could not remain on the sidelines. Francisco Granados, the government delegate in Valencia, informed the media about the first hypotheses being weighed up:

At first everything seemed to indicate that the minors could be in some kind of club, although, as four days have passed since their disappearance, it hasn't been ruled out that some criminal organization is keeping them in a roadside brothel, having kidnapped them to force them to work as prostitutes.[14]

---

11. Alcaina, interview.
12. Alcaina, interview.
13. *Informe Semanal*, "¿Dónde están las chicas de Valencia?"
14. *El Levante Valenciano*, November 18, 1992.

The hypotheses investigators were considering at that time could essentially be divided into three types: the girls had voluntarily run away, and, having spent time away, were afraid to return; abduction; and, lastly, published in *El Levante Valenciano*, "perhaps the girls hitchhiked to the club, the driver had a fatal accident, and the vehicle hasn't yet been found."[15]

After a few days, mere descriptive facts became uninteresting in and of themselves; media outlets thus began to come out with their own interpretations of what had happened. Subtly, a means of recording and producing news focusing attention on emotions rather than facts began to take shape. Emotionality would be used to generate a feeling of identification with the girls. To achieve this—to get people to identify (with) the girls and see themselves in them—emotionality was to be configured as an exceptionally precise bodily technology. This was to be one of the main tools used in the sexual danger narrative. In the *Informe Semanal* report, the journalist shows images of one of the girl's classrooms and asks one of her classmates whether people were fearful. She replies, "Mothers don't want us children to go out late now. . . . They want us home before it gets dark."[16] The shot closes with the empty desk of the teenage girl. Subtly, fear filters through. Together with not knowing what could have happened to them, the fear constitutes a call for caution, lest one's desk be the next to be left empty. Their testimonies, reproduced below, were filmed in the street, surrounded by other people from the town. According to one local, the danger was becoming a reality: "The girls don't want to follow that route."[17] Intimidation was setting in, and these were the first warning signs.

However, there was also a contradictory idea at play: the notion that three girls together could not just disappear. This fostered further mistrust and gave traction to the idea that they

---

15. *El Levante Valenciano*, November 19, 1992.

16. *Informe Semanal*, "¿Dónde están las chicas de Valencia?"

17. *Informe Semanal*, "¿Dónde están las chicas de Valencia?"

could be playing a bad joke on everyone. Part of the groundwork of the narrative was thus laid out, and the teenage girls' conduct began to receive criticism. A close friend of the girls recalls a high school teacher in class openly saying,

> "Bah, they're probably out there partying."
> "The three of them! How could they disappear?"
> "Those girls have gone out partying."
> And we got angry, me and a friend, and we said, "Stop talking about it, you don't know what you're talking about."
> Knowing them, you know, we were like, "It's impossible, it's impossible that they're just out partying, impossible."[18]

They were presumed guilty, even before the information required to assess what had happened was available. After the first week, conjecture and speculation of all sorts about the whereabouts of the teenagers filled newspapers and table talk in equal measure. Stopping the media from dropping the story could mark the difference between all available resources remaining mobilized, or the investigation going through more ordinary channels. As Alcaina recalled:

> At night, the monitoring team gets set up in the mayor's office. I watch the news on all the channels and, depending on where I see the story has died down a little, I simply have to comment on two reports. . . . I mean, if there is not enough coverage in Catalonia, but you have twelve calls from Catalonia, well, that day, in the press, you comment on three from Catalonia, and it [the issue] comes up again there. I mean, like I keep telling you, I hoped to find them alive.[19]

---

18. Marta de la Fuente, interview, October 26, 2011.

19. Alcaina, interview.

Going through the ordinary channels would have meant running the risk of the case being forgotten—precisely what happened with the enforced disappearance of the Aguilar de Campoo girls.[20] The fact that the press and TV did not forget Alcàsser meant that neither did the state security forces, nor institutional representatives, nor even the government itself.

Teresa Domínguez, the accident and crime editor of *El Levante – El Mercantil Valenciano*, covered the Alcàsser case practically in its entirety. During the search, this journalist was in contact with the families' spokesperson (the father of one of the girls). She remembers a conversation that took place a few weeks after the disappearance. In a routine phone call to find out if there was any news, the spokesperson asked her,

"Do you think we'll be able to keep this in the limelight for long?"
She replied, "Look, I'll be honest with you: it's going to depend on you. On whether you know how to work it."[21]

Initially, the instrumentalization of certain marketing strategies to ensure the case would not be forgotten was part of a

---

20. When the Alcàsser crimes came to light, the newspaper *La Vanguardia* recalled the disappearance of some young women from Palencia. At the time the bodies were found, the young women from Aguilar de Campoo had been missing for nine months. The newspaper gave the story the headline, "Un pueblo de Palencia teme que sus dos desaparecidas corran la misma suerte" [A town in Palencia fears their two missing girls have suffered the same fate]. With the exception of this newspaper, which cites this news item in order to make a comparison, the case of the girls from Aguilar de Campoo had no media coverage in the press at the time.

21. Teresa Domínguez, interview, December 16, 2011. Teresa Domínguez has worked for *El Levante – El Mercantil Valenciano* since 1989. *El Levante* is one of the newspapers with the largest circulation in the community of Valencia. In her first four years there, she was an accident and crime subeditor, and she later became section chief. She covered the Alcàsser case from the date of the enforced disappearance until the coverage of the trial.

maneuver considered necessary to guarantee the continuation of the search. As the celebrated French sociologist Pierre Bourdieu puts it,

> You can only break out of the circle by breaking and entering, so to speak. But you can only break and enter through the media. You have to grab the attention of the media, or at least one "medium," so that the story can be picked up and amplified by its competitors.[22]

What at first appeared to be an effective tool in the search for the teenage girls would later transform the whole physiognomy of the Alcàsser case.

As the weeks passed, a broad swath of society became increasingly involved in the investigation. The president of the Valencian government, Joan Lerma, met with the families to offer them resources and support. After the meeting, the father of one of the teenagers said, "We're going to pull out all society's stops to find our daughters."[23] Indeed, every sector of the population was mobilized; they knocked on every door, and no stone was left unturned. During the first week of December, a brigade from a specialized division of the Guardia Civil, the Central Operative Unit (UCO), arrived in Alcàsser to restructure the investigation. The archbishop of Valencia visited the girls' families and asked the faithful, even if they could not attend mass, to pray "three Hail Mary's of the Angelus daily, petitioning the Virgin for each of the girls."[24] The interior minister, José Luis Corcuera, who was in direct contact with the families, publicly promised to do everything he could to find them. The president of the government, Felipe González, met with the parents on Noche Buena, the most important day in the Spanish Christmas

---

22. Pierre Bourdieu, *On Television*, trans. Priscilla Parkhurst Fergusen (New York: The New Press, 1998), 26.

23. *Las Provincias*, November 27, 1992.

24. *Las Provincias*, December 1, 1992.

calendar, which falls on December 24. Hundreds of calls placing the girls all over Spain were received by the Guardia Civil and town hall offices.

The media gave coverage to all kinds of speculation—for instance, that "the police are investigating whether the Alcàsser girls traveled in a Granada FC coach."[25] At the same time, the idea that the teenagers were being held against their will took hold: "Corcuera believes that the girls have been kidnapped," or even, "They have been taken to a harem."[26] The news of the disappearance traversed borders. It became an international story. The idea that the girls might not be in Spain prompted the Ministry of Foreign Affairs to distribute twenty thousand posters with photographs of the teenagers to its embassies. Alcaina recalls they were "posters in color, in French and English, German, Flemish, Russian, and Moroccan: in seven languages."[27] He added that at the height of the fruit and vegetable season, lorry drivers leaving for Europe put "the poster on all the motorways and highways."[28] Meanwhile, the newspaper *Diario 16* reported that "Interpol is looking for the Alcàsser girls in Algeria despite the Pamplona trail."[29]

In parallel to the investigation, the girls' lives were topics of conversation: news of them, and about them, generated social participation. The media were constructing protagonists whose silence did nothing more than stoke anticipation for an exclusive about their return. And such a return would have set the media calculating how that scoop could boost their audience shares. On the TVE program *¿Quién sabe dónde?* journalist Paco Lobatón gave the floor to the father of one of the girls. As journalist Joan Manuel Oleaque reported, "He told viewers to pay

---

25. *El Levante Valenciano*, November 24, 1992.

26. *Las Provincias*, December 1, 1992; *El País*, January 3, 1993.

27. Alcaina, interview.

28. Alcaina, interview.

29. *Diario 16*, January 16, 1993.

attention to the *De Tú a Tú* program with Nieves Herrero the next day because he was going to give them a surprise."[30] The idea of offering something unexpected as bait to bolster curiosity and expectations not only worked on the audience but also established competition between programs. According to Oleaque, in truth, "the people in charge of Lobatón's program" were the most surprised of all and "were worried about whether [the father] knew where the missing girls were and had decided to tell the story on Antena 3 TV."[31] The return of the teenagers began to be discussed as an exclusive. However, the surprise the father had been talking about was in fact the on-set appearance of the musical duo Platón (who were well known and a big hit with teenage girls at the time) and a professional skater the girls (who were keen on the sport) admired. A friend of the girls also took part in the program. She was the focus of much attention because she was one of the last people to have seen them.

The reason for getting people the girls admired on the program was to convince them to return. The professional skater sent them a message encouraging them to go back home. And, in a short presentation of the musical duo, Nieves Herrero explained that they had gone through a similar experience in which both members—who were brothers—had run away from home because of family problems. As one of the duo said:

> I think that if they're listening to me, they ought to realize, they shouldn't be so silly that they wait two years. I mean, there's always another way to go about it, an alternative, instead of disappearing, or running away from something.[32]

---

30. Joan Manuel Oleaque, *Desde las tinieblas: Un descenso al caso Alcàsser* (Barcelona: Diagonal, 2002), 153.

31. Joan Manuel Oleaque, *Desde las tinieblas*, 153.

32. Transcribed fragments of Nieves Herrero's *De Tú a Tú* special, broadcast live from Alcàsser on January 28, 1993, on Antena 3.

Thus, what was supposed to be an appeal to promote the search for the girls ended up reprimanding them. Moreover, both singers were convinced that the teenagers' problems had probably been blown out of proportion. One added, "Whatever's happening to them has probably happened to all of us here too, just perhaps worse, I mean, I don't think it's such a big deal it can't be dealt with, right?"[33]

On the basis of such statements, it would be difficult to infer that the teenagers might be being held against their will. Instead, the TV program's guests made it sound like it was all some kind of childish game—just some kids cooking up a tempest in a teakettle. Moreover, the idea that they might be in trouble at home cast suspicion on the families and put them on the defensive. They had to look for their daughters and, at the same time, make it clear that the teenagers had no problems at home and therefore could not "fear going home," because they were not strict parents and "have never beat" them.[34]

By the end of January 1993, even before the appearance of the lifeless bodies of the teenage girls, the media maelstrom had got completely out of control. In the seventy-six days of the search, the media had effectively managed to answer the question "Who were the Alcàsser girls?" but not the fundamental question, "Where are the girls from Valencia?"[35] The process of society's identification with the teenagers was intense and sustained; it was as if a net had been flung over society at large, with patches sown from each individuals' emotions. Not only was the sexual danger narrative produced thanks to this initial symbiosis, but its viability was also ensured.

---

33. *De Tú a Tú*, special live broadcast, January 28, 1993.

34. *El País*, November 17, 1992.

35. This is the translation of the title of the *Informe Semanal* episode "¿Dónde están las chicas de Valencia?" aired November 21, 1992, on TVE, and an article in *Las Provincias* published on December 13, 1992—Trans.

"Bodies That Matter"[36]

On the morning of January 27, 1993, two beekeepers informed the Guardia Civil that, while on a routine walk near the beehives on their property, they found the half-buried lifeless remains of what they thought could be a human body. After a few hours, once its relevance became clear, the press was unofficially informed.

Even before the families were notified, the media reported that three corpses had been found in a municipality near Alcàsser. The appearance of the lifeless remains of the three girls set off a bout of fierce competition between different media outlets. In the absence of information about what had happened, the exclusive focused on the suffering. First came the pain, the indignation, and the thirst for revenge; the gaze rests elsewhere, past the bodies. Afterward, there was no turning back: the girls are public, their pain is public, their lives and their voices are public, their story is public. Above all, their bodies are public.

In the early afternoon, the news reached the *Las Provincias* editorial department. Teresa Laguna, a subeditor at the newspaper, remembered it clearly: "That day, at about 4:30 p.m., the editor in chief said, 'They've just called with a tip-off. It seems they've found the Alcàsser girls.' It was top secret."[37] This was the outline of the first exclusive. The rest of the media would hear the news within three to four hours. At around seven or

---

36. The title of this section is borrowed from Judith Butler's book *Bodies That Matter* because the significance of the corpses' discovery does not stem exclusively from the terrible outcome, but also derives from the material and discursive limits that, from that moment onward, begin to be defined. Another, perhaps more import, reason is that, as we shall see, the Alcàsser sexual danger narrative cautioned a whole generation of women in a bodily sense.

37. Teresa Laguna, interview, December 14, 2011. Teresa Laguna has worked for different media outlets. She began her career as a journalist on a radio program on *Cope*. Later, she continued her career alternating between radio and print journalism. She covered the Alcàsser sex crimes for the newspaper *Las Provincias*, from the enforced disappearance of the teenagers until the trial was held.

seven thirty that evening, the news agency EFE distributed the teletype of the discovery of the bodies. Teresa Domínguez, a subeditor at the newspaper *El Levante Valenciano*, explained:

> The story was going to be another newspaper's exclusive. The smart thing the Guardia Civil did—a particular Guardia Civil officer, in fact, but I'm not going to give you his name—was to cut off that exclusive. He called EFE, the EFE correspondent, and said, "All I'm saying is this: they've been found, the three girls have appeared. Officially it hasn't been confirmed, but you can say that the bodies of three people who look like teenagers have been found."[38]

Las Provincias was the first newspaper and the first media outlet to arrive on the scene:

> They told us, "The Tous area. You're on your own."[39] We couldn't ask too many questions in case we raised suspicions. So we took the car and drove through totally unlikely places, lost in the mountains, until we came across the Land Rover of the Guardia Civil on one of the roads and we thought, "Well, we're on the right track."[40]

A few hours later, a whole procession of different media outlets headed for the scene. The first reports were confusing, but rumors spread, and the story was confirmed on the 9:00 p.m. news programs.

The town had a protocol for informing families in the event of a sudden development. However, in some cases, the

---

38. Teresa Domínguez, interview, December 16, 2011. EFE is the leading news agency in Spanish—Trans.

39. The place the bodies were found is the La Romana ravine, in the municipality of Tous (Valencia).

40. Laguna, interview.

media were the first to pass on the news of the discovery of the bodies. Carme Miquel, a teacher and principal at a school in Alcàsser, recalled,

> When I found out, I went to Míriam's mother's house. She didn't know anything about it. I went there to see what was going on. And at that moment, Nieves Herrero called to ask if she knew anything.
>
> She said, "Do you know anything?"—Nieves Herrero already knew—"Have you heard anything?" she asked.
>
> I hadn't said anything, because I didn't know how to tell her, and I thought someone would have to prepare her for it.
>
> Míriam's mother said, "Well, no, no, I don't know anything, my daughter's teacher is here, I don't know. . . . I haven't heard anything. . . . What do you mean?" she asked.
>
> "Well, they say that . . . I don't know, I don't know."
>
> Then, in the end, of course, the town council gave her the news, with the psychologist, in a different way.[41]

Obtaining testimony, in this case from Míriam's mother, appeared to take precedence over any consideration for the sheer shock families would face on finding out about the death of their daughters from journalists. However, both the tip-off about the discovery of the bodies and Nieves Herrero's phone

---

41. At the time of the interview, Carme Miquel had been a teacher and a principal for twenty-two years at the state school in Alcàsser, with a three-year break in which she worked at the Department of Education helping promote teaching the Valencian language in schools. In 1964, with a group of young teachers, she was part of the driving force behind what she defines as "the first postwar movement of pedagogical renewal in Valencia." She has published several books and articles and contributes to different publications including *El Levante Valenciano*. With regard to the Alcàsser crimes, she was active in combating the most reactionary discourses on the death penalty and is firmly in favor of education and schooling. She was also close to the family of one of the teenage girls and taught two of them for several years.

call to the mother appear trivial in comparison to what would later appear in print and broadcast media.

Within a few hours, the town had been invaded in equal parts by the police, the media, and members of the public. As Joan Manuel Oleaque recounted:

> The police were everywhere when it was made public, with the whole town cordoned off. It was like a film. I had never seen so many police, not even when the pope comes. It was unbelievable. It was also the first time this sort of thing was televised.[42]

Once again, the town square served as the place for the population to channel their uncertainty and consternation. The relatives went to the town hall, where the authorities and a team of health workers were waiting to give them the news. The town square was the stage where mourning and spectacle came together: the former a sign of respect, of accompaniment; the latter an overwhelming, unchanneled sorrow that was to reach new depths when apprehended through the camera lens. As Carme remembered, "There was a sepulchral silence in the village square. It was the day the bodies had been found. But when a camera popped up and anyone got started—'Kill them! Kill them!'—that's where all the cameras flocked."[43]

What was once a square was to be transformed, little by little, over the days, into a gallows. To my mind, the square suggests a space in which social forms and norms are breathed. This terrain was to metaphorically represent the place where two forms of violence against women were to take shape: torture and explicit

---

42. Joan Manuel Oleaque was forty-five years old at the time of writing and lived in Catarroja, where he was born. He is a journalist, writer, and lecturer at the Valencian International University. He covered the Alcàsser crimes for the magazine *El Temps* and authored articles for *El País*. Oleaque is also the author of the book *Desde las tinieblas: Un descenso al caso Alcàsser*.

43. Miquel, interview, October 27, 2011.

cautioning. In this sense, the square evokes the place of public spectacle, where the torture of the body was inflicted as punishment in full view of everyone. And, as the story progressed, the violence enacted on the body was to merge with the discipline of the cautionary tale.

The very next day, January 28, headlines "about the end of the Alcàsser girls" sprawled across newspapers' front pages. *Las Provincias*, the newspaper with the exclusive, showed the first photographs of the scene: "The Alcàsser girls found murdered. Handcuffed and marked by violence: they were found buried, wrapped in a rug."[44] Without verifying the information, sensationalist, incredibly morbid headlines appeared in quick succession. *El Levante Valenciano* read: "The Alcàsser girls found dead. The girls were buried in a pit, piled up, tied up and in an advanced state of decomposition. Two of the girls' heads had been separated from their trunks and one's watch had stopped at 11:10."[45] The appeal to meanings with close ties to mystery and morbidity captured the curiosity of those who wanted to resolve the enigma of the "watch that stopped at 11:10." This was the beginning of a story that was to trivialize sexual violence while constructing a political narrative about sexual danger.

In those early days following the crime, journalists were desperate not to be left behind in the news race. Domínguez remembered, "When they appeared, you can imagine the media frenzy that story could generate. It was like the newspaper was about to blow and we had to start running stories."[46] Running stories took precedence over any ethical code. Another journalist recounted:

> What's more, newspapers even copied each other. At that time, you couldn't do it on the internet, but at one in

---

44. *Las Provincias*, January 28, 1993.

45. *El Levante Valenciano*, January 28, 1993.

46. Teresa Domínguez, interview.

the morning the first copy was already being sold in that square in Valencia. I remember we copied each other.[47]

Neither the lack of information nor the absence of first-hand sources appeared to constitute much of an impediment to running stories: "*Las Provincias* published some nonsense: if they had found a rug, well, we copied them."[48] In those first two days, the newspapers with the highest circulation at the state level and some of the regional papers sidestepped the more lurid headlines. But, as competition between media outlets increased, all of them ended up making indiscriminate use of any attention-grabbing media or rhetorical recourse.

The place the girls had been found was shown: the pit, the map of the area, and the coffins. The position of the corpses, the arm sticking out of the ground bearing a huge watch, and the objects found at the site were all drawn up as a vignette. The state in which the bodies had been found was described. There was no shortage of shots of the families approaching the town hall, where they were told the news, and of the coffins being taken to the forensic pathologist, accompanied by the first statements from relatives and friends.

Of particular interest are the hours between the moment of discovery and the point when details of the autopsies were first made public. Against a background of total chaos, the meanings conveyed at that initial stage went even more unnoticed. It was, however, during this exact interval that the whole corporal ordering of the narrative took shape. While waiting for official news of the details of what had happened, the sobs, the grief, and the emotionality were to pave the way for the body to become the recipient of the discipline of sexual terror.

47. Interview with anonymous print journalist, December 13, 2011. At the express wish of the informant, their personal details and those of the media outlet to which they belong are omitted.

48. Interview with anonymous print journalist, December 13, 2011.

Television, to no one's great surprise, was to replicate what had been done in the print media in its own sphere of influence. In this respect, it seems particularly important to focus on the *Pasa la Vida* afternoon program, presented by María Teresa Campos on TVE. In this program, conversation centered on the panelists' "red lines"—those boundaries that should not have been crossed. Their discussion maps neatly onto the struggle between progress made by the feminist movement and nostalgia for a past society that ought to be resuscitated. At the time the program was broadcast, the only information available was that three bodies showing signs of violence had been found. In the absence of facts, the discussion was supposed to address concerns sent in by dozens of parents: "María Teresa, tell us, what do we do with these children?"[49] It was with this question that Concha Galán, the program's copresenter, opened a debate that was supposedly about what had happened in Alcàsser. This talk show, and the statements made on it, do not constitute inconsequential utterances; rather, they deal in meanings that reveal society and its entire functional and organizational structure.

In the first place, the Alcàsser crimes were to open the door to a revision of the institution of the family. As a rule, this was almost always accompanied, and in fact preceded, by the looming shadow of a younger generation who had been given too much freedom. *Pasa la Vida* was a program viewers thought of as representing family values, and this was why they asked for its position on the case:

> Parents have called in saying, "Your show's a family show. It's a show that makes us feel united, that makes us feel like part of the family; please discuss this issue. We're

---

49. *Pasa la Vida*, presented by María Teresa Campos, aired January 28, 1993, on TVE.

scared to death, we don't know what to do with our boys, we've given them too much freedom. We need a sort of state of exception for the boys. What do we do with our daughters? Because it seems like the world's gone mad."[50]

For the sake of clarity, it makes sense to highlight the gendered distinction articulated above. The first statement, "We need a sort of state of exception for the boys," uses the masculine (*niños*, which can be translated as *children* or *boys*), whereas the anguished question "What do we do with our daughters?" refers directly to girls. Let us examine and reconstruct this fine analytical distinction through metaphor: for the daughters, a cautionary message; for the sons, a state of exception, which, in the framework of this study, entails having the capacity to incorporate *bare life* as an originary political element. Moreover, the recurrent use of the term *freedom* gets entangled with concerns about the youth not being brought up properly—a youth that, inexplicably, seems to be running wild. But, in addition to the doubt surrounding what to do with the youth, the statement also points to the anguish produced by not knowing exactly what to do with your daughters. It is young women who are, almost explicitly, placed at the center of all the suggested corrective measures.

The presenter, for her part, stressed the importance of approaching the issue from the perspective of defending family values: "This is the issue we are going to deal with today, from the point of view of family."[51] This perspective alone forced a considerable narrowing of the field of analysis. The starting point for the sexual danger narrative was framed in terms of healing the institution of the family.

Before the discussion began, there was a live phone call with Francisco Granados, the government delegate in Valencia. Granados provided an overview of the investigations

50. *Pasa la Vida*, January 28, 1993.

51. *Pasa la Vida*, January 28, 1993.

being conducted to determine the causes of death. The work, Granados said, was in the hands of a team made up of three professors of forensic medicine and two forensic experts. The government delegate also confirmed that, at midday that same day, the relatives had identified the bodies. Finally, Granados stressed that it was still too early to give details. In this conversation, Campos, who was particularly concerned with the results of the autopsies, persisted in asking:

> "Can't you say anything, or give us any news, Mr. Granados? I mean, is it that we don't know how the girls died, if they were beaten to death or, well, I don't know, strangled, or shot? Hasn't anything about that been leaked?"
>
> "At the moment it isn't possible. Besides, it's not a question of it leaking out. It's now a question of providing the public with conclusions based on a serious autopsy, carried out by professionals."[52]

The government delegate thus called for seriousness and caution, so as not to pass on erroneous details or misconceptions.

What was truly significant about the program, however, was the debate that followed. The talk show began by conveying the idea of a deep-rooted concern in society and the family in relation to youth freedom: "Tell us what to do; I'm letting my son go out and come back whenever he wants. Should we go back to having a curfew?"[53] Pilar Sánchez, a social worker specialized in working with young people, thought the priority ought to be raising awareness and talking to teenagers openly about the existing danger, rather than imposing martial law. According to this expert, setting boundaries was of no use if young people did not know what to do when something happened to them. For example, she added that women

---

52. *Pasa la Vida*, January 28, 1993.

53. *Pasa la Vida*, January 28, 1993.

are always more aware. If something happens to you:
Where should you go? What should you do? I would like
to tell all the parents out there to stay calm and, above
all, not to play it up; to be realistic about the fact that we
have to show them that danger exists and that kids have
to learn to measure it, because it's there.[54]

Her reasoning essentializes fear and danger. That is to say, danger
exists per se, as neither subject to anything nor a consequence of
anything and must be submitted to. What the social worker did
anticipate, quite accurately, was that after the Alcàsser sex crimes,
young people, particularly young women, would in-corporate
new information about sexual danger that was to be extremely
effective.

Based on the idea that youth was synonymous with excess
and, therefore, with the absence of authority, the debate
focused on associating the dangers new generations faced with
insufficient family discipline and organization. Campos suggested, as a direct consequence of this, "I suppose that many of
you will feel deeply frustrated as mothers."[55] Thus, the TV presenter placed the responsibility for the Alcàsser case on women
in equal parts: on the youth, and specifically on the behavior
of young women; and on mothers, who were supposed to raise
young people.

The concern, then, was how to regain the power over young
people that had been lost. As Sánchez argued, "Authority, when
established progressively, allows the child to get used to living
by the rules, and to the fact that rules exists, and that if you do
not comply with the rules, you get in trouble."[56]

When the discussion focused on the lack of authority, it
became clear that this absence was seen to have potentially led

54. *Pasa la Vida*, January 28, 1993.

55. *Pasa la Vida*, January 28, 1993.

56. *Pasa la Vida*, January 28, 1993.

to the horrendous turn of events. In this sense, the message being conveyed was that failure to follow the rules might have put the teenage girls in mortal danger. This somehow sanctioned the implicit—sexist—convention, by which three women are seen to put themselves in danger merely by being on their own in a given place at a given time.

In the program, the main issue at stake was not what to do about sexual violence. Instead, taking its existence as a given, the question was how to convey accurate information about it without creating panic: "'If you want to go out at night and stay out until the morning,' tell them, 'You can't drink, you can't come back by car, you can't hitchhike.' Is this the right message? Yes, it is."[57] Thus, the only practical solution was for women to give up certain spaces and activities in order to ensure their protection: "They shouldn't be going to clubs. They'll have time for that. But if they do go, go and pick them up; it doesn't cost you anything."[58]

The renowned journalist Antonio Álvarez Solís, on the other hand, brought a very distinctive idea of freedom to the debate:

> I believe we have to educate them to exercise their will, not just to exercise freedom. Freedom is also an idea of renunciation, of order . . . of achieving things, a certain noble order in one's own life. They have to be educated in the exercise of will, but they need to know that they are in their own world; the world shouldn't be presented to them as something external.[59]

Álvarez Solís here presents freedom as the internal logic of the established order itself. In other words, the rules define

---

57. *Pasa la Vida,* January 28, 1993.

58. *Pasa la Vida,* January 28, 1993.

59. *Pasa la Vida,* January 28, 1993.

freedom, and this disappears when anyone's will goes against the rules. Therefore, you have the freedom to *not* deviate from the norm. In fact, that the term *will* is closely tied to the category of "woman." It was not so much a question of discussing the absence of family authority, but of the nonexistent respect for the will and authority of women.

On this program, which had dedicated significant airtime to the Alcàsser crimes, there was no mention of the hypothetical perpetrators of the crimes, nor of their motive or under what structures they could operate: there was nothing about violence against women, and nothing about what allows it to happen. The focus of the debate was young people and how badly they were being brought up. In this context, Sánchez concluded by stating, "Nobody alters their conduct unless that type of behavior has negative consequences." In a way, this expert had laid down both the foundations and the objectives of the sexual danger narrative in this statement. In other words, what was expected of the Alcàsser crimes was that they would serve as punishment; that they would force young people to mend their ways; that they would encourage a return to the family. And a return to the past would mean a step backward for women's individual liberties.

Paco Lobatón or Nieves Herrero?: The Restitution of the Public Body

> *In editorial rooms, publishing houses, and similar venues, a "rating mindset" reigns. Wherever you look, people are thinking in terms of market success.*
>
> **Pierre Bourdieu,** *On Television*

In the brief period of time between the discovery of the bodies and the publication of the autopsies, a series of events took place that were to rend a decisive breach in the media, in society at large, and in the construction of the narrative itself. The initial chaos was nothing more than the bulwark against which the subsequent coverage of the crimes was justified. The spectacle and the exclusive on grief functioned as a catalyst and, also, as a neutralizer for crimes of sexual violence.

The programs broadcast live that night, *¿Quién Sabe Dónde?* with Paco Lobatón and *De Tú a Tú* with Nieves Herrero, are particularly important for the elucidation and analysis of these issues. These programs transformed a case of sexual violence into a soap opera that trivialized sexist violence, turning it into a consumer product. To borrow an idea from Judith Walkowitz's historical study: all the myths of the day were brought together in a story published in installments. The Alcàsser serial was just beginning.

In my opinion, that night was the beginning not only of the reality show but also of an incipient simulacrum—a concept I borrow from sociologist Jean Baudrillard to ground a description of the episodic spectacle the Alcàsser crimes became.[60] Baudrillard argues that in advanced societies, any

---

60. Natalia Fernández Díaz has carried out a study on sexual violence and its representation in the Spanish press. Her research covers the period from 1989 to 1993, including some news items published at the beginning of 1994. In her investigation, she highlights the key role of the media in the reproduction and creation of sexist prejudice. Díaz also makes a brief assessment of the introduction of the *reality show* and the *snuff film*, which is of great relevance to this investigation. The author states: "The fashion for debate on sexual harassment was soon overtaken by rape as spectacle, packaged by the media in reality show formats, and later by domestic violence which, up to the time of writing (2003), is still a constant feature in the society pages of Spanish newspapers. A constant, by the way, in which the focus is placed on the spectacle rather than condemnation, in this way we see the perfect process of hybridization of genres such as pornography, *snuff*, or reality show, if not open hyperrealism." Natalia Fernández Díaz, *La violencia sexual y su representación en la prensa* (Madrid: Anthropos, 2003). On reality shows, see also: Rosa María Ganga, "El *reality show* a la hora de la merienda," *Revista Latina de Comunicación Social* 26 (February 2000); and the blog post by María Jesus

event tends to get degraded such that it becomes a spectacle or an object of consumption.[61] For this to happen, it is irrelevant whether what happened is true or false. Representations, information, interpretations, and broadcasts are equalized as mere simulacra of reality. The Alcàsser crimes were put on stage as a social simulacrum: a spectacle with a script adhering to a system whose structural logic is the rape, torture, and murder of women. Given their sheer brutality, the details of sexual torture recounted directed the viewers' gaze toward the horror and away from the analytical, away from any possibility of perspective. These programs contributed to the construction of a narrative that sought to undermine a generation of young women's individual and sexual freedoms.

Both programs' effectiveness stemmed from the fact that they supplemented the visceral exposure of pain with testimonies that could be interpreted as "objective." The appearance on set of specialist doctors, institutional representatives, and witnesses who had been present the moment the bodies were found gave the programs a degree of credibility. This supposed objectivity also served the function of concealing the very sexist subjectivity that shaped the programs.

My starting point is the idea that one of the results of the Alcàsser sexual danger narrative was the construction of a socially cemented *public body*—that of the teenage girls. *De Tú a Tú* and *¿Quién Sabe Dónde?* made possible the restitution of the public body for a whole generation of young women, in such a way that cautioning and chastisement constituted both explicit and implicit messages.

Lamarca Lapuente, "El *reality show* en España: Definición, características, tipos, antecedentes y claves del éxito; Cine y *reality show*," *Artes Digital*, November 3, 2009.

61. Jean Baudrillard, *Simulations*, trans. Phil Foss, Paul Patton, and Paul Beitchman (New York: Semiotext(e), 1983).

Debts and Dividends on the Pain and Suffering Scoop

On the afternoon of Thursday, January 28, 1993, hundreds of people gathered in the town square, where the media joined them. Producers, councilors, directors, and cameras were finalizing the details before the broadcast. This is how Andrés Domínguez remembered it:

> My sister asked me to go with her and I went. So, they organized them and placed them on stage in a specific way. I stayed below, watching the program. I remember that they told them all, "Come and stand like this, everyone," giving more prominence to their closest friends and, above all, to one girl, the one who was ill, who was also going to go to the party, but didn't in the end.[62]

The props were thus organized, the chairs that the protagonists were to occupy prepared. And a special place was left for the central character: the teenage girl who did not go out on the night of the crimes, who was to become the figure used to construct a lesson to chastise and caution all the other young people. The rest was simulation, decoration. As Teresa Laguna recalled, "Olga Viza and the team were choosing the people to stand at the back, creating the banner for them to stand behind, to make the set for the news, for the live TV broadcast."[63]

From the outset, competition between the different media outlets made consistency in information an exclusively aesthetic requirement. The manipulation to which the teenagers' closest friends were subjected can only be understood in the context of a debt, and also as a consequence of a feeling of responsibility toward the family members. Elisabet Pla, a friend of the teenagers, explained:

---

62. Andrés Domínguez, interview, December 17, 2010.

63. Laguna, interview.

The impression of those who were targeted more at some point, or participated in something, was that it was out of goodwill. It could even be that some of the families, at some point, asked one of my friends to do it. . . . At that point, you say of course you want to help. And you can't do anything about how you are treated, because, on top of it all, you're just a fifteen-year-old kid.[64]

It was the media's perception and indications that a debt had been accrued over the search period that solidified the identification with the girls. One of the reasons why relatives and people close to the girls participated in the programs that night, putting their own mourning aside, was precisely because of this false idea of a debt owed. Journalist Genar Martí observed:

Their parents got used a lot, and they, who'd been torn apart by what had happened, were taken from set to set. I even have the feeling they were told they had to do it because of all the help they'd got before, giving the disappearance of their daughters a chance. It made them feel a bit like they had the responsibility to be there, instead of at home at a time like that.[65]

The great scoop that consisted of sitting the teenagers' relatives down on set the very day their bodies were identified

---

64. Elisabet Pla, interview, October 26, 2011.

65. Genar Martí, interview, December 16, 2011. The journalist Genar Martí has worked mainly in the accident and crime section and the courts section of Canal 9. He covered the news of the enforced disappearance of the teenage girls when he was working for Onda Cero and, after the trial, as chief accident and crime editor for Canal 9. A few years later, he made an investigative report with a hidden camera entitled "Alcàsser, vides marcades," which was widely broadcast and had a considerable impact, and which aimed to condemn the economic irregularities of the foundation created as a result of the Alcàsser crimes. He continues to work for Canal 9 and covers current affairs reports.

could only have been brought about through a sort of binding obligation. On this vein, Carme Miquel recalls the gratitude that the mother of one of the girls expressed toward Herrero in particular:

> They had a feeling of gratitude toward the media. Because, of course, according to them, they'd done a lot. It's true: they'd shown the image of the girls a lot and, because they felt grateful, they collaborated with the media.[66]

The families, we must understand, were receiving in their homes not just a journalist but the person who, in the search process, had mobilized all the resources of broadcast media to help find the girls. In this sense, the families were opening their doors to someone they understood as an intimate acquaintance, with whom they had maintained a close and constant relationship spanning the preceding months.

The TV channels set up their sets in Alcàsser: TVE in the town hall itself, and Antena 3 in the concert hall, a venue that could host a large number of people. *¿Quién Sabe Dónde?* and *De Tú a Tú* were broadcast live in the same time slot.

Herrero kicked off the *De Tú a Tú* program. The first image showed a scene made up of the family members of two of the teenagers—dads, siblings, and the mother of one of the girls. Behind them came the rest of the relatives—uncles, aunts, cousins, grandmothers. The journalist, seated in the center, commenced.

> Good evening. This is not going to be a normal *De Tú a Tú* program today. I think I owe it to the families of Alcàsser because week after week, after that November 13, we have shared, I think with the same intensity as their friends and relatives, the families' distress.[67]

---

66. Miquel, interview.

67. *De Tú a Tú*, special live broadcast, January 28, 1993.

This "same distress" Herrero said she shared with the families was, it seems, what led to the excessive zeal for access to information. As José Gil, municipal psychologist in Alcàsser, recalls,

> I remember on the day of the funeral [January 30] a journalist from Antena 3, who was very well known then, was sitting at one of the parent's houses to stop the others getting interviews. It wasn't Nieves Herrero; it was her assistant, who was also very well known.[68]

Like Herrero, Lobatón began *¿Quién Sabe Dónde?* with a show of solidarity that disguised a yearning for the exclusive scoop:

> The hearts of all the citizens of this country are today in Alcàsser. And that is the reason why we're here. Beyond any journalistic agenda, having stood beside these families in the search from the beginning, seventy-five days ago, we wanted to be here, and we're here today.[69]

Through it all, Lobatón retained his relative credibility. Society at large was extremely critical of Herrero, but Lobatón came off much better, his reputation bolstered by the sense that he had guided the program, and the interventions in it, with greater seriousness and respect. However, save a few of the boundaries Herrero crossed on air, for the most part Lobatón conducted himself in the same way. Genar Martí recalled:

---

68. José Gil, interview, December 17, 2010. As of this writing, José Gil remains the Alcàsser municipal psychologist. He was in charge of coordinating and treating the families, as well as to those close to them and locals in need of psychological help. He participated in a few media outlets and wrote op-eds condemning the role of the press in the case.

69. Transcribed fragment from Paco Lobatón's *¿Quién Sabe Dónde?* special broadcast live from Alcàsser on January 28, 1993, on TVE.

I remember going from one place to another and being amazed to see the sets that had been put up at the concert hall and the town hall. And then the producer, I think it was Lobatón's producer, who went around grabbing people, like, by the arm, taking them to his program and trying to steal them from the other one. I remember that recruitment drive above all.[70]

Getting the first statements while stopping the relatives from talking to other media was a widespread practice, especially among those media outlets that had given the issue lots of coverage during the enforced disappearance. Lobatón's performance was endorsed by a misogynist society that saw Herrero's interventions as an abominable malpractice, while perceiving Lobatón's—macho—journalism as rigorous. And yet, that afternoon, before the programs were broadcast, a vicious battle had been brewing over the exclusive and the documents, along with the trafficking of testimonies.

Lobatón began his program by going through footage of the relatives he had interviewed that morning. Here, he explained the reasons he did not have footage of one of the families:

We were also able to visit Desireé Hernández's parents. Of all the parents, they are probably the ones who have had the most difficulty in coping with the situation. They accepted our visit but begged us to leave the cameras and microphones outside.[71]

Lobatón put forward this idea in a context in which the other two families—who had in fact committed to Herrero's program—had granted him interviews so that *¿Quién Sabe Dónde?* could be broadcast that same night. Interpreting, on air,

---

70. Martí, interview.

71. *¿Quién Sabe Dónde?*, January 28, 1993.

that the Hernández-Folch family's refusal to appear on the program was a product of their struggle to cope with the news was a way of reappropriating part of the suffering and incorporating it into the show. Otherwise, Lobatón could well have omitted his personal assessment of how the family was handling the news and respected their express desire not to cave to the emotional (and televisual) blackmail of having to provide testimony of their grief.

The anatomy of pain and the scoop on suffering were an indispensable part of the construction of the sexual danger narrative and its incorporation.

The Ritual of Pain and the Stolen Testimonies

Several commentators on the Alcàsser crimes and the story's handling suggest that this case marked a turning point in the media: in Nieves Herrero's *De Tú a Tú* special, they see the birth of *telebasura* (literally, trash TV).[72] Confirmation of this genesis was largely based on those elements that contributed to the morbid presentation of the story, as well as to the broadcast of distressing images and testimonies without ethical qualms. To my mind, what these elements were doing was pushing for social change rather than a shift in the media. It was not the media that instituted changes to the way it operated but society that was

---

72. For more detailed information on the concept of *telebasura* and its different interpretations from a journalistic perspective, see Carlos Elías Pérez, *Telebasura y periodismo* (Madrid: Libertarias/Prodhufi, 2004); Lorenzo Díaz, *Informe sobre la televisión en España (1989–1998)* (Madrid: Ediciones B, 1999); and Lorenzo Díaz, *La caja sucia: Telebasura en España* (Madrid: La Esfera de los Libros, 2005). For a more general overview of the media, see Ignacio Ramonet, *La tiranía de los medios de comunicación* (Madrid: Debate, 1998). Several authors cite the Alcàsser crimes as a case that changed the way television was produced and the press. Íñigo Marauri, *Evolución en el tratamiento de los sucesos en la prensa diaria de información general en España (1977–2000)*, unpublished thesis.

to construct the sexual danger narrative, using the media as its main means of dissemination. Therefore, I reject the idea that the turning point happened on TV with the birth of *telebasura*. The issue was not that the media suddenly veered toward reality TV; it was that reality TV served as a tool for the preservation of the sexual status quo and helped stop the crimes being considered in political terms. The shift introduced by the narration of the Alcàsser crimes took place in the social sphere, and specifically, I argue, in the bodies of women. It was women who were directly affected by the story.

Throughout the Alcàsser sexual danger narrative, the acute sense of identification with the suffering of the teenage girls is clearly a defining characteristic of the pain experienced. Moreover, the fact that this took place by way of a spectacle furthered its perpetuation in collective memory. *¿Quién Sabe Dónde?* and *De Tú a Tú* made this sense of identification their discursive banner. Herrero provided the image; Lobatón gave it a voice. Together, they built the body of a whole generation—a generation of people obliged to keep remembering that their lives had been saved. Identification with the girls constitutes a way of producing truth in which the story of the young women's lives was complemented, in equal parts, by the story of their deaths.

The voice gives the story emotions; the scoop Lobatón offered the viewers of *¿Quién Sabe Dónde?* that night is the subjective sound of existence, a proof of life, an act of existence:

> Now, at 9:36 a.m., I would like to invite you to listen to one of the voices that are absent today. We came across it, by chance, when we were visiting the family of Toñi Gómez. Her mother, evoking the memory of her daughter and the last day she spoke to her, that Friday, just before the disappearance, told us she had been on the local radio and had given a shout-out to all her friends and, of course, Desi and Míriam. She herself had made a recording of that speech, of which she was immensely

proud. And you can see, in the recording you are about to hear, that she was really happy; she had great plans for the weekend.[73]

In the recording, the teenager can be heard requesting a song and talking to the program's presenter, "Toñi says that she wants to dedicate the record to her friends and then lists and mentions—among others—Míriam and Desireé."[74] The radio presenter asked her what she was going to do that weekend, to which she replied there was no way she was staying at home. The video montage combined the voice-over of the recording with images of the family shot that same morning. In them, one of her brothers and her sister appear sitting in her room, listening to the recording. When the recording reaches the point at which Antonia tells the announcer there was no way she was staying in, her sister, who was in a crouch, burst into tears. The voice (Antonia's own) had the ability to bring the "absent voice" back to life. Clearly this is a recording that can be identified as a prescriptive text, proposing rules of conduct—a recording that, like the story, worked as a warning, a reminder of what might not have happened if she had not been so eager to go out the day before.

The exploitation of suffering was often disguised as solidarity with the families. In a night of intense speculation, pain was camouflaged as aid: "We are going to try to get all the testimonies here," said Herrero, "all the people with relationships to Míriam, Desireé, and Toñi. Because we want to get as close to them as we can. To join in their pain."[75] Almost the whole first part of the two programs was devoted to the suffering of the relatives, while another large portion was dedicated to description of what had happened, that is, how and where the events

73. *¿Quién Sabe Dónde?*, January 28, 1993.

74. *El País*, January 29, 1993.

75. *De Tú a Tú*, January 28, 1993.

took place. This was followed by explicit questions about the state of the bodies. They traced the life history of the girls, in the broadest sense.

Thus, pain acquired an objectively relevant meaning in the narration of sexual danger. The graphic document that came to represent the pain scoop—in big letters—was broadcast live, at minute seventeen of Herrero's program:

> *De Tú a Tú* has spent twenty-four hours with the people of Alcàsser, with the families, and we've witnessed a meeting that I think had been eagerly awaited for hours: the meeting of Fernando and his wife. His wife had been aching to hold him. He was aching to hold her. I'd like you to share the pain, the intense pain of these families. We captured this moment, but I'm sure it was the same for all the other families. Let's share their pain.[76]

The encounter to which the journalist refers is the moment when, for the first time after hearing the news of their daughter's murder, the father and mother of the teenager met. A troubled Herrero invites us to "share their pain" and, as if it were a documentary, the cameras and photographers chase the father along the corridor of the house, until he hugs his wife, at which point the flashes start going off, and the cameras pick up the sound of what the two of them say in each other's ears.

The broadcast of that moment marked the culmination of the relentless search for the girls that, for almost three months, had been at the epicenter for the media, society, and relatives. Sharing this pain, the program added the finishing touch to a seventy-six-day search. On set, Herrero asked Fernando García:

> How many times have we spoken? You thought about talking to the king. You spoke to Felipe González, to

---

76. *De Tú a Tú*, January 28, 1993.

Corcuera.[77] You talked to Matilde Fernández, to the ombudsman. You even talked to people close to Hassan II. You went to London because you knew you could make contact with the TV there, and that information could be sent to other countries through that channel. I think you have a clear conscience, don't you, Fernando?[78]

To which the man replied, visibly dismayed, "Well, the truth is I . . . I think there's always going to be something more that could've been done, but . . ." This idea of what could have been done but was not, the doubt as to whether or not they had been mobilized enough, broadened the range of suffering for all to see on live TV. Sitting to the left of the presenter were Antonia Gómez's father, brothers, and sister. The presenter asked Luisa, Toñi's sister, to hold the microphone for her father. "He probably won't be able to," Herrero said. Then, adopting a totally different approach to the one she had used with Fernando García moments before, the journalist asked Toñi's father how he was coping with the fact that he had been less involved in the search:

Perhaps because of your work, you were unable to fight as hard as Fernando has fought, but your daughter [Luisa, Antonia's sister] has fought just as hard . . . just like Desireé's parents. I'd like you, who didn't go on TV because you couldn't, to tell us what it was like experiencing what was happening from behind the scenes? How was it?[79]

Apparently, not appearing on set was synonymous with not having fought hard enough to find their daughter; it also

---

77. At the time of the events, Felipe González was the Spanish prime minister, José Luis Corcuera was the Spanish minister of the interior, and Matilde Fernández was the minister of social affairs. Hassan II was the king of Morrocco 1961–1999—Trans.

78. *De Tú a Tú*, January 28, 1993.

79. *De Tú a Tú*, January 28, 1993.

appeared to turn them into mere observers who suffered their own misfortune from the second row. Toñi's father, who is also called Fernando, could barely speak, yet he responded with piercing clarity to Herrero's subtle question, "Well! We were . . . on a par with him. The only difference is that we always trusted his way of expressing himself. And, more importantly, we did the other tasks he told us to do."[80]

This answer did not satisfy the journalist, who decided to interrupt him to ask, "Fernando, what's it like? What's the pain of losing a child like? What's it like? What's it like? What's it like?"[81] What the father's response would be was plain to see, as were the emotions the journalist was stirring up with her question. Suffering as spectacle made revenge, and the death penalty, an extension of itself. Understandably, if a family member appears on screen grief-struck and broken over what happened, the underlying tone is not one of serenity. The emphasis on grief exacerbated the thirst for revenge and, as a consequence, there was a widespread demand for the death penalty. Journalists' questions, in large part, served to play up an emphasis on the death penalty. In the heat of what they were witnessing, the population acted accordingly.

Lobatón, for his part, after playing the recording of the radio program with Toñi's voice, showed Toñi's grandmother on the TV screen, who, totally devastated and in tears, said, "I can't believe they died like this. They should do to them what they did to my granddaughter. They should be killed. They should be burned, covered in gasoline or whatever they find."[82]

Apparently, Lobatón did not agree with capital punishment. Scruples that had seemed absent when it came to respecting the families' mourning reared up to reproach a teenager who expressed his indignation on set:

---

80. *De Tú a Tú*, January 28, 1993.

81. *De Tú a Tú*, January 28, 1993.

82. *¿Quién Sabe Dónde?*, January 28, 1993.

I think the person or people who committed these crimes—well, like when we all collaborated in the search, now anyone who wants can collaborate to find the person or people who brought this tragedy about and kill them by any means, but no prison. Leave him in the middle of the village and burn him.[83]

Lobatón challenged the teenager, "Do you realize that what you are saying is appalling? Appalling?"[84] The presenter distanced himself from the very images that he and his team had broadcast. Evidently, it was easier to reproach a visibly agitated teenager for his intervention than to acknowledge that broadcasting the families' suffering had fed into what was becoming a breeding ground for death penalty demands.

In fact, the call for the death penalty reflected a shared desire to bring to justice those who had indiscreetly rendered visible the social contract—a social contract that legitimizes and protects sexual torture. For exposing this pact, the perpetrators had earned the death penalty. Any sentence not involving the death of the offender would be deemed unsatisfactory by a society that was in no position to reflect on sexual violence; capital punishment was thus seen as the only possible solution. Any chance that the crimes would spark debate or any discourse situating the murders as the product of a society that permits everyday violence against women had to be snuffed out.

The instrumentalization of the girls' friends was yet another way of staging suffering. Gemma, one of the teenagers' friends who did not participate in the live program, still holds a vivid memory of a tough interview Herrero had conducted with a close friend of one of the Alcàsser girls:

---

83. *¿Quién Sabe Dónde?*, January 28, 1993.

84. *¿Quién Sabe Dónde?*, January 28, 1993.

I don't remember exactly what she said, but I do remember that she went too far with him. She asked him some pretty tough questions, and I saw a clip of it and I was like, "That's enough." It was enough, because I felt so bad . . . no, no, no, I couldn't watch it. It was outrageous. It was at the point when everything had just happened, when people were so upset, so hurt, when you still couldn't accept it. And . . . like, at that moment, they've just told you, and you don't even believe it, and to be attacked like that.[85]

Gemma was referring to the interview Herrero did that night with the boyfriend of one of the girls. The teenager was treated like an important document that, in addition, represented pain from a distinct perspective: love. That agitated boy struggled to hold himself together through every question. The journalist presented him as an extraordinary piece of testimony:

I'd like you to meet someone who's never spoken, it turns out. Talking to the relatives, we found out he's someone who, perhaps in silence, without anyone knowing, also cried a lot when he found out about the condition in which Míriam had been found. We could say that he was an important guy friend, her best guy friend; the more classical among us would say "boyfriend." But I would like him to tell me how he feels, as a person who had a great friendship with Míriam. What does it feel like? Are you feeling empty? How are you?[86]

The boy hesitated and replied that yes, he felt a great void. The voice-over merged with an on-screen image of the teenager. Finally, Herrero asked him, "So, now what? Because when

---

85. Valero, interview.

86. *De Tú a Tú*, January 28, 1993.

you are in love and, suddenly, your love is cut off. It was so brutal. What are you feeling?"

"Hate," answered the boy. "First of all, immense hatred, enormous rage, and also very intense hatred."

"Do you think that you will ever be able to say, 'I forgive you?'" Herrero insisted.

"Yes. Yes, I think so."

Having no use for this rational response, the journalist went on, "When you think of Míriam, what do you think of?"

"Well, of all the good memories we had together, she and I," replied the teenager, on the verge of losing his composure. His voice and the hand holding the microphone trembled.[87]

One question, in particular, that the journalist asked the teenager—"So, now what?"—brings us to the idea of change. It constituted an important element that came through in both presenters' questions that evening. Questions about what was going to happen after those events were common and, in the specific case of this investigation, recurrent. The idea of *change*, at that time, was not articulated from a premise of breaking with social attitudes and forms but was instead linked to a (pre-)existing fear that had to be confronted through corrective measures rather than a collective response. Corrective measures imply the imposition of new boundaries, borders that represent a return to a place where things were supposedly done better. The questions about potential change are in fact aimed at reproducing immobilism: a reactionary social process that saw in the Alcàsser crimes a clear path toward a definitive resolution.

The Metaphor of the Cautionary Tale

Identification with the girls through suffering was complemented by bodily identification. Both Nieves Herrero and Paco

---

87. *De Tú a Tú*, January 28, 1993.

Lobatón brought forensic experts, undertakers, and the bee-keepers who had found the bodies on set with the sole purpose of picking up on all the minutiae as quickly as possible. This is relevant because, as the first anatomical-forensic details—which were mostly pure conjecture—were being articulated, a warning appeared on the screen; alarm bells rang.

The body represented (the tortured body) and the lived body (that which receives the cautionary reminder) mutate almost imperceptibly into one figure: the fourth friend. The girl who did not go out that night, because she was ill, became the representation of a generation of young women who were spared. The cautionary message was to materialize through this individual, an individual who had been distinguished from the start but was given even more prominence that night. I focus my attention on this teenager because it is through her image, as captured on screen, and in the suffering her words convey in her interview with Herrero, that a whole generation of young women was able to feel her life being spared. Esther thus represents what I call *the metaphor of the cautionary tale.*

Despite the fact that relatives and friends were present, discussion proceeded to the condition in which the bodies had been found. The same witnesses who would sit in court for the 1997 trial were testifying on set the night of January 28, 1993. To add to the gravity of the message, both presenters had also invited either prestigious forensic experts or expert psychiatrists—neither of whom refrained from contributing to speculation.

The interview Herrero conducted with the deputy mayor of the town, José Manuel Alcaina, offers another example of the frequent recurrence of attempts to obtain information on the state of the bodies. The first question asked of Alcaina aimed at finding out the latest official information. In a lengthy intervention, the institutional leader called for more calm and less melodrama. He also reminded them all that the investigation was secret and pointed out the importance of verifying information to avoid unnecessary unpleasantness. Nevertheless, the

journalist dug deeper:

I'd like to ask: I know it's very rough and that in front of so many people here tonight, it's extremely difficult, but are you able to tell me if, with the results of the autopsy, the bodies were found to have been mistreated and raped?[88]

An awkward silence ensued: an obligation to talk. In a clear attempt to sidestep the question, Alcaina discussed the difficulties in establishing such matters in bodies after so much time. With this intervention, the deputy mayor sought to exercise control over the situation—a fact that the presenter overlooked.

She insisted, "Okay, just one question. You didn't answer me. Were the girls mistreated?"

"Visually, you can't tell," Alcaina answered again.

Lobatón did something similar at the town hall. The presence of forensic experts, specialists, hunters, and the beekeepers who found the bodies was justified because "they could help to understand what had happened a little better." Lobatón interviewed the employee of the funeral home who had been involved in the removal of the bodies. Again, the state of the bodies became the focus of analysis: "Do you have anything to say about the position the bodies were in?" Lobatón asked.

"About what? What?" answered the puzzled undertaker.

"About the way they were found," replied the journalist.[89]

The undertaker went on to describe the exhumation order and how the bodies had been found in the pit. This was followed by an interrogation about the objects found, the worker's own feelings, and whether the pit had been properly dug, which could help to determine the number of perpetrators.

In an incessant reshuffling of testimonies, the same people who were seated on Herrero's set appeared minutes later, or minutes before, on Lobatón's, except for those considered exclusive—that is, direct relatives or close friends. Thus, the

---

88. *De Tú a Tú*, January 28, 1993.

89. *¿Quién Sabe Dónde?*, January 28, 1993.

beekeepers went from one stage to another, recounting the discovery. Both men, who were visibly affected, particularly in the presence of the teenagers' families, answered the questions as best they could. As they talked on screen there was a fade-in to one of the girls' mothers hugging a photograph of her daughter and being hugged in turn by her husband, as she breaks down upon hearing the beekeepers' account. The beekeepers' statements added gratuitous suffering that did not shed light on what had happened. Quite the contrary: the seed was being sown of a form of entertainment based on the sexual assault and torture of women.

In *De Tú a Tú*, grief and the recounting of events combined in equal parts. Rarely have the relatives of people subjected to such raw violence had to witness all the explicit, gory details of the events surrounding the discovery of their loved ones— much less on live TV. Near the end of the program, there was a live link to the studio in Madrid. Waiting there were psychiatry professor Enrique Rojas and forensic anthropologist José Manuel Reverte, who had already participated in the talk show *Pasa la Vida* on TVE.

On the face of it, the presence of these experts might have been expected to bring some degree of rationality to the program. But this was not the case. Psychiatrist Enrique Rojas made an initial assessment of how the family might cope with their grief:

> I think that, at this point, there's this immense sadness. I suppose feelings of sadness are flooding in. I'd say two basic things here. Firstly, we have to let these feelings in. It's inevitable. Sadness is, at this point, an accordion of subjective feelings: melancholy, sorrow, upset, and anger. On the other hand, I'd say there's an important theme, and that's the theme of transcendence. I mean, *transcendence* comes from the Latin *transcendere*, "to go through by rising above." Everything that rises converges. I think it's very important, at this moment, not to lose sight of this aspect. In this way, we move from the law of retaliation to

the law of love. I believe that there are two great loves in life: the love of a mother, which nothing can take away— it's a pure love—and the love of God: for believers, this is a great vibrant love that's full of goodness. Between the two, there's this really crucial bridge. I believe we ought to invoke the two aspects. First, a deep, intense, solid, abundant sadness is unavoidable. But at the same time, it's important to look upward in search of transcendence.[90]

The psychiatry professor thus proffered a preamble to befit a bishop. In a speech devoid of scientific logic, Rojas appeals to God and the family as balms for recovery: the pure love of the mother, who will protect the family, under the watchful eye of the father in heaven—a mother, let us remember, who is "deeply frustrated," in the words of María Teresa Campos. The dangerous thing about this intervention is how tremendously subjective it is. In theory, it was coming from the field of science, in which logic and rationality are supposed to be a given. However, the psychiatrist exposes prejudiced, subjective feelings, with a complete bias toward his own reactionary thinking.

On the other hand, according to the psychiatrist, criminal acts of a sexual nature have long been typified by psychiatry. Therefore, in his opinion, when it comes to defining the characteristics of the perpetrator or perpetrators, we would be talking about

both a psychopathic personality and an unbalanced personality. And this personality is defined as an anomaly of formation with four traits. Aggressiveness: out and out aggressivity that is forceful and intense. Secondly, impulsivity. Normally, human behavior moves between two facets: the reflexive—I think, then I act—and the impulsive—I carry out an action, and then I think about it. Thirdly, coldness of mind: the coldness with which the acts are committed. And fourthly, the absence of guilt. These people do not feel guilty. There's an important thread running through these four points, which is what the French call "malignity," that is to say, the relish, the pleasure felt in doing harm.[91]

In fact, the professor's definition could be used to describe any person in a given context. And what the psychiatrist's reasoning certainly does not resolve is the question of the subjects toward whom the malice, coldness, apathy, and lack of guilt are directed, who are young women, teenage girls; nor why the girls were subjected to sexual torture. Somehow, psychiatry establishes a justification for the attacker's behavior while assuming its exceptionality.

The forensic anthropologist then intervened, trying to piece together the puzzle of what had happened. The body speaks as an excellent piece of evidence; and, in conjectures and hypotheses, this expert's imagination was given free rein, blending anthropological theory with his own moral prejudices. The presence of the anthropologist, who had previously participated in and successfully solved several cases, was justified by the discovery of the bodies. The position in which they had been found led the presenter to believe that it had not been the work of just one person. The forensic expert, in agreement with the presenter, replied, in a half-joking tone, "I am convinced that to get the better of three Valencian women, you need at least three Valencian men." In his opinion, it would have taken no fewer than three individuals. He went on to say,

> I think it'd be difficult because girls always know how to defend themselves well. And if they haven't learned judo or karate, well, they must have done, because it's the way

91. *De Tú a Tú*, January 28, 1993.

to defend themselves against sexual assault nowadays, when it seems that some want to see the dignity of women trampled on with the pornographic films, on the one hand, and vice, with the *litrona* [liter of beer], the nightclubs, where there is nothing but alcohol, drugs, and all kinds of carbonated vices. Clearly there's no way a Nobel Prize will be coming from there, but it's now, at this time, that we need to carry out this type of investigation and work.[92]

First of all, the demagogic argument that it would take three men to overpower three young women essentially placed responsibility for the aggression on the women's inability to defend themselves. Thus the antiquated idea that a woman can be assaulted only if she does not resist rears its ugly head. Reverte also seized the opportunity to discuss his thoughts on young people, which in themselves can be seen to offer a justification for the crimes. Without any data on the case, what the forensic scientist knows for certain is that crimes of these characteristics could only have occurred in a morally corrupt society. The image he conveys of the youth is that no Nobel Prizes can be expected from this generation and that it is corrupted. There is no mention, on his part, of the sexism that pervades this new generation, the product of an education in which he also played a part. The anthropologist's take on the situation can hardly be seen to be based on data or theories of forensic anthropology, but was, instead, conditioned entirely by his own point of view. The expert exhibited his utter contempt for the social context surrounding him. Without prior analysis, disgruntled by men and women's new ways of doing things, Reverte sees these crimes as an opportunity to both reformulate and criticize the society of that time.

Thus, the two representatives from the scientific world who appeared on *De Tú a Tú* that night did nothing to elevate the

---

discussion of the crimes, nor did they help viewers understand them. Science was invoked to describe a man capable of committing such crimes. Yet, to assess the behavior of young people, particularly young women, a simple moral assessment would do. In short, if they went to the nightclub and got in the car, there could be no doubt they were being irresponsible. If the aggressors did what they did, it was because they were ill and, as such, had to be scientifically categorized.

I would like to highlight something extremely significant from the *De Tú a Tú* special that went completely unnoticed at the time. At one point in the special, the presenter showed footage in which she interviewed three hunters from the area. A few seconds before the journalist and the hunters appear on screen, the blown-up photographs of the murdered teenagers are shown in such a way that they take up the entire screen. Astonishingly, a fourth photo is also shown: an image of Esther, the friend who had not gone out that night. Their images remain frozen on the screen for a few seconds each. Meanwhile, off screen, the voice of Nieves Herrero can be heard at the scene:

> "We're going to try to follow"
> —*shot of Desirée Hernández, with her name in big letters*—
> "a similar route to that taken by the murderers"
> —*photo of Míriam García*—
> "to hide the bodies of the three girls from Valencia"
> —*shot of Antonia Gómez*—
> "I have been able to gain access"
> —*uncaptioned shot of the friend of the teenagers who did not go out that night and was the last person to see them*—
> "to one of the hillsides near to where this event took place."

The image of the teenage girls' young friend appears next to their own, as if she, like them, had suffered the same fate.

I interpret this moment as the turning point that was to delimit the subdued body, the *docile body*. I understand this moment as the point at which the cautionary reminder gives way to the creation of docile bodies: the fourth friend whose life was spared is the symbol of the generation of young women whose lives were spared and who have to learn the lesson in order to live. Like nothing else, the fact that her image was shown next to those of her friends represents the force of the discipline of sexual terror and indoctrination striving to condition a whole generation of women. The image said: This is what can happen to you—*photograph of the tortured bodies with first and last names*—to you who have been spared—*photograph of the docile or cautioned body*—personified in the figure of the friend who did not go out that night and who appears with neither first name nor surname.

To make this materialize, in addition, the young friend—Esther—was sitting there on live TV. It is important to bear in mind that when Nieves Herrero interviewed her, she had already seen herself sharing the screen with her friends. She had heard about the state the bodies had been found in, the positions they were in, the route they had taken, everything. She herself had identified what could have happened to her. The journalist presents Martínez, saying, "Here's someone who's in a very bad way. If it hadn't been for the fact that she was ill, Esther could've been one of the girls. Instead of three, there would've been four of them."[93] And, in fact, it could still happen to her, to her or any of the young girls watching the program: that is the message. The image is edited to place the teenager exactly where she might have ended up: a pan shot with her friends fading out to the place where the bodies had been found. Moreover, the presenter concludes without a doubt that there would have been four of them, assuming nothing could have prevented it.

"Esther, now, you just received news of the arrest. What are you feeling?"

---

93. *De Tú a Tú,* January 28, 1993.

"About what?" replied the teenager.[94]

"What are you feeling?" was not a very nuanced question in a context in which Herrero had introduced her by reminding her that she could have been the fourth. The presenter asked her about the arrest, and the teenager replied only that she hoped that it was their killer and that justice would be done. The opportunity to discursively materialize what had already been perceived in images came in the next question:

"How many times, Esther, have you thought that if you hadn't been ill, you might have been one of them? How many times have you thought that?"

The teenager looked at the floor. She replied, "Many times."

"Many times?" insisted Herrero.

"Many times," confirmed the girl.

"Can you sleep at night, Esther?" the journalist asked.

The teenager shook her head. "Before, I mean, when they had disappeared but . . . before it was known that they were dead, I don't know. . . . I used to think about them a lot, but I could sleep. But since I found out, I can't sleep. I just can't stop thinking about them."

"Do you think it won't be the same?" The journalist ended the interrogation, once again, with the idea of change.

"No. Nothing will ever be the same. Nothing. Nothing," replied Esther.[95]

The portrayal of Esther encapsulates perfectly *the metaphor of the cautionary tale*. The friend who did not go out represented those whose lives were spared, those who behaved well, those who did not transgress and therefore got a second chance. She is the *body of the cautionary tale* made explicit. The media narrative sends a clear message to a whole generation of young women who have been symbolically and metaphorically spared.

---

94. *De Tú a Tú*, January 28, 1993.

95. *De Tú a Tú*, January 28, 1993.

The Sexist Microphysics of Power

If you wish to understand and perceive events in the present, you can only do so through the past, through an understanding—carefully derived from the past—which was specifically developed to clarify the present.

Michel Foucault, *Language, Counter-Memory, Practice*

The Alcàsser sexual danger narrative is a story of boundaries to be observed, of out-of-bounds territories: the border comprising the tortured body and the *docile body*. Alcàsser is a political narrative that was to imprint—from the body, onto the body—all manner of limits and boundaries; that is, *corporal borders*.

The Alcàsser crimes, constructed as an account of sexual danger, is a truth society can understand; it ties in with the structures of meaning from which the *social body* reaffirms its continuity.

Now, from a perspective rooted in feminist theory, what does the production of the truth about the Alcàsser sex crimes really involve?

It is in the sex crimes themselves that the truth of the Alcàsser case is hidden. This truth is not to be found in discovering how they happened, or where the crimes were committed, but in questioning why it could happen, who could commit the crimes, and why there is a place where crimes of these characteristics could materialize. In this vein, Michel Foucault argues:

> Rather than ask ourselves how the sovereign appears to us in his lofty isolation, we should try to discover how

it is that subjects are gradually, progressively, really and materially constituted through a multiplicity of organisms, forces, energies, materials, desires, thoughts etc.[1]

The Alcàsser crimes show how a case of sexual violence served to ignite the flame of social anxiety about society itself, yet failed to call into question the foundations that allow crimes of this kind to take place, much less talk openly about the body that suffers them. What matters is the *social body*, not women's bodies, which are constructed as public.

An Account That Produces (Its) Truth

> *The exception is more interesting than the regular case. The latter proves nothing; the exception proves everything. The exception does not only confirm the rule; the rule as such lives off the exception alone.*
>
> **Giorgio Agamben,** *Homo Sacer*

Decades later, the Alcàsser case is a clear example of an account that is still being honed. The mechanism that sustains it is the production of knowledge that continuously fabricates *truth* about sexual danger. This mechanism is inherent to social structure. As Foucault writes,

> Power never ceases its interrogation, its inquisition, its registration of truth: it institutionalizes, professionalises and rewards its pursuit. In the last analysis, we must produce truth as we must produce wealth, indeed we

---

1. Michel Foucault, *Power/Knowledge: Selected Interviews and Other Writings, 1972–1977*, ed. Colin Gordon, trans. Kate Soper et al. (London: Vintage, 1980), 97.

must produce truth in order to produce wealth in the first place.[2]

Social survival depends on the production of a coherent truth, a reflection of society itself, which, as such, defends it. The strength of the prevailing power in the narrative's construction stems from the conflict around proving this power exists and thus harms, through its effects, everyone who produces and receives the narrative. This is the difficulty of understanding the consequences of the narrative, as Foucault notes:

> Power would be a fragile thing if its only function were to repress, if it worked only through the mode of censorship, exclusion, blockage and repression, in the manner of a great Superego, exercising itself only in a negative way. If, on the contrary, power is strong this is because, as we are beginning to realise, it produces effects at the level of desire and also at the level of knowledge. Far from preventing knowledge, power produces it.[3]

The impact produced by the sexual torture to which the teenagers were subjected is overt power and is perceived immediately. The effect produced by the description of such torture, in contrast, goes unnoticed, and it is this that contributes— efficiently—to the entrenchment of the *docile body*. Thus, *the discipline of sexual terror* unites fear of physical punishment and self-regulation of risks, as mechanisms learned and internalized in women's everyday practices.

For this mechanism of power to be truly effective, it has to be decentralized, blended into the narrative, kept out of plain sight. Accordingly, Foucault suggests that power must be analyzed

---

2. Foucault, *Power/Knowledge*, 93–94.
3. Foucault, Power/*Knowledge*, 59.

as something which circulates, or rather as something which only functions in the form of a chain. It is never localised here or there, never in anybody's hands, never appropriated as a commodity or piece of wealth. Power is employed and exercised through a net-like organisation. And not only do individuals circulate between its threads; they are always in the position of simultaneously undergoing and exercising this power. They are not only its inert or consenting target; they are always also the elements of its articulation. In other words, individuals are the vehicles of power, not its points of application.[4]

This power dynamic is what makes the narrative of sexual danger so effective, as well as rendering it an elusive, complicated mechanism to grasp. This, in turn, makes it difficult to confront. With this in mind, every detail, every meaning produced by the account—which might go unnoticed a priori—must be scrutinized.

In order to extend its reach, the narrative makes use of what Foucault defined as *the microphysics of power*. Using this concept, I understand the account of sexual danger in Alcàsser as the resultant product, as he writes, of a diffuse power

being exercised. No one, strictly speaking, has an official right to power; and yet it is always exerted in a particular direction, with some people on one side and some on the other. It is often difficult to say who holds power in a precise sense, but it is easy to see who lacks power.[5]

In this sense, the microphysics of power is the instrument that triggers the entire system of knowledge production. Thus, the

---

4. Foucault, *Power/Knowledge*, 98.

5. Michel Foucault, *Language, Counter-memory, Practice: Selected Essays and Interviews*, ed. Donald F. Bouchard, trans. Donald F. Bouchard and Sherry Simon (Ithaca, NY: Cornell University Press, 1996 [1971]), 213.

process of crafting the account is an integral part of a whole, of a power "that profoundly and subtly penetrates an entire societal network."[6] The structure in which the microphysics of power dwells is society as a whole.

I would like to point now to a failure in the concept of *the microphysics of power*. It is a shortcoming signaled by Silvia Federici when she argues that Foucault

> is so intrigued with the "productive" character of the power-techniques by which the body has been invested, that his analysis practically rules out any critique of power relations. The nearly apologetic quality of Foucault's theory of the body is accentuated by the fact that it views the body as constituted by purely discursive practices, and is more interested in describing how power is deployed than in identifying its source.[7]

It is this need to identify the origin of power that drives me to incorporate the variable *sexism* into the concept of *the microphysics of power*. And it is in this sense that I reformulate the notion into *the sexist microphysics of power*. The idea is to rupture the concept at the very heart of its enunciation; sexism is inserted in such a way as to make it pivotal to the concept. This is why I speak of *the sexist microphysics of power*, rather than *the microphysics of sexist power*.

Using the sexist microphysics of power as an analytical tool allows me to establish that the knowledge and truth being disseminated, however diffusely, are sexist. If the sexist microphysics of power works in such a sophisticated way, it is because, on some level, individuals obtain or preserve given privileges through it. Depending on the position they occupy socially,

---

6. Foucault, *Language*, 207.

7. Silvia Federici, *Caliban and the Witch: Women, the Body, and Primitive Accumulation* (New York: Autonomedia, 2004), 15.

privilege refers to the maintenance of an advantage, or at least not suffering a disadvantage, in relation to another individual. This idea is at the core of the sexist microphysics of power and is pivotal to making it an infallible mechanism. A form of "humanism" constitutes the sublime part of the machinery, the gentler side of power that cannot be trusted. Given that these crimes had such a far-reaching emotional impact on society, it appears hard to fathom that behind all the solidarity and empathy extended to the families and the victims themselves, there could be a social structure that sought to safeguard sexual violence as a mechanism of domination. Foucault defines humanism as

> the totality of discourse through which Western man is told: "Even though you don't exercise power, you can still be a ruler. Better yet, the more you deny yourself the exercise of power, the more you submit to those in power, then the more this increases your sovereignty."[8]

Thus, it is of crucial importance to be alert to the humanism running through the narrative, because it could interfere with our understanding of the sexist microphysics of power. This concept is therefore the torch with which to illuminate those areas where there is always light: this is, after all, the reason they are neither illuminated nor explored. Knowing how to identify this humanism in the narrative is crucial because society expresses itself through it: "The theory of the subject (in the double sense of the word)," Foucault reminds us, "is at the heart of humanism."[9] It is also worth noting that Foucault's definition of humanism is riddled with sexism: to no one's surprise, the subject who is to be sovereign is the Western man.

At the same time, this device comes with a strategy: to construct the Alcàsser sex crimes as an isolated and, therefore,

---

8. Foucault, *Language*, 221.

9. Foucault, *Language*, 222.

exceptional incident. Thus constructed, the narrative showed an emotionally shattered society that, on the basis of its "humanism," rejected any responsibility for what had happened. The present study will try to show that, to the contrary, as Giorgio Agamben proposes, the exception "reveals the essence of State authority most clearly."[10]

The sexual violence that cements society is thus the norm that the strategy of the exception protects and perpetuates. The narrative constructed from the Alcàsser crimes views rape as a political element that is absent from the analysis but, nevertheless, shapes and configures reality. The very concept of rape is at the heart of the exception—the configuration of which, in the Alcàsser case, functioned as an emergency device, activated to allow for the reestablishment of social norms and standards. At the time, the crimes shook society and managed to reestablish physical and sexual violence against women as its very cornerstone, not to be tampered with under any circumstances.

In short, the sexist microphysics of power, on the basis of which knowledge dissemination takes place, holds society responsible for everything: for all the things from which the exception had allowed society to dissociate itself. Instrumentalization of the exception and the sexist microphysics of power together, as analytical tools, can help neutralize the distortion conveyed by the account of sexual danger from the Alcàsser case.

Corporal Geographies and Performativity

> Territory is no doubt a geographical notion, but it's first of all a juridico-political one: the area controlled by a certain kind of power.
>
> Michel Foucault, *Power/Knowledge*

---

10. Giorgio Agamben, *Homo Sacer: Sovereign Power and Bare Life*, trans. Daniel Heller-Roazen (Stanford: Stanford University Press, 1998), 16.

The abundant meaning-production witnessed through the discursive analysis of the Alcàsser case's newspaper archive is objective proof of how society produced a single—sexist—truth about the Alcàsser sex crimes. The space in which the narrative operates is, essentially, women's bodies. The body is, in this sense, a surface on which to locate what I call *corporal geographies.*

Corporal geography, as a concept, maps the idea of territory—with all its connotations of power and occupation, as well as struggle and resignification—onto the body. This territory I am referring to is a political, and undeniably social, space. The concept of corporal geography allows me to position women's bodies in a specific territory in which certain inscribed rules and obligations hold sway. Thus, the forbidden, out-of-bounds spaces of the exterior are transferred to the body, shaping the power of corporal geography. Similarly, the description or graphic representation of the body constitutes what we could call a *corpo-graphy.* In this vein, the analysis of the *border* also offers important insight. I understand the border as a series of boundaries that, rather than being geographically placed, represent the existence of physical violence on women's bodies and offer a cautionary reminder of those boundaries women should not cross. For women, these borders carry a weighty symbolic load and represent the restrictions set by a society whose functioning is grounded in and supported by sexual violence. Moreover, using the corporal geographies concept (and associating all emerging meanings with a bodily territory-terrain) means that, when we speak of sex crimes—in the literal, descriptive sense—we may speak of their effects on the body too—also in the literal sense. For this very reason, corporal geographies must be situated in relation to the *corporal border.* After all, that is where the boundaries imposed by the territory described in the narrative materialize.

Also of interest here is Judith Butler's concept of *performativity,* which they understand "not as a singular or deliberate 'act,' but, rather, as the reiterative and citational practice by which discourse produces the effects that it names."[11] Through using this concept, the Alcàsser narrative can be interpreted as an account of the body that was to produce the effects it names in the bodies of women. In addition, it establishes the narrative as a product of the sexist microphysics of power that, by repeating the same discourse and the same meanings and myths, produces the desired effect.

Social Climatology and the Perfect Discursive Storm

Social climatology masked the set of strategies defining the channels through which the narrative was to unfold. In the first phase, immediately after the crimes, the focus was on the details relating to the evidence on the bodies of torture. Social discourse tried to decenter the debate. The most straightforward way to do this was to categorize the crimes as an "incident" and drive discussion toward the issue of violence in general.

Across the media, after the discovery of the bodies and the (in)appropriate live broadcasts from Alcàsser, the murder of the teenage girls was latched on to as if it were each outlet's own private media struggle.[12] The crimes' categorization as an incident made it easy to divert attention away from much-needed reflections on society, and toward spectacle and morbidity. In fact, the use of the accident and crime section, called the *sección de sucesos* (literally, incidents section) in Spanish newspapers was the most effective way for the sexual danger narrative to hide its function. Madrid's *Asociación de Mujeres para la Salud* (a

---

11. Judith Butler, *Bodies That Matter: On the Discursive Limits of "Sex"* (London: Routledge, 1993), 2.

12. This play on words calls attention to a double meaning: it was "inappropriate" according to critics and public opinion (and here Foucault's *humanism* makes itself known), and yet it was a broadcast of "appropriate" content for the purpose of constructing a sexual danger narrative.

women's health association) highlighted this issue in its monthly periodical, *La Boletina*:

> To call the rape, torture, and death of a woman at the hands of a man an "incident" clearly reveals the direct representation this occurrence has in the mind of the person who designates it as such. The term "incident" refers, in effect, to a particular relationship between offender and victim, to an occurrence that can be explained in terms of the relations of a male individual who, because of his particular psychological history, would have fixated on women. Sexist aggressions at their highest level are thus stripped of all political significance.[13]

Disavowal of the sexist nature of sex crimes is society's way of disassociating sexual violence from the social. If the crime is not political, if sex crime is just something that happens, society dissociates itself, and Alcàsser becomes, as the feminists report in their article, "the misfortune of that particular woman because she crossed paths with a sex maniac."[14] This line of argument is the criterion guiding part of the newspaper archive; it is one of the pillars underpinning its entire structure. As Pierre Bourdieu argues,

> Human interest stories create a political vacuum. They depoliticize and reduce what goes on in the world to the level of anecdote or scandal. This can occur on a national or international scale, especially with film stars or members of royal families, and is accomplished by fixing and keeping attention fixed on incidents without political consequences, but which are nonetheless dramatized so as

---

13. Asociación de Mujeres para la Salud, "Violadores, psicópatas y discurso patriarcal," *La Boletina* (Madrid) (May 1993): 13.

14. Asociación de Mujeres para la Salud, "Violadores, psicópatas, y discurso patriarcal," 13.

to "draw a lesson" or be transformed into illustrations of "social problems."[15]

The programs broadcast live from Alcàsser were the focus of criticism from all sides. Thus, what became a social problem was not the sexual violence that structures social relations but the way in which these two programs covered the topic. However, the scandal produced by the way the journalist Nieves Herrero conducted the program, far from offering foreclosure, served to provide a wider opening. I interpret the barrage of criticism received by Herrero's program as, in a way, a consequence of the sexist microphysics of power itself; it was, as Baudrillard puts it, "a simulation of scandal to regenerative ends."[16]

Illustrative of this paradox are the publications that filled the front pages of the main newspapers after the first forty-eight hours. Criticism of the journalist's performance shared space with the first leaks from the autopsies. Focusing all the attention on the presenter's activity and labeling *De Tú a Tú* the most perverse program ever broadcast gave the other shows and publications free rein. In this way, as Baudrillard notes, "the denunciation of scandal always pays homage to the law"[17]—that is, to sexist regulations.

Therefore, in the framework of the present study, the—journalistic—theories proclaiming the Alcàsser crimes to be a turning point constitute yet another maneuver to shift attention away from sexual violence. Television was not entering a new era of broadcasting; television was entering a new social era. The turning point was inscribed on the social body, and specifically on women's bodies. Indeed, the "incident" had its first

---

15. Pierre Bourdieu, *On Television*, trans. Priscilla Parkhurst Fergusen (New York: The New Press, 1998), 51.

16. Jean Baudrillard, *Simulations*, trans. Phil Foss, Paul Patton, and Paul Beitchman (New York: Semiotext(e), 1983), 30.

17. Baudrillard, *Simulations*, 27.

chastening effects on women: "about Nieves Herrero's program, I think it's cruel. I'm an eleven-year-old girl, and today I'm very scared to go out in the street."[18]

Lobatón's and Herrero's programs gave rise to talk about the explicit violence broadcast on TV and arguments that this could negatively affect viewers' behavior. A member of the public told the "El Cabinista" section of *Las Provincias*,[19]

It's amazing that nobody protests about everyday television, which for me is much more harmful [than Nieves Herrero's program], as it is a continuous drip feed of films about killer dolls, immoral men, murders, rape, drugs, and sex on steroids.[20]

The institutional authorities, which were in the social spotlight, also interpreted the depictions discussed from a cause/effect perspective. Matilde Fernández, then the minister of social affairs, stressed the importance of reflecting on whether "certain violent films or messages may be fueling these paranoid behaviors."[21] The fact that rape was a fairly common plot in any TV series or film only became relevant in the context of the triple crime. It was as if, up to that point, rape had occurred exclusively in fiction.

All the details of what happened went into the construction of the Alcàsser narrative; the same was not true of responses to it. The search for explanations and answers focused, first, on interrogating the teenagers' bodies through a detailed disclosure of the autopsies, and. second, on discussing the reasons—in general—behind violence of such proportions. Some pointed

---

18. *Las Provincias*, February 3, 1993.

19. The "El Cabinista" section of *Las Provincias* took the form of a column compiled from information and opinions volunteered by members of the public via telephone—Trans.

20. *Las Provincias*, February 19, 1993.

21. *Las Provincias*, January 31, 1993.

out the fact that "the conduct of the alleged murderers of the Alcàsser girls has a sexual motive whose origin lies in a sick society, not in the individuals who constitute it."[22]

Without a specific disease to treat and target, others were in favor of eliminating the specific evil and avoiding unnecessary contagion: "This soulless vermin must be made to disappear to stop them repeating their criminal acts and to preserve common good in society."[23] Maite Larrauri contributed, in *El País*, a different discourse highlighting the importance of sexism in crimes of sexual violence:

> Those who call for the death penalty think of surgical solutions because they defend the idea of a social body with rotten parts. They don't see, or don't want to see, that sexism is the air we breathe, it's a cultural trait on which the acts that are considered most ordinary are founded.[24]

In this counter-discourse, the author highlights the existence of everyday sexist violence. She points out the recklessness of the desire to see the Alcàsser crimes as an incident in isolation from society as a whole. Thus, describing the offenders as "vermin" can be seen as an attempt to separate "civilized men" from their responsibility for the crimes. All responsibility was focused on the perpetrators, reducing the scope of the analysis of sexual violence and absolving completely the rest of society. The attempt to obscure the perpetrator by neutralizing them is a key part of the construction of exceptionality. Society focused on looking for culprits, not for those responsible, and this issue was basic to the construction of the exception. The *Asociación Española de Mujeres Juristas* (Spanish Association of Women

---

22. *Levante Valenciano,* January 30, 1993.

23. *El Levante Valenciano,* February 6, 1993.

24. Maite Larrauri, "Frente a la violación," *El País,* February 14, 1993.

Jurists) was forceful when it came to holding society to account for protecting sexist violence: "The acts surrounding the rapes and deaths of the Alcàsser girls are the result of a misogynist society without which the type of monsters that are created in such a society would not exist."[25]

Gradually, the image of a society in jeopardy became the focal point of public debate and explanations for the murder of the teenage girls were sought in the most pressing social problems of the day. The news went from flooding the accident and crime section to filling the culture pages. The discussion then focused on violence in its most general sense. The director general of the police, in an article entitled, "Why Is Society in Such a State?" analyzed similar crimes and concluded that there is "a very worrying degree of latent violence in society. Spanish society is on edge, not relaxed, and at the drop of a hat, significant levels of aggressivity emerge."[26]

In his opinion, violence is generally provoked by some movement that is out of the expected, out of bounds. Specifically, in the Alcàsser case, the provocation came from the exercise of freedom that hitchhiking represented for the teenage girls. Remarkably, in *El País*, Tina Alarcón, president of the Asociación para la Asistencia a las Mujeres Violadas (Association for Assistance to Raped Women), stated, "This is a time of social violence. I put all this down to violence, to a competitive society generating frustration that, in turn, is being channeled through sexual brutality."[27]

Frustration and competitiveness found an outlet in women's bodies. This same analysis could not, however, answer the question: Why do women's frustration, pain, or competitiveness not find an outlet in men's bodies? Finding fault in women's conduct was a simple task and, indeed, more consistent with the

---

25. *El Levante Valenciano*, February 5, 1993.

26. "¿Por qué está fatal la sociedad?," *El Correo Español*, January 29, 1993.

27. *El País*, January 31, 1993.

sexist regime. However, when it's men's actions and attitudes in question, the debate turns to the social: society is sick, and violence is generalized. Where the subject dissolves, so too does the act committed by the subject. In other words, not only is the sexist microphysics of power a mechanism of disclosure; it is also a tool of concealment. So, the debate on sexual violence focused on questioning the meaning of violence in general and on raising metaphysical questions about the evolution and nature of humanity. In *El Correo* newspaper, the director general of the police declared, "If we could ever know why a man can end up attacking mankind, we would have in our hands the ideal solution in which peace and harmony would be the ordinary rule of trust."[28] This nostalgia for the sacred text of Cain and Abel shows how far the debate was from analyzing the Alcàsser case from a political perspective.

These reflections on the evolution of "man," which allow the subject to be diluted, are directly related to the strategy that articulates humanism as a concept. For Foucault, "humanism reinforces social organization and these techniques allow society to progress, but along its own lines."[29] Unsurprisingly, the humanism that structures the sexual danger narrative is sexist. Behind this concept, which is supposed to promote solidarity, lies society's permissiveness toward society itself. I refer here to the social maneuver that diverts attention from sexism's responsibility in order to strengthen and perpetuate sexism itself, in order, in Baudrillard's words, "to save at all cost the truth principle, and to escape the specter raised by simulation—namely that truth, reference, and objective causes have ceased to exist."[30]

28. *El Correo Español*, February 2, 1993.

29. Foucault, *Language*, 221.

30. Baudrillard, *Simulations*, 6.

The Sexist Microphysics of Power

Some recountings of the incidents placed special emphasis on the teenagers' responsibility therein. Through this kind of argument, meanings that tried to restrain women's behavior were transmitted. Consequently, the practice of hitchhiking was used as an excuse to raise a further set of social issues relating to the levels of freedom women were beginning to experience.

Some voiced opinions containing suggestions that there was a problem with authority and family responsibility. The mayor of Alcàsser, the socialist Ricardo Gil, said it like this, "The crimes have served as an incentive for families to fulfill their parental obligations. We should try to spend as much time as possible with our children because that is always a good thing."[31]

Coming from a representative of the established order, his argument implies that what caused the crimes was the families' failure to fulfill their obligation to keep their daughters at home. The mayor stated openly what it was, in his view, that society had lost and needed to regain responsibility and family life. Inevitably, he was also making the point that it was inappropriate for young girls to be out and about at unseemly hours hitchhiking.

In the 1990s, the changes brought about by the feminist struggle started gaining visibility. This progress and new openness was taking its toll on a misogynist society that saw in the Alcàsser crisis the pretext to return to a past in which women were kept in their rightful place. That backward glance lingered long enough to raise questions about existing structures. A shopkeeper from Alcàsser expressed his concern, saying, "I'm not saying that democracy's a bad thing, but for cases like these, democratic laws aren't much use."[32] He equates democracy to a certain lack of authority, understanding this term as a synonym

---

31. *El Levante Valenciano*, January 29, 1993.

32. *El Mundo*, January 30, 1993.

for licentiousness—an attitude that, in his opinion, had consequences that were reflected in the crimes. Responsibility for the crimes was extended to a political system perceived to be too permissive, with an absence of authority and an excess of fundamental rights. And it was precisely the curtailment of rights that was indirectly demanded of women. The truth is that advocating a return to a more authoritarian regime meant endorsing the return of men and women to their rightful places.

The murder of the three teenage girls brought to light existing fears about social disorder and tapped into the idea that life had been safer in the past. In this context, young people were the target of most moral judgments:

> It's time to give serious thought to the new trends and behaviors contributing to a whole series of extremely negative developments; from the weekend release of those in prison for sexual offenses, to the absurd total confidence of young girls. Instead of the campaigns to stop you getting pregnant if you don't want it, we need to start with campaigns for a life with normal—let's say European, since it's fashionable—schedules. And let's see if we can banish the "movida hasta que amanece" [on the scene 'till dawn], the "litrona" [liter of beer], and "todo vale que la vida son cuatro días" [life is short, so anything goes]. The painful chronicle of car and motorbike accidents on Fridays and Saturdays, and rapes, would cease.[33]

In other words, nights out had always been a male experience, and it was men who had had exclusive purview of the early hours. Weekend partying, drinking alcohol at night, and getting home in the early hours of the morning started to become a problem when women joined in. It is no coincidence that when women took to frequenting spaces reserved for men, conflict

---

33. *El Mundo*, January 30, 1993.

emerged. That was, therefore, the right time to reflect on certain attitudes, activities, and practices. As a member of the public told the press,

> The sale of alcoholic beverages, inappropriate schedules, families where parents and children hardly see each other or talk, houses more like hotels for eating and sleeping than like homes where families take stock of the good and bad of each of its members. We have to come to our senses and get the authorities to do something.[34]

The aim was, therefore, to safeguard the family unit and all its members. As the archbishop of Barcelona saw it, the underlying issue was the image of "man" that society was promoting:

> How long will it be before we can come up with another model for man, another way of educating the youth? The problem is one of inner formation and of human and family values. We have to restore man's integrity.[35]

Certainly, getting *man*'s integrity back could help to keep things in their proper place, and thus allow *woman*'s integrity to be restored.

A few days after the three young women's bodies were found, a group of young people walked out of their classes to hold a spontaneous protest:

> As young people, we want to show our absolute condemnation of the murder and rape of our friends in Alcàsser. The lives of three young people have been snuffed out, and it isn't coincidental that they were three young women.[36]

---

34. *Las Provincias*, January 29, 1993.
35. *La Vanguardia*, January 30, 1993.

36. *El Levante Valenciano*, February 4, 1993.

In a short press release, they gave the crimes a gendered reading. Days before, feminist associations in Valencia had called a demonstration whose turnout exceeded all expectations. In a square packed with people, the crowd expressed their opposition to the death penalty and stressed the importance of "raising social awareness to put an end to chauvinism and the perception of women as sexual objects."[37] Likewise, in Madrid, a total of fifteen women's associations issued a press release in which they expressed their "rage and impotence in the face of incidents that laid bare the most brutal form of misogynist rape."[38]

Impotence is perhaps the most apt word to describe this point in time: the mass disclosure of the details of the ordeal the teenagers had endured pushed to disarm any feminist arguments that might have urged women not to stay at home. In letters to the editor of the newspaper *Las Provincias*, a teenage girl published her opinion of the crimes and their consequences:

> To all the boys and girls of my age [fifteen]. It seems over the top when our parents tell us to be incredibly careful, to not go out at night, and to not trust anyone. Sometimes we think it's no big deal, that we're grownups and can take care of ourselves, but I say, wouldn't Míriam, Toñi, and Desireé have thought the same that evening when they left their houses never to return again?[39]

Restricting access to public spaces deemed unsafe meant, in the end, strengthening the institution of the family.

Arguments for placing limitations on women's freedom were widespread, and criminal lawyer Amparo Buxó spoke out against them in the newspaper *El País*:

---

37. *El Levante Valenciano*, February 1, 1993.

38. *El País*, January 31, 1993.

39. *Las Provincias*, February 19, 1993.

As if on instinct, all sexual offenses turn against women's freedom of movement. After the case of the elevator rapist in Alarcón, women were advised not to go out alone at night, to go upstairs in the company of other people, and not to open their doors.[40]

Feminist discourse was focused on counteracting a whole range of symbols of terror and fear that, at that time, were at their most prominent. What the lawyer had put into words was the initial effects of the sexual danger narrative.

A scathing open letter addressed to the minister of the interior, José Luis Corcuera, was published in the editorial notes of the journal *Mientras Tanto*:

I implore you, minister, to carefully consider the possibilities of a strategy for combating sexual violence based on the following hypothesis: women's empowerment is the only effective response to rape. Do you follow me, minister? I'm talking about women's freedom in earnest. I see no other way for women to emerge from impotence and gain power than for us to lose it. Look at the paradox: you are taking advantage of the tide that has turned with the Alcàsser crimes to take power away from judges and give it to the penitentiary institution and the police. This is a mistake. What we should be discussing is the role women play in our society.[41]

The voices that called sexual violence by name were neither muted nor vague. Far from it: they were forceful, openly stating what the crimes meant and how deeply entrenched the

---

40. *El País*, January 31, 1993. Pedro Luis Gallego, known as the "elevator rapist," was convicted in 1996 for the rape and murder of two women, along with numerous other sexual attacks. —Trans.

41. "Notas editoriales: Miremos cara a cara al violador, *Mientras tanto* 53 (1993): 7.

problem of sexual violence was. However, most of the articles written from a feminist perspective were published as opinion pieces in newspapers, periodicals, and the feminist movement's own media. None of these outlets were frequented by teenage girls and young women. But TV *was* reaching them, and with it, the transmission of images of the bodies and descriptions of the abuse suffered. The feminist loudspeaker, therefore, struggled to reach this group—a group that was particularly permeable to the discourses and meanings produced by the sexual danger narrative.

Territory and Boundaries: The Restructuring of the Corporal Border

Orography: An aspect of physical geography that deals with the study, description, and representation of land relief.

Corporal orography is the strategy the narrative would use to (in) corporate the border. Indeed, an excavation of the boundaries that the narrative began to establish enables us to consider how the metaphorical, the apparently inoffensive, becomes substance, becomes corporeality. The links that bind the narrative together and give it a veneer of social acceptability are myths that function as instruments of vigilance and chastisement. The myths also operate as networks, with connections to the past in which society recognizes itself.

The narrative is an amalgamation of explicitly and implicitly stated boundaries, spaces, and territories in which women's lives and bodies are resignified. There are clear thresholds, on the basis of which the whole case is structured. All these limits—which are summarized in what the teenage girls should not have done—were to be subsequently in-corporated by women. This infiltration was reinforced by the disclosure of the autopsies, a cautionary reminder associated with an extremely specific sort of pain.

133

Women's breaching of the border is an act that, in itself, implies the preexistence of boundaries. All walls have cracks, and the narrative's main objective was to plug the gap through which women's bodily autonomy had slipped. By hitchhiking, the teenagers broke the rules and put themselves in the danger zone, experiencing, in the words of Giorgio Agamben, "the absolute capacity of the subjects' bodies to be killed."[42] The warning about the practice of hitchhiking establishes a call for social vigilance over the behavior of teenage girls. This space is the political site in which the sexist system attempts to reassert its rights to the body-territory that belongs to it.

As the investigations continued, the media reconstructed the incidents, and, as with Jack the Ripper in nineteenth-century London, "the social meanings of melodrama were also responsive to the patriarchal and democratic expectations of its popular audience."[43]

Holding the Trial: Hitchhiking, the First Boundary Breached

The narrative establishes its foundations on the guilt of the women. Hitchhiking constituted the first limit to be overstepped, but also the motive behind the celebration of what I consider to be the only trial of the Alcàsser crimes.

The challenge now is to interrogate the narrative, to ask it: Who are you judging? Who are you watching? Who is doing the watching? Who are you going to condemn? This analytical perspective is based on the assertion that the only trial in relation to the Alcàsser crimes was the one that held the women responsible for what happened. Indeed, the entire Alcàsser trial

---

42. Agamben, *Sovereign Power*, 125.

43. Judith Walkowitz, *City of Dreadful Delight: Narratives of Sexual Danger in Late-Victorian London* (Chicago: University of Chicago Press, 1992), 178.

is an amalgamation of cautionary messages and social surveillance and punishment.

According to Agamben, "Everyone is inwardly innocent, but the only truly innocent person is not the one who is acquitted, but rather the one who goes through life without judgment."[44] In other words, only those who go through life without trial are truly innocent; the teenage girls are thus guilty because they themselves, as well as their actions, were judged. This reasoning transforms the whole meaning of the narrative. For a narrative about sexual violence to emerge, a tale of guilt had to be constructed in a roundabout way, and it had to be made clear that the teenagers alone were responsible for their situation.

The account of the incidents was reconstructed by newspapers in different ways; in retrospect, everything seemed to indicate that the teenagers could have avoided their fate. According to *El Levante Valenciano*,

> The night she disappeared, Míriam had asked her father
> to drive them to a nightclub less than two miles from
> Alcàsser. Míriam's mother told her daughter that her dad
> wasn't feeling well; she also gave her a scolding and told
> her it was far too late to be at a nightclub.[45]

Though it was far too late, the three teenagers hitched a lift to the club; according to the media, this was an unnecessary risk because, after all, "the three girls, didn't have 500 pesetas between them, so they couldn't even have gotten in to the nightclub."[46] As if this were not enough, "when they barely had a ten-minute walk left, they got into the car instead of walking."[47] This way of narrating the news does not merely describe the

---

44. Giorgio Agamben, *Remnants of Auschwitz: The Witness and the Archive*, trans. Daniel Heller-Roazen (New York: Zone Books, 1999), 19.

45. *El Levante Valenciano*, January 28, 1993.

46. *El Levante Valenciano*, January 28, 1993.

47. *El Levante Valenciano*, January 28, 1993.

facts; it perpetuates the idea that the girls took unnecessary risks. The account does not question why such risks existed but, rather, suggests that the girls put themselves in harm's way.

The most pronounced—but not the only—manifestation of this idea can be found in a book about the crimes called *Sin piedad* (literally, "ruthless"), written by Fernando Martínez Laínez. The book is essentially a novel crafted out of the newspaper archives of the case which the context and events of the teenagers' lives are woven into, without much rigor. In his account, the author sets up a situation in which a journalist goes to Alcàsser to investigate the incidents and has a conversation with a police officer there. Here, the author gives himself full license to pass moral judgment on the behavior of the young women:

> [Take] the case of those girls, for example, they could have walked a little further, they were close to the night-club, and yet, to avoid walking another ten minutes, they chose to put themselves in the hands of fate. Female victims have a tendency to minimize their exertion (cutting through wasteland, trusting a stranger, hitchhiking, underestimating nighttime dangers) that facilitates the murderers' actions.[48]

When it comes to the teenagers, the author's reasoning borders on the contemptuous: he accuses them of cutting through dangerous places out of sheer laziness. Indeed, the girls had apparently put themselves in the hands of a "fate" that murders, rapes, and tortures. The text is basically a misogynist "they asked for it."

Other newspapers, such as *El País*, also recounted the day of their disappearance with a focus on blaming the teenagers, albeit in a more subtle way: "The party at Coolor had already started. Nirvana and Guns N'Roses were playing. Their gang—girls who

---

48. Fernando Martínez Laínez, *Sin piedad* (Madrid: Ediciones B, 1993), 24.

look like women dressed in jeans and platforms—are waiting for them, as they have before, by the speakers."[49] In the collective imagination, this description of the girl/woman comes dangerously close to the idea of provocation, the seductive "Lolita" that drives older men crazy. Thus, the image of teenage girls dressed as women, in the bodies of girls with their thumbs out, placed the burden of proof back on the girls, who were once again, in a way, blamed.

In the aftermath of the crimes, public attitudes shifted in favor of increasing security measures around women. Inevitably, this also meant bolstering the role of men as protectors of women and, consequently, consolidating the image of the woman as public. In a narrative built on blaming the teenage girls, little room was left for rejecting male protection. Moreover, the rhetoric used by journalists at that time emphasized alarmism. As one newspaper article warned, "According to expert psychiatrists, a phenomenon of pathological contagion may be occurring in persons with clinical problems. Incidents that get as much publicity as that of the girls from that Valencian town end up promoting emulation phenomena."[50] All this contributed to the creation of a hostile environment in which daring to go out alone at night was seen as utter madness; thus, the responsibility of women for any aggression was also successfully restored.

The need for protection, coupled with parents' concerns about what might happen to their daughters, increased the emphasis on the labor behind the discipline of sexual terror as a practice. Mothers went to pick up their daughters in the early hours of the morning outside nightclubs, and even walked them to bus stops. In an article in the newspaper *Las Provincias* entitled "We Want to Go Out without Dying," a teenage girl of the victims' age declared, "It could just as easily have been

---

49. *El País*, January 31, 1993.

50. *El Correo Español*, January 29, 1993.

us. I'll never hitchhike again in all my life."[51] This statement is directly related to the live metaphor of the cautionary tale I describe in the previous chapter. The effectiveness of the narrative was precisely that it transformed the warning into self-restriction. Feli, Susana, Belén, and Maria José, students in the University Orientation Course—equivalent to twelfth grade in the US—said that despite the fact that they rarely went out, they had received numerous warnings and a lot of advice from their parents following the murder of the three teenagers: "My parents tell me to be careful about who I hang out with, not to go out alone, to take a taxi when necessary, and to be wary of strangers."[52] Risk control became a legitimate step preceding all ordinary activities. The practice of hitchhiking was the element through which punishment was extended to young women at large: "It serves as a lesson, but we have paid a very high price."[53] *Hitchhiking* was the word that channeled the idea of danger, of threat. Under the headline "Fear Grips the People," a group of teenage girls declared that they had decided never to hitchhike again, because "it's too dangerous."[54]

Fortunately, the adoption of self-imposed restrictions did not affect all young women in the same way. The "escape" route is visible in residents' complaints that, even in the wake of the disappearance of the girls, a number of young people had not learned their lesson and had kept on hitchhiking. Thus, when someone from the area stopped, it was to scold the hitchhiker. In other words, if the discipline of sexual terror had not achieved its purpose, the young people would face a second reprimand. Iterative practices form the medium through which discipline finds expression. Society's systematic correction of young

---

51. "Queremos salir a la calle sin morir," *Las Provincias*, February 4, 1993.

52. *El Levante Valenciano*, February 3, 1993.

53. *El Mundo*, January 29, 1993.

54. "El miedo se apodera del pueblo," *El Levante Valenciano*, January 29, 1993.

women are a form of surveillance and punishment which is both hard to locate and difficult to ignore. Therefore, punishment must be seen "as a complex social function."[55]

In those days, all eyes were on the teenagers' group of friends and, above all, on the friend who did not go out that night. The newspaper *La Vanguardia*, with a photo of the teenager right in the middle of the page accompanied by the headline "A Nightmare All Too Near," pressed the group to talk about whether they would have gotten into a car with three or four people in it. This line of questioning reflects the discursive violence that abounds throughout the newspaper archive. And it is a trap, because it is hitchhiking itself that is the basis for guilt, for doling out responsibility for what happened to the teenagers. In response, one of the teenagers recalled she had done it on the odd occasion; another said she would never have gotten into a car with more than two people. *La Vanguardia* was very clear about who was spared and who was not, who was prudent and who was not.

The discussion on hitchhiking called for young people, particularly teenage girls, to forgo such practices, which were considered unsafe and inappropriate. But hitchhiking had until then been widespread and regarded as safe. Gemma remembered,

> Yeah, it was really quiet here. Nothing had ever happened, nothing at all. And it was really close, and, yes, yes, my friends used to hitchhike. Yes, the truth is they did. Well . . . I don't know. . . . People had always hitchhiked. Always.[56]

The proximity of the nightclub made the place a known, "familiar" territory. The municipalities were close together, the

---

55. Michel Foucault, *Discipline and Punish: The Birth of the Prison*, trans. Alan Sheridan (New York: Vintage, 1995), 23.

56. Gemma Valero, interview, October 25, 2011.

communities close knit. The narrative omitted the actual experience of what hitchhiking entailed and used it as a pretext to blame the teenage girls.

Under the headline "Friday the Thirteenth in Alcàsser," the newspaper *El Mundo* published a fabricated dialogue worthy of a soap opera—"Hey, your name is Miguel, right? Well, thanks for giving us a lift."[57] In this reconstruction of events, the newspaper hinted that the girls might have known one of the vehicle's occupants. If true, this conjecture would reinforce the idea that the girls had taken precautions, that is, that they had not got into a stranger's car. In any case, the most important fact, which destabilizes any possible accusation of recklessness, is that there were three of them—*they were not alone.* This important detail seems to go unnoticed by those who suggest such obvious precautions as: never return home alone, never cross open terrain or empty plots alone, and, of course, never hitchhike alone. Although the teenagers did everything that could have been expected of them, in the end, the narrative starts and finishes with the same point: their guilt and responsibility.

The practice of hitchhiking is synonymous with freedom and mobility for women. It is a metaphor for the ability to take on public space, to move, and to cross the threshold of nightfall. To move from one place to another with the same freedom as men—a freedom that is harshly punished and repressed.

A 1993 opinion article entitled "Who Rapes Who?" mentions Golda Meir, Israeli prime minister from 1969 to 1974.[58] According to its author, at a meeting she was asked to order a curfew for women to stop them from being sexually assaulted. To which she replied, "But who rapes who?" and was told matter-of-factly, "Men rape women." The prime minister was said to have proposed that a curfew should be decreed from 10:00 p.m. onward for men only. This response turns the pattern

---

57. "Viernes 13 en Alcácer," *El Mundo*, January 31, 1993.

58. "¿Quién viola a quién?," *El País*, January 31, 1993.

of responsibility and guilt on its head. If the judgment passed on the teenage girls had focused not on their responsibility but on the power structure that permits such acts of sexual violence, we would be talking about a vastly different society today.

Hitchhiking was, ultimately, the space in which borders were redefined. Hitchhiking is the metaphor of transgression, a liminal place akin to a *no-man's-land*. To hitchhike is a decision, a voluntary decision that, in a sexist regime, can have consequences. The trial that took place prosecuted the girls and enacted a sentence, publicly exposing their tortured bodies as punishment.

Myths, Exemptions from Responsibility, and the Construction of the Nonman

The driving force of the narrative is largely built on what the girls had done wrong, rather than the behavior of the perpetrators. The discourse becomes detached from the offenders' responsibility for the incidents. The penal system condemns their acts, but this does not mean that they are considered guilty. Those guilty of what happened had already been judged. The distinction I make here between the judicial and the social is of fundamental importance: the former pertains to the norms that allow society to justify itself; the latter, to the norms that regulate the sexual status quo.

It was medical science, particularly psychiatry, that afforded legitimacy to men's violent behavior, creating binaries such as the civilized man versus the animal nonman. These myths were to contribute to the fluidity of the narrative, lending it credibility, because society recognizes itself in such categories. This was a major problem with which feminist discourse had to contend.

How can myths about sexual violence be dismantled when it is science itself that confirms them? Myths are schemes of meaning that most people recognize or internalize. Those articulated through science are the more dangerous because, in theory, they stem from supposedly impartial practices, making them appear true, or even irrefutable.

In line with the arguments made so far, the first step toward establishing exoneration of responsibility is to strip the crimes of their political significance, turning them into an incident. This is how they put it in *La Boletina*:

> Once a sexist act has been stripped of all political signif-
> icance, and responsibility for it has been imputed exclu-
> sively to the perpetrator, the next step is to attenuate, if
> not totally eliminate, the latter's personal culpability. To
> do this, it is but a question of declaring him sick, unbal-
> anced, abnormal, psychopathic, or any other adjective
> that allows us to attribute his behavior to uncontrollable
> impulses firmly embedded in his personality.[59]

This dichotomy allows two things to happen: on the one hand, it exempts the civilized man from all responsibility; on the other, it makes it difficult to distinguish the perpetrator, rendering him unrecognizable. If he is not a man but a beast, how can he be identified? The minister of the interior forcefully stated that, although there was no room for extenuating circumstances, we were undoubtedly in the presence of "a few of the beasts that sometimes live among good people and that, unfortunately, sometimes bite, or go further, as in this case."[60] Myths contribute to social stability; they are society's way of understanding and codifying what happens. However, belief systems also adhere to patriarchal norms that entrench certain myths—those that align with them—to the detriment of others, which are ignored. "My brother and his friend used to say that all women were whores,"[61] said Enrique Anglés, brother of one of the perpetrators of the

---

59. Asociación de Mujeres para la Salud, "Violadores, psicópatas y discurso patriarcal," 15.

60. *El Mundo*, January 30, 1993.

61. *El Mundo*, January 31, 1993.

three crimes. These statements put another great myth on the table. Following this argument, an editorial in the periodical *Mientras Tanto* urged the interior minister to reconsider his statements:

> By limiting the scope of guilt to the criminals themselves, and by emphasizing their status as beasts, or werewolves, you are not acting coherently as interior minister to prevent the recurrence of such cases. You only promote the death penalty, you only promote the impunity of your police, who are capable of hunting down criminals but not of preventing crimes. Don't you think you should, at the very least, make a public statement that henceforth anyone who says all women are whores will be regarded as suspect?[62]

The predominant discourse tended to frame the behavior of the perpetrators as exceptional. Yet other voices, such as that of Maite Larrauri, warned against "forgetting that the one frightening us each day, saying degrading things to women and bringing his body close to ours without consent, is nothing more than a peaceful citizen."[63]

The divide that separates the exceptional from the everyday is the same divide that distinguishes the beast from civilized man. The state of exception is, in fact, that zone in which civilized man acquires all the rights to attack like a wild beast or, as the interior minister put it, to go further. But both are the same man. The narrative came with the caveat establishing the man/ nonman duality because, as observed in *Mientras Tanto*,

> it would be unacceptable if the equal status of women as rape-able were to lead us to think, by an elementary

---

62. "Notas editoriales," 5.

63. Maite Larrauri, *El País*, February 14, 1993.

symmetry, that we men also share the condition of rapists. That is not the case. Your statements—Mr. Corcuera— have set the record straight. All men are not equal. You said it yourself, minister, that there are inhuman beasts incapable of controlling their lowly instincts and good, upright men who are prepared to use the strength of our sex to protect the weaker sex.[64]

On the day of the teenagers' funerals, a middle-aged man pondered aloud, trying to understand what had happened: "I could understand if the killers had raped the girls in a moment of blindness. But then . . . who can understand what happened afterward?"[65] As can be seen here, rape as alienation had a degree of social currency. Once again, Larrauri emphasized those socially permitted attitudes that, depending on the circumstances, could become very serious acts:

> The fact that no man is ashamed to boast to other men about what he has done or would like to do to this or that woman, or the fact that few men show contempt for such attitudes, is extremely serious because many things can cause barriers to disappear—including, for example, the certainty of impunity, as shown by the mass rapes in Bosnia. Then comes the horror, the generalized condemnation, and the search for atonement in the belief that there's no one to blame but the perpetrator. The chain of necessity that links what's achievable because it's possible and what's possible because it's thinkable is then ignored.[66]

And if the beasts are not men, where do they live? This was a

---

64. "Notas editoriales," 3.
65. *El Levante Valenciano*, January 31, 1993.
66. Maite Larrauri, *El País*, February 14, 1993.

question to which psychiatry seemed to have an answer. In an interview in *El Levante Valenciano*, psychiatrist Francisco Chelós explained that the reasons such crimes can be committed are related to the environment in which people live. Regarding the Alcàsser crimes, he explained,

> We're talking about a rural environment. There's a gap between the mentality of the urban centers and the towns. In rural areas the social vehicles of the big cities promoting stable and normal relationships between men and women are absent.[67]

The idea that rural environments harbored murderous rapists, and that civilization was a place where this kind of thing happened less, was a throwback to the forest/city dichotomy. This argument was also applied to the profile of the killer. The newspaper *La Tribuna* published the following: "[Antonio] Anglés is illiterate, perverse, and primitive, despite his skill at surviving in rural environments and his primitive intelligence."[68] He was portrayed as a beast, an irrational illiterate guided by instinct and impulse. The fact that psychiatry gave murderers and rapists the profiles of animals for the media made it impossible to identify them. In this sense, the cloud of confusion surrounding the figure who commits such crimes obscures the ideology behind them and provides safe haven for perpetrators.

Another argument that was legitimized by the press was the idea that the man-animal existed thanks to terrible family upbringing. In *La Vanguardia*, an article entitled "Psychiatry Places Sadistic Crimes on the Border of Madness" contained an interview with the psychiatrist Estela Weldon, who offered answers and explanations for how male obfuscation could lead to crimes with the characteristics of those at Alcàsser

---

67. *El Levante Valenciano*, January 30, 1993.

68. *La Tribuna*, March 8, 1993.

These atrocities are like retaliations against that female figure who hurt them, albeit unconsciously. Some experts
believe that sex may not even be the motive for the crimes
but, rather, a mere vehicle, a way of humiliating and hurt-
ing the woman they attack in the place of the one against
whom they want to enact vengeance. It's possible that the
mothers unconsciously treated their sons in a sadistic way,
with continuous beatings, no tenderness, and sometimes
even seductive behavior.[69]

In this case, it was a question of blaming another woman—the
mother—who, besides being an unconscious sadist, failed to fulfill her role. The seduction the mother inflicted on the defense-
less child is transformed, in their maturity, into the capacity to
rape all other women, who are, of course, born provocateurs.
All pathways depicted in the narrative delimit women's behavior
in terms of guilt, whether they are homemakers, teenagers, or
mothers. Furthermore, it's worth noting that one vector of the
narrative about sexual danger in Alcàsser aimed to promote the
restoration of authority in the place of licentiousness. And it
might reasonably be concluded that the authority that needed
to be restored was that of the father. After all, where the mother
exercises authority, she either ends up falling into sadism or traumatizing her children so much they grow up to be murderers.

In *El País*, psychiatrist Luis Rojas Marcos, of the New York
City Health and Hospitals Corporation, provided an explanation for understanding sexual violence. In Rojas's words, sexual
aggression has

a biological and cultural basis. Behind the rapist there
is a psychopathy, an inability to feel the pain he causes
his victim, a superego with an absence of guilt, and one

---

69. "La psiquiatría sitúa en la frontera de la locura los crímenes sádi-
cos," *La Vanguardia*, January 30, 1995.

fundamental element is hatred toward women, an irrational hatred, almost always the product of the abuse or humiliation he has suffered as a child at the hands of a female figure who is very dear or close to him.[70]

The "biological" basis would thus refer exclusively to an inability to restrain sexual instincts. And the "cultural" basis would be the hatred of women based on the humiliation inflicted by a woman who was dear. The psychiatrist describes an abused boy who channels his irrational hatred toward women, a hatred that is just as irrational as his biological inability to repress his sexual desires. Dr. Rojas says,

> Some men channel this hatred in the domestic sphere, and others go outside, attacking other women, sometimes sharing their misdeeds with others. In the case of the alleged killers in Alcàsser, there may also have been a group orgy.[71]

As it stands, the rapists' attitude is almost depicted as a matter of self-defense. It is a matter of making up for past humiliations. It does not explain, however, why women do not defend themselves in the same way for the humiliation of being sexually abused by their fathers. Rojas also argues that men who do not channel their hatred toward their wives go after other women. If they are able to restrain themselves with their wives, why can they not restrain themselves with other women?[72]

---

70. *El País*, January 31, 1993.

71. *El País*, January 31, 1993.

72. These arguments, defended by psychiatrist Luis Rojas in *El País*, are also found in his book *Las semillas de la violencia*. In it, the author states that the seeds of violence are sown in the first years of life and that "these malignant seeds are nourished by the cruel aspects of the environment and grow stimulated by the social conditions and cultural values of the period." Luis Rojas, *Las semillas de la violencia* (Madrid: Espasa, 1995), 187. On the other hand, in the chapter entitled "Violación de la mujer," Rojas

Medicine, as an empirical science, is difficult to refute and, as expressed in the periodical *La Boletina*, it offers a basis for values by which "the sexist attacker is not in fact seen as a subject guilty of committing an aggression but rather as a poor fellow, himself the victim of a repressive society."[73]

When it comes to sexism, science is only as empirical as the meanings that underpin society, as the historian Thomas Laqueur rightly states,"Science does not simply investigate but itself constitutes, the difference [it explores]."[74]

In short, myth becomes science and science becomes myth; "science and melodrama met again, this time locked in a deadly embrace."[75] The idea that psychopathy is what is behind sexual violence, and that it goes hand in hand with a tragic childhood history, has been upheld for years. Virtually all reconstructions of the crimes in subsequent years alluded to the terrible childhood of the offenders.

The notion of a generalized pathology gave way to the figure of the main defendant. The investigation into the character of Antonio Anglés—whose whereabouts remain unknown to this day—functioned as a vehicle to justify his actions. For example, several media outlets reported that Anglés was sexually deviant, gay, and liked to dress as a woman. All these traits, together with a difficult social context and a hard childhood, forged a profile and an answer as to why he had committed the crimes. Both categories, gay and crossdresser, actually revealed a homophobic, misogynist society rather than the profile of an attacker. Society

---

reviews rape in the "history of humanity," in addition to reviewing the work of feminist authors who deal with the subject in their works. Rojas acknowledges the existence of sexism and the patriarchal structure but emphasizes the difficult childhood of sexual offenders as an explanatory element.

73. Asociación de Mujeres para la Salud, "Violadores, psicópatas y discurso patriarcal," 19.

74. Thomas Laqueur, *Making Sex: Body and Gender from the Greeks to Freud* (Cambridge, MA: Harvard University Press, 1990), 17.

75. Walkowitz, *City of Dreadful Delight*, 169.

found in sexuality an apparatus of control from which to justify the physical and sexual torture of the three young women.

First, it was the fact that Anglés liked to take care of his physical appearance that supposedly demonstrated his homosexuality: "He uses creams, oils, and other skin care products; he also waxes, showing a tendency and a certain facility for cross-dressing."[76] Here, the narrative and the myths contradict each other: the idea that Anglés took great care of his appearance is radically opposed to him being akin to a beast or an instinctive animal. Indeed, to the contrary, he had the capacity for self-control, Joan Manuel Oleaque recounts "Unlike his other friends, who spent their time drinking and smoking, Antonio had decided to take care of his body as a teenager. He ate healthily and played *frontón*" (a squash-like sport with Basque origins).[77]

Anglés's alleged homosexuality made room for another set of responses to the crimes. While the association of his behavior with femininity supposedly identifies him as gay, the comparison of a man to a woman is seen to definitively separate him from his manhood. The investigation into Anglés's alleged homosexuality began to flood newspaper pages. In an interview, his former cellmate was asked whether Antonio really liked men, to which he replied "A macho man rapes a woman and, if necessary, kills her, but he does not beat her up, break her teeth, and tear off her nipple like he did."[78] According to this informant, Anglés had killed the teenage girls out of rage, because he saw them as beautiful and successful. Supposedly, since he knew he

---

76. Juan Ignacio Blanco, ¿Qué pasó en Alcácer?, n.p. Available online, the publication was withdrawn from bookshops and from the publisher's catalog following a court order.

77. Joan Manuel Oleaque, *Desde las tinieblas: Un descenso al caso Alcàsser* (Barcelona: Diagonal, 2002), 57. Many towns in Valencia have courts that are open to the public for playing the Valencian variant of the game—Trans.

78. *El Levante Valenciano*, February 6, 1993.

liked men, a kind of impotence took hold of him because he could not be like them and have all the men he wanted. "He would say: 'Those girls go around provoking men, I'm going to fuck them up, but properly.'"[79] What interests me in this informant's arguments are the meanings he uses to express himself: That "a macho man rapes," "girls . . . go around provoking men," and, above all, that murder, torture, and rape were explained by alleged homosexuality. Following the framework of signification set out in the testimony, the flip side of this argument that Anglés's torture of his victims can be attributed to his homosexuality is that sexual assault and murder could be attributed to any heterosexual macho male: "because a macho man rapes and, if necessary, kills."

Anglés's homosexuality also served as grounds for those who, later on, argued that Anglés and the only successfully captured defendant in the crime, Miguel Ricart, had not participated in the Alcàsser crimes. The argument used was that because Anglés was gay, he could not have raped them. Depending on the claim being made, the same discourse was used to support different arguments: for those who believed in Anglés's guilt, he was gay; for those who argued that Anglés was a scapegoat, he was also gay. Yet, subliminally, it seems that both arguments claim that rape is only complete when it happens within the framework of heterosexuality; because rape is not macho if a gay man does it.

The newspaper *El País* had already warned that Anglés could hardly be a normal man: "Those who know him compare him to a panther, and it is known that he practices sadomasochism at its roughest and that he gets aroused by adverts for women's underwear."[80] Although at first sight nothing appeared to hint that the perpetrators of the crimes were primitive savages, as the owner of a bar where they used to go regularly told it, "I

---

79. *El Levante Valenciano*, February 6, 1993.
80. *El País*, January 31, 1993.

couldn't believe it was them, what with how polite, smart, and well-dressed [they were when] they came in to eat."[81] The sexual danger narrative was based on the premise that the rapists had a profile that differentiated them from the rest. However, as highlighted in the editorial "Look the Rapist in the Face," in the journal *Mientras Tanto*, dissociation of these men from their "normal" peers is incredibly difficult:

> I looked the rapists in the face, I read their records published in the newspapers. And my dismay grew. If I had crossed their path, would I have recognized the unmistakable rapist instinct in Miguel Ricart's good looks? How could I tell him apart from all the other nightclub hustlers who make aggressive boasts, not out of malice, but just to show the girls they are strong enough to defend them from other men?[82]

This conceptualization presents us with the portrait of the shifting man, that is, the man who fluctuates between beast and rational man; it also exposes the explicit trap of the "civilized/uncivilized man" dichotomy. According to Judith Butler,

> There is no singular outside, for the Forms require a number of exclusions; they are and replicate themselves through what they exclude, through not being the animal, not being the woman, not being the slave, whose propriety is purchased through property.[83]

That is, identification of perpetrators as vermin, beasts, or psychopaths excludes the rational man from all responsibility. Yet—and here comes the interesting and truly political

---

81. *El Levante Valenciano*, February 1, 1993.

82. "Notas editoriales," 5.

83. Butler, *Bodies That Matter*, 52.

part—it includes him through his exclusion, just as the exception includes the norm through its own suspension.

In the end, what the media did achieve was to make Anglés a famous man. For years, his psychological profile and the reasons why a man like him would come to commit such barbarities filled newspaper pages. This was compounded by the fugitive's adventures on the run. The press began to call him the "angel of death" and to plot all the points through which he was known to have passed on maps. Wherever he was suspected of hiding, the local population was terror struck. As he made his way to the United Kingdom, neither the state police, nor Interpol, nor the customs offices through which he passed managed to arrest him. Anglés became an elusive hero who managed to reach Ireland, escaping before disembarking by throwing himself into the icy waters, where he was presumed to have died. Years later, some remains washed up on a beach; a skull made the front pages. Whether Anglés is alive or not does not matter so long as his legend has a life of its own, and the angel of death continues to feed into the story of Friday the thirteenth in Alcàsser.

Cartography of the Body: The Discipline of Sexual Terror and the Physical Fear of Punishment

Cartography: the art and science of map drawing and the science concerned with maps and their making

The never-ending proliferation of anatomical literature that filled newspapers, magazines, and TV programs represent coordinates on the corporal map produced by the sexual danger narrative. The images were not censored at all: each representation references a specific pain that the body registers, marks, notes down, and stores away. In this way, the discipline of sexual terror maps the body, establishing one route that is safe and others that are not—unapproachable spaces, unnavigable places. The detailed dissection of the physical punishment enacted on the bodies of teenage girls gave way to a social dissection in which everyone participated.

In this part of the account, the public dissection of the teenagers' bodies begins, triggering the definitive restitution of women's bodies as public bodies; they go back to being public, situated in the public domain. Torture in public view has a juridical-political function. It is a ceremonial act that aims to reconstitute a sovereignty that had been momentarily flouted. Michel Foucault writes "It restores that sovereignty by manifesting it at its most spectacular. The public execution, however hasty and everyday, belongs to a whole series of great rituals in which power is eclipsed and restored."[84]

The First Anatomy "Lesson": The Public Body

> *Power here is conditioned on a regularly dramatized public*
> *exhibition of a predatory action against a woman's body.*
>
> **Michel Foucault,** *Discipline and Punish*

Details of autopsies, photographs, and images were released indiscriminately. Preliminary studies provided the first details, and the impact the unveiling of these data had produced a corporal effect that would be difficult to dispel in the long term. With teenage girls' bodies on the front page, it was hard to lay out any temperate feminist or political analysis. By then, society as a whole, and women in particular, were already feeling a form of identification with every act of torture and abuse the teenage girls had endured. The disclosure of forensic details began, at this point, to consolidate the discipline of sexual terror. In Butler's words,

---

84. Michel Foucault, *Discipline and Punish*, 48.

The boundary of who I am is the boundary of the body, but the boundary of the body never fully belongs to me. Survival depends less on the established boundary to the self than on the constitutive sociality of the body. But as much as the body, considered as social in both its surface and depth, is the condition of survival, it is also that which, under certain social conditions, imperils our lives and our survivability. Forms of physical coercion are precisely the unwilled imposition of force on bodies: being bound, gagged, forcibly exposed, ritually humiliated.[85]

In the Alcàsser case, the account of sexual torture revealed the workings of coercion. However, the ritual of humiliation did not end when the teenagers' physical suffering was over. Far from it, the public dissection to which they were subjected, with attention to all the circumstances, all the marks on them, configured a binding, almost perpetual humiliation. In this sense, the public presentation of the girls' bodies and the eyes of society on them, on every inch of them, was the preliminary step required to begin restoring women's bodies to the position of public bodies. With the Alcàsser case, the bodies of the teenage girls took on an unprecedentedly public profile, and this time, it was society as a whole that dissected the bodies.

The bodies speak, and citizens listen. The bodies interrogated by the media are not silenced; they are present, down to every last detail. Media competition was frenetic, and the information circulating was not necessarily factual. According to Teresa Domínguez, a journalist for *El Levante Valenciano*, the silence from those responsible for the investigation led to an even bigger mess: "The mistake from headquarters was to clamp down on the flow of information, which pushed journalists

---

85. Judith Butler, *Frames of War: When Is Life Grievable?* (London: Verso, 2009), 54.

to get it from whoever they could find. And that makes for a shoddy product."[86] The truly noxious headlines were not long in coming. In a matter of days, the whole of society knew all about the girls' last moments. The teenagers' bodies were made just as public for their attackers as they were for a society that watched the bodily dissection from their sofas.

All the newspapers published the details. At the time, having contacts in forensics might mean an advantage. And, if this was not possible, to stop circulation dropping, giving the appearance of having information was a must. One journalist recalled,

> We put in the autopsies at the time because we copied them from *Las Provincias*. It's sad but true. By order of the editor, they were printed, and we left them as they were. On top of that, I remember that the headline was particularly nasty. . . . The protection of privacy wasn't seen as important.[87]

This competition between media outlets had a direct impact on the disproportionate increase in details. Joan Manuel Oleaque recalls,

> People who were there were told, "If that guy said they removed a nipple, that they amputated this and that . . . you go further: the details, the blood, the stab wounds, everything that was cut off."
>
> And she [the journalist] said, "But, come on."
>
> "Do it, dammit. If they say something, you double it." And it was like that. It's true, it was like that.[88]

---

86. Teresa Domínguez, interview, December 16, 2011.

87. Interview with anonymous print journalist, December 13, 2011. At the express wish of the informant, their personal details are omitted, as well as those of the media outlet to which they belong.

88. Joan Manuel Oleaque, interview, December 14, 2010.

The debate about the autopsies focused solely on the ethical question of whether they should have been published. That is, the debate centered on something that was already inevitable. It did not focus on the effects their publication had on women's bodies. The impact of the necropsies was doubly effective because they were accompanied by visual representations. The image, as Butler argues, is a meaning in itself: "The photograph is not merely a visual image awaiting interpretation; it is itself actively interpreting, sometimes forcibly so."[89] The impact of the image is not necessarily determined by the content but by what it suggests. Butler explains, "The photos are not only shown, but named; the way that they are shown, the way they are framed, and the words used to describe what is shown, work together to produce an interpretive matrix for what is seen."[90] Thus, combining visuals of the road where the teenagers hitchhiked, photographs of the La Romana site, and texts with the details of the autopsies forges a direct link between physical territories that already have a specific image association and bodily spaces that already have a pain threshold inscribed on them. And all this was to enable the discipline of sexual terror to become both a corporal practice and a practice of territory-place.

The media described in detail the place where the incidents allegedly took place. In diverse ways, using various visual techniques, they reconstructed the roads traveled. The site of La Romana and the bumpy road leading to it were shown. The pit. All the objects scattered around the site were photographed. The atmosphere of the space where the aggressions took place was saturated with drawings showing the position and the exact spots occupied by the teenagers in the pit. The post, the beam that was supposedly used in restraining the girls for torture, occupied a central position in the image. The recreation of

---

89. Butler, *Frames of War*, 71.
90. Butler, *Frames of War*, 79.

the map of how the place was reached merged with the layouts of the house's interior. A photo of old mattresses crowned the spectacle; in Butler's words, "This is torture in plain view, in front of the camera, even for the camera."[91] The media is sexual violence. The images that went with the details of sexual torture were stored in collective and individual memory. And this made it possible to recreate the scene of the incidents again and again, and to remember them through the body. The interest in autopsies and the way they were leaked and narrated fostered the internalization of sexual terror. The public dissection of teenagers' bodies was both an object and a social objective. One part of society recounted it, and the other watched attentively.

The dissemination of forensic details triggered the discipline of sexual terror's first effects. In the early days, the corporal dissection brought about states of terror and psychosis, especially among women. This widespread fear was interpreted as a direct, if short-lived, effect of the shocking story. However, in reality it signified the large-scale introduction of the discipline of sexual terror. The narrative brought people into direct contact with the existence of awfully specific, concrete, and individualized physical and sexual violence.

The emotional impact of this was compounded by physical pain. The account provoked corporal fear that allowed women not only to put images to what had happened but also to feel it. The early cautionary effects produced by this form of discipline are obvious within the narrative itself. One woman who called the "El Cabinista" section of *Las Provincias* to show her solidarity with the families said,

> Hello. I am incredibly sad, indignant, angry, and scared because what happened with the Alcàsser girls was too much. They had to give me a pill, and I don't have any

---

91. Butler, *Frames of War*, 84.

relationship or family links with these families, but it gave me a nervous breakdown. I mean, this is too much, this is too much, it's unbearable.[92]

The emotional aftermath was intricately linked to the consequences provoked by the dissection of the bodies. The girls—and some boys—in the town of Alcàsser needed psychological assistance to deal with the impact of the story. In the opinion of those who treated them,

> The deployment of the media has aggravated the fears of Alcàsser's young people. They said that when the bodies were found, there was a hand with a watch sticking up above ground, and this hand appeared in the nightmares of many. They described the heads separated from the bodies, and this scene also appeared in many dreams.[93]

As described above, the people affected—including the women interviewed as part of this investigation—had very precise data and images about the details of the agony suffered by the teenagers. The girls and boys of the town "were overloaded with negative images, a hand sticking up, rapes, shots in the head, they go to bed and cannot sleep"; "they close their eyes and see mangled bodies."[94] According to *El País*, the pupils from the state school where Desireé Hernández studied "had to have medical treatment after suffering hysterical crises."[95] Six of the girls' classmates recounted the images that assaulted them at night, "in which arms that wanted to escape from the earth, suffocating black holes, and inert bodies wrapped in paper made frenzied

---

92. *Las Provincias,* January 29, 1993.

93. *La Tribuna,* March 29, 1993.

94. *El País,* January 31, 1993 and *El Levante Valenciano,* February 5, 1993.

95. *El País,* January 29, 1993.

appearances."[96] The teenagers of the time unconsciously witnessed their own bodily defragmentation.

Fear of punishment and physical suffering was coupled with the panic of sexual threat. Particularly unpleasant headlines covered the front pages of newspapers, and the warning of what could happen to any woman was extremely concrete. But the triple crime also confirmed the existence of the tortured bodies, of the physical torture inflicted on them, which was a direct threat. At the burials, anonymous leaflets were thrown into the air saying, "Yesterday it was them, today it could be you."[97] Not only did this bring a blatantly cautionary message to light; it also revealed a whole social system of punishment enacted on women's lives and bodies. Consequently, as Foucault notes, in terms of the sexist regime and sexual danger narratives, "'the whole of society' is precisely that which should not be considered except as something to be destroyed. And then, we can only hope that it will never exist again."[98] The resulting product of Alcàsser's narrative took the form of a dissected body that was to become public, thus returning to the beginning—to the place where the teenage girls hitchhiked. In this way, the *border* is restored, the sexist regime reinstated.

96. *Diario 16*, January 29, 1993.

97. *El Levante Valenciano*, January 31, 1993.

98. Foucault, *Language*, 233.

From Public Bodies to Dissected Bodies: The Penal Process

In the years following the January 1993 discovery of the teen-agers' bodies, a conspiracy theory took root. According to this theory, the suspects, Miguel Ricart and Antonio Anglés, were mere scapegoats: the crimes had actually been committed by high-profile individuals and top politicians. The Alcàsser case becomes a group portrait: in the image reflected back at us, I see the bodies of the young women with a throng of hands prodding their insides. Rembrandt's *Anatomy Lesson* provides the metaphor: there is the teacher (or patriarch), in this case the indiscreet TV camera, who shows a body opened up on a dissection table. A spotlight illuminates it and, just as the pub-lic does, students observe with interest or enthusiasm: some involve the spectators, bringing them in; one looks away; one stares into the middle distance. But they are all present; they smell, touch, explore, and plunge their hands into the bodies of the teenagers.

The Trial Is the TV; the TV Is the Trial

During the nearly four years that elapsed between the discovery of the bodies and the trial, a plethora of hypotheses arose regard-ing what had really happened. The theory that Ricart and Anglés had not acted alone, and that others had been involved, led to a mediatized trial that reopened the controversy.

The Alcàsser case proceedings began in court in May 1997. The real trial, however, as discussed above, had taken place ear-lier. I am interested in the criminal trial only insofar as it was to be configured as an extension of the sentence or punishment imposed on the women. I adopt a definition from Giorgio Agamben's work, with a view to inverting the terms used to approach the analysis: I propose that, regarding the Alcàsser sex crimes,

> the punishment does not follow from judgment, but rather that judgment is itself punishment (*nullum judicium sine poena*). "One can even say that the whole punishment is in the judgment, that the action characteristic of the punishment—incarceration, execution—matters only insofar as it is, so to speak, the carrying out of the judgment.[1]

That is to say, the process that physically and disciplinarily punished the teenage girls—and, by extension, all women— occurred prior to the legal process to which Miguel Ricart was subjected. The judgment that was made concerning the guilt of the girls was, in itself, the imposed sentence. And the criminal proceedings against Ricart were to be an extension of this sentence. In this sense, the trial was to become yet another act of violence against the young women. The Alcàsser trial, which became a season of a soap opera, released episode by episode, only interests me insofar as it constituted the prolongation of the women's trial.

Moreover, I conceive the idea of *bodily dissection* as vital for a consideration of how the Alcàsser trial, in its prolongation, was able to continue enacting a sentence on women. The media once again opened up the bodies of the teenage girls, inspecting and dissecting them. Society speaks with propriety, and proprietarily, about some part or other; expounding on mutilations with a hand inside the bodies: recording, removing parts, commenting, and proffering opinions. All the parts of the bodies are signified

---

1. Giorgio Agamben, *Remnants of Auschwitz: The Witness and the Archive*, trans. Daniel Heller-Roazen (New York: Zone Books, 1999), 19.

by sexual torture in one form or other. This is the punishment that is prolonged: the cautionary tale of what can happen to any woman.

The Alcàsser criminal trial lasted from May to July of 1997. After the sentence had been handed down condemning Ricart to 170 years in prison, some refused to accept that this had brought the Alcàsser case to a close. On camera, a young man in his twenties announced

> This sentence, for me, wasn't very fair, because, come on . . . this man does not deserve it, he was just part of the cover up, he had nothing to do with the rapes or the murders. He simply covered up the facts, and that's it."[2]

This characterization of Ricart aroused pity: not only did the sentence appear unfair and disproportionate, but a cover up of the sexual torture and murder of three young women was considered a minor offense. Thus, from a certain societal perspective, the perpetrator started to be seen as someone who had been misfortunate. To cover up sexual violence is sexual violence, and so is the suggestion that cover-ups should go unsanctioned.

Indignation over the sentence was rooted in conspiracy theories. Before the official trial was held, detractors of the official version got a great deal of TV time to delve into who the real killers of the teenage girls were. In the days prior to the proceedings, in relation to a trial described as "farcical," the public was already expressing opposition. The newspaper *El País* reported, "At dusk, an angry crowd thronged to the streets clamoring against the alleged millionaire murderers at large and the 'ineptness' of justice in a demonstration that had not received authorization from the government."[3] The belief that the crimes had been committed by high-ranking public officials was a factor that contributed

---

2. "Polémica sentencia," *Dossier*, aired September 9, 1997, on TVE.

3. *El País*, May 10, 1997.

to the sex crimes' characterization as class crimes. The father of one of the teenage girls was the main supporter of this hypothesis. In a TV report on Antena 3, the explanation was proffered that, "He accuses the ones at the top, the ones with power and influence, the ones nothing sticks to no matter what. Who could resist taking his side?"[4]

The transformation of sex crimes into a struggle between high-ranking officials and lowly workers made it possible to frame sexual violence within a power structure that emphasized class differences rather than sexism. Moreover, it conceived of women as property that belonged to a given class. In other words, it was the working class who were wronged, rather than women. From the conspiracy theory emerged political demands denouncing different social ills and abuses of power. The Alcàsser trial acted like an escape valve for issues causing social unrest.[5] On the other hand, the idea that high-ranking officials were involved in the crimes had its origin in a classic theme that Judith Walkowitz spotted in nineteenth-century London in relation to Jack the Ripper: "the seduction of poor girls by vicious aristocrats."[6] The conspiracy theory forestalled closure, keeping the process open. But, above all, it let loose the "bad man"—he who is everywhere and can be anyone.

The parameters introduced to demarcate the conspiracy theory shifted the focus of the debate away from the sexism and sexual violence crosscutting all social classes. It was this theory that sparked pity for Ricart, a man who had raped, tortured, and

---

4. *Alcàsser, enganchados al misterio*, aired July 27, 1997, on Antena 3.

5. As Foucault writes, "Once again, we can ask how did the judicial apparatus, and more generally the penal system, operate? My answer is that it has always operated in such a way as to introduce contradictions among the people." Michel Foucault, *Power/Knowledge: Selected Interviews and Other Writings, 1972–1977*, ed. Colin Gordon, trans. Kate Soper et al. (London: Vintage, 1980), 21.

6. Judith Walkowitz, *City of Dreadful Delight: Narratives of Sexual Danger in Late-Victorian London* (Chicago: University of Chicago Press, 1992), 85–86.

murdered three teenage girls. Paradoxically, the contradictory universe in which society attempted to problematize sexual violence was home to the conspiracy theory that debunked the monstrous, primitive, anti-social, psychopathic depiction of the perpetrators. It revealed that those behind such atrocities can wear ties and live in the best houses in town. Ultimately, both the conspiracy theory and the official version widened the gap dissociating the crimes from sexism: the poor blame the rich, and the rich look to the poor, to the beast in the forest. Both ways of thinking form part of myths contributing to the entrenchment of patriarchal norms. In the years leading up to and following the trial, the conspiracy theory that contested the official version gained a great deal of support. In the eyes of society at large, the autopsies, the dissected bodies, were irrefutable sources of information. The different interpretations of the forensic account created an aura of mystery that meant any hypothesis could be thrown into the mix. In the program *Dossier*, a few months before the Ricart's trial, viewers were invited to watch the "narration of events that took place four years ago, through the experiences and diary of the father of one of the girls."[7] In this program, the viewer accompanied the father on a tour of the scene of the events. The interior of La Romana house and the pit in which the teenagers had been buried were shown. In these places, the father discussed his doubts about the burial and the state of the bodies, and violated publication bans. Interspersed with these clips, the undertaker appeared to detail the state of the bodies on the day they were found. The program replayed footage from the day of the funerals, where the grief of friends and families was once again palpable. The last shot hovered over the graves as one by one the names and surnames of the young women appeared in a continuous restitution of the women's (dissected) bodies as public.

---

7. "Alcàsser, diario de un padre atormentado," *Dossier*, aired November 19, 1996, on TVE.

The legal process was thus to begin against a background of heightened anticipation. The Alcàsser trial commenced, and this was the point at which sexual violence was firmly established as a source of entertainment and recreation. The trial, as Jean Baudrillard proposes, was the setting:

> The transition from signs which dissimulate something to signs which dissimulate that there is nothing, marks the decisive turning point. The first implies a theology of truth and secrecy (to which the notion of ideology still belongs). The second inaugurates an age of simulacra and stimulation.[8]

Simulacra or The Social Snuff Film Script, Setting, and the Fan Phenomenon

On May 12, 1997, a lengthy trial began. A great many people were summoned to testify, and anticipation was running high. The media coverage gave the public the chance to attend the trial every day. As reported in *Dossier*, "The trial was broadcast live with a degree of mandatory censorship. Two media outlets in Valencia broadcast it live, and one national and one regional channel held daily debates on the proceedings."[9] This censorship related to the sessions in which the autopsy videos were shown and recounted.

The reason for granting the media and the public access was, in fact, to avoid further suspicions about the trial. A number of interested parties were present, including the public prosecutor and the teenage girls' families' representative. Another prosecuting party was led by the Clara Campoamor Association, a

---

8. Jean Baudrillard, *Simulations*, trans. Phil Foss, Paul Patton, and Paul Beitchman (New York: Semiotext(e), 1983), 12.

9. "Polémica sentencia."

group founded in 1985 with the aim of defending women's rights, particularly in judicial proceedings. The association was represented by Virgilio Latorre, a renowned progressive criminal lawyer who, throughout the proceedings, was conspicuous for his ethical scruples and discretion. Witnesses, experts, and the public filled the Provincial Court of Valencia to capacity.

Outside, crowds of people gathered every day in hopes of gaining access to the courtroom. Numbers were handed out at a kiosk out front. For many, attendance of the sessions became a fixed routine, part of their daily agenda. As one regular explained, "I get up every day at 3:00, 4:30 a.m. and come to the trial. Then I eat, take a little nap, tidy up the house a little, go out a bit in the afternoon, and I do the same the next day."[10] The incidents recounted and the interventions of the different parties generated much suspense among fans; every day new facts were revealed, and new intrigues emerged, "It's like a drug. In the end you get hooked in a way . . . because it gets you interested, and it's not like it's them telling you about it. You see it for yourself, you make up your own mind, you make your own judgment."[11]

The ever-present conspiracy theory operated like a parallel trial. The same witnesses who testified in the morning in the provincial court had testified the night before on TV. Televised debates and programs analyzing each day's session were an enduring presence. The trial and the TV, the TV and the trial; their roles were constantly swapped. For journalist Teresa Laguna, "There were two trials: the trial all the media were watching inside the courtroom, and the trial we were watching on television. They were two different trials."[12]

The way I see it, rather than a parallel trial, it makes sense to think of it as a *simulacrum* that affected all the parties involved and that, as Baudrillard puts it,

---

10. "Polémica sentencia."

11. "Polémica sentencia."

12. Teresa Laguna, interview, December 14, 2011.

reveal[s] to us that "reality" is never more than a world hierarchically staged (*mise-en-scène*), an objectivity achieved according to the rules of depth; that reality is a principle the observance of which regulates all the painting, sculpture, and architecture of the time. But it is a principle and a simulacrum and nothing more, put to an end by the experimental hypersimulation of *trompe l'oeil*.[13]

In other words, the legal process and its broadcast formed part of the construction of the Alcàsser sexual danger narrative. They interacted with each other. They are a single system producing the same thing through different discourses. Therefore, the conspiracy theory and the authorized version, the official and the parallel trial were two sides of the same coin. For this investigation, both form part of the trial that prolongs the sentence handed down to the teenagers, and to women at large.

Generally speaking, it can be said that all programs broadcast about the trial sought to fill their slots with more than just verbatim representations of the hearing. As it was such a long procedure, the court drew up an agenda including all those summoned to testify. From the beginning of the trial, the media therefore knew when witnesses would be testifying. This made it possible for journalists to synchronize the trial sessions with the broadcasts of the programs. Thus, it was quite common for the same witness, expert, or figure to testify on the TV programs the night before or the same day he or she testified in front of the court. As journalist Genar Martí explains, "Take the beekeeper, for example, on the day he had to go to testify. If we wanted to put more emphasis on that story, we would go a few days before, talk to him, and put together a report."[14]

---

13. Jean Baudrillard, "The Trompe l'oeil," in *Calligram: Essays in New Art History from France*, ed. Norman Bryson (Cambridge, UK: Cambridge University Press, 1988), 57.

14. Genar Martí, interview, December 16, 2011.

The sex crimes were transformed into the transferal of characters paraded across different sets. The relatives of the main defendants were a fixture in the media. "The Anglés family," recalls Martí, "we did a report on them when the events happened at the trial, all of them."[15] The outside world had consequences for the trial and vice versa. In this loop, the line between reality and fiction was what was being revealed. And this very subtle demarcation was to sustainably entrench the simulacrum. In the course of prosecutor Enrique Beltrán's interrogation of Enrique Anglés (the brother of the accused), planes of reality and fiction overlapped:

"Your brother wasn't normally violent, was he?"
"He wasn't violent, no."
"But, when he wanted something and he couldn't get it, that's when he was violent, right?"
"No."
"Not even then?"
"Not even then."
"But that's what you said on TV last night."
"But we're in court, not on TV."[16]

Statements made outside the courtroom could be debated by the public, but those made inside the trial were implicated in the process itself. This double role, this double mask concealing the same reality, was a component that facilitated the transmission of the Alcàsser crimes alongside the ever-present question of discerning what was real and what was interpretation. Baudrillard provides an interesting definition of fiction and reality that I believe may encompass the narrative construction process here:

15. Martí, interview.
16. *Alcàsser, enganchados al misterio*, aired July 27, 1997.

To dissimulate is to feign not to have what one has. To simulate is to feign to have what one hasn't. One implies a presence, the other an absence. But the matter is more complicated, since to simulate is not simply to feign. "Someone who feigns an illness can simply go to bed and make believe he is ill. Some who simulates an illness produces in himself some of the symptoms." (Littré) Thus, feigning or dissimulating leaves the reality principle intact the difference is always clear, it is only masked.[17]

The thoughts shared in the programs not only broadcast the public's different perspectives on the crimes but also reciprocally influenced the way in which the witnesses and experts themselves interpreted what happened in the trial. This is how Virgilio Latorre, one of the prosecution lawyers, explains it:

I don't care if someone goes on TV and says whatever comes to mind. The problem is when an expert comes and tells you something. And that calls into question other evidence as to who the accused is and, therefore, their guilt.[18]

The trial was the place, the metaphorical stage on which the media, citizens, theories about the crimes, anatomical-forensic details, and interpretations of it all came together. Latorre draws attention to the importance of using objective evidence to reveal the inconsistency of some theories:

We had to explain the difference between what it means to speak on television and what it means to speak in a trial, and how there were certain errors they'd been pushed to make, and we were able to get them out of them by

---

17. Baudrillard, *Simulations*, 5.

18. Virgilio Latorre, interview, October 25, 2010.

comparing what they were saying on television and what was in the criminal investigation.[19]

The criminal courtroom was a grand forum for debate that contributed to the creation of knowledge: sexual violence seen as spectacle. The trial condemned Ricart but let sexual violence off, behind the smokescreen of spectacle. The trial as a whole—TV versus court of justice—constituted the culmination of one of the phases of the sexual danger narrative in which we can see the true meaning of simulacrum. In Baudrillard's words:

> Whereas representation tries to absorb simulation by interpreting it as false representation, simulation envelops the whole edifice of representation as itself a simulacrum. This would be the successive phases of the image: it is the reflection of a basic reality; it masks and perverts a basic reality; it masks the absence of a basic reality; it bears no relation to any reality whatever. It is its own pure simulacrum.[20]

In other words, the sex crimes were a reflection of an underlying reality. The mechanism of the sexist microphysics of power and the strategy of the exception masks and denaturalizes this underlying reality: sexual violence dissociated from the narrative and transformed into TV, film, and spectacle ends up concealing the absence of the deeper truth. The judicial procedure no longer had anything to do with reality; it was already a simulacrum.

The conspiracy theory managed to discredit the judicial process and focus attention on its main protagonist, Miguel Ricart, whom part of the public already saw as a scapegoat. Thus, one of the perpetrators of the triple crime came to have two lines of defense: his lawyer and public opinion. On the other

---

19. Latorre, interview.
20. Baudrillard, *Simulations,* 11.

hand, the victims remained in the background; their bodies the only source of information, they were kept in anticipation. The private prosecution, which represented one group of the families (that of the father who had put forward the conspiracy theory), suggested, in its interventions, that Ricart was not the only one responsible for what had happened. In a trial in which what was being judged was precisely Ricart's participation in the events, the private prosecution was singled out for working for the defense instead of for the prosecution. Virgilio Latorre pointed this out in the trial itself:

> There was this moment, it was one of the most critical moments of the trial, when, after a series of questions from the private prosecution, I interrupted. I asked for the floor and said that the private prosecution was working perversely, since it was doing the work of the defense rather than the prosecution, and it was disturbing.[21]

This allegation put the actions of the private prosecution under the spotlight, as they were carrying out defense work on Ricart's behalf, rather than accusing him. Latorre recalls:

> And what a commotion there was. There was great uproar because, as a result of that, the defense got very offended. They said they were withdrawing. At that time, we were almost halfway through the trial, and it would have meant a mistrial. The private prosecution didn't care. The Bar Association intervened, there were meetings where I tried to explain what I meant in order to calm things down. In addition, at that time, the association sent observers who were at the trials. I mean, it was all pretty deplorable. Then, little by little, things began to return to normal.[22]

---

21. Latorre, interview.

22. Latorre, interview.

The threat of abandonment by the defense would have resulted in a mistrial, which, for the defendant, was in itself an advantage. A mistrial would also have benefited the parties defending the conspiracy theory.

In addition, the different hypotheses broadcast on TV gave the defendant arguments to which he could refer. In this sense, the conspiracy theory provided Ricart with alibis that he himself began to use in his defense, Latorre recalls,

> no matter how much he later denied these things and declared his innocence. Moreover, he even supported it with arguments from TV. If they said, "The hairs don't bla bla bla, or whatever . . ." on TV, then he would say, "No . . . and besides, those hairs are of no consequence," and he would follow the trail of the discourse the press had used.[23]

What we know for certain is that Ricart gave extensive details of the torture suffered by the teenage girls. Whether or not there were more people involved, or whether the events occurred in one order or another, such brutal details are not incompatible with the evidence of his participation and collaboration in the execution of the crimes. Pretending to cover up for someone, or pretending to have knowledge about matters he was not supposed to talk about, did not absolve him of responsibility for the acts. The fact that TV provided him with an alibi exposes the workings of the social system itself.

The trial of Ricart gave carte blanche to the snuff film theory. One of the conspiracy hypotheses concerned the potential existence of a recording of the sexual torture. This idea became quite widespread. However, without wading in on the question of its existence, what I can confirm is that, up to now, the only existing snuff film was that which was shot and viewed by society itself. Consuming images; downloading, viewing, and publishing the

---

23. Latorre, interview.

photos and the autopsy reports; or debating the most lurid parts of the criminal investigation are all modes of accessing the snuff film of the Alcàsser crimes.

Before the trial was held, some of the media already had access to documents from the criminal investigation into the triple crime. Particularly noteworthy at this stage was TV presenter Pepe Navarro's polemic program, *Esta Noche Cruzamos el Mississippi*, on Telecinco, in which the father of one of the teenagers appeared every night. On the show, no part of the teenagers' bodies was spared dissection, analysis, or exhibition. Rosa Folch, Desireé Hernández's mother, found out about the content that was going to appear in the program from watching TV:

> I turn on Telecinco and I hear them say, "We have the scoop on the Alcàsser criminal investigation."
>
> I said, "For God's sake, the Alcàsser investigation scoop? What is this? What is it?"
>
> That's when the soap opera started, and they just started saying stuff, like what they had done to the girls. Besides, lots of it was lies.[24]

The idea of dissection, of the fragmented body, of explicit violence shown on TV, became the snuff film of a whole society—a society that avidly watched the sexual torture to which the teenagers had been subjected, day after day, live and direct. The forensic details became a media superstar in their own right. Access to the investigation was partial, and not everyone enjoyed the same privilege as Telecinco. The father of one of the girls, Fernando García, had given exclusive access to Navarro's program on that channel; to the rest of the media, he only revealed bits and pieces of information. As Genar Martí explains,

> We interviewed him in the office. He had the criminal

24. "Polémica sentencia."

investigation documents and showed you a few things but wouldn't let you take anything away with you. . . . It was a bit like an investigation managed by him.[25]

As was the case with the first details of the autopsies, the fact that only a couple of media outlets had access to the criminal investigation documents prompted the dissemination of poorly verified information and fierce competition between outlets.

Every night, society watched a film reenactment in real time: the brutality of the images and the suspense provided by the bodily dissection made the program one of the most successful primetime TV shows. The program contributed to the debate's resurrection in the streets, and rumormongering took center stage. As Rosa Folch recalled, it was like a serial that society at large appeared to be hooked on:

> I was going to work, and even my coworkers, the ones I wasn't so close to, started saying, "Did you see this or that yesterday?" And it really hurt me, because they brought stuff up and said things they shouldn't have said. Because the criminal investigation documents are for the parties involved, for the three families, for the lawyers. But not to take to a TV show as if it were a soap opera.[26]

The social reappropriation of girls' bodies, and their management as a scoop, enable a particularly violent heteropatriarchal logic to persist: others may disclose, make decisions on, touch, observe, and talk about women's bodies without permission.

All kinds of theories came out of the woodwork to complement the conspiracy hypothesis; some mentioned satanic rites, others diabolical sects. The fascination provoked by the Alcàsser fable took hold of the public. And the conspiracy theory had

---

25. Martí, interview.

26. "Polémica sentencia."

additional appeal: not only did it go against the official truth, but it also confronted power. In his book *Toda la verdad diez años después*, journalist Francisco Pérez Abellán writes:

> Television had come across an exciting case that, for the first time, was daringly covered live. The country browsed its mysteries. On Pepe Navarro's program, a group of the best investigative journalists prepared a special every day to debate all the murky parts live.[27]

The author of this book (discussed in detail below) thus characterized the Alcàsser crimes using two words: *fascinating* and *mysterious*. However, there is nothing mysterious about the murder of women. The freedom of expression that was so celebrated clashed head on with the right to privacy of the families and the teenage girls themselves, as well as the women who had been directly affected by the sexual danger narrative. What was being defined as exciting was, essentially, the sexual torture of three young women. Folch once again highlighted the contradictions of this process: "They took pictures of my daughter, and it hurt me even more. My other daughter recognized her when they took the photo of my daughter as they had left her there."[28] The teenage girls became public once again, as they had been for their executioners. The reproduction of the snuff film was only possible in a society that consented and endorsed it. Let us return to the image of a whole society around a dissection table. There is the anatomist, who cuts, shows, teaches, and a light that illuminates the body to be dissected, leaving the rest of the painting in semi-darkness.

---

27. Francisco Pérez Abellán, *Alcácer, punto final: Toda la verdad diez años después* (Barcelona: Martínez Roca, 2002), 89. Francisco Pérez Abellán was a regular contributor to María Teresa Campos's program *Día a Día* and Pepe Navarro's program *Esta Noche Cruzamos el Mississippi*, as an investigative journalist specializing in the world of crime.

28. "Polémica sentencia."

Such banalization, and the "TV series" that was essentially produced, can best be analyzed by looking to the stream of devotees the Alcàsser crimes mobilized. The fans were, after all, the most visible part of the spectacle, of the simulacrum. As one broadcast described it, "For some, attending a session of the Alcàsser trial was a holiday highlight. To see Miguel Ricart up close, to see those who tried him, to breathe the air of the Valencian courtroom was just another tourist attraction."[29] Indeed, Antena 3 featured a segment dedicated exclusively to the fan phenomenon and the regulars who filled the courtroom every day. A fan explained, smiling at the camera, the reasons why he and his family were at the trial:

> I've come from Zaragoza. I'm attending the trial for national interest and because of the hype surrounding the issue. I'm on holiday, and because my daughter and wife were interested in the issue, I've come to the trial. For them, more than anything, you know? I'd go further: my daughter is a staunch fan of [the rock band] El Último de la Fila, and my daughter wouldn't swap this trial for an El Último de la Fila concert.[30]

TV programs began to focus on the fan phenomenon and to interview fans at the entrance to the courtroom. "We did a report on the regulars," recalls Martí. "There were about fifty people who went every day."[31] The most enthusiastic fans talked about the trial and each other with alarming flippancy:

> I come to the trial because I like it and because, I don't know . . . every day . . . you want it . . . like a drug. You get up and say, Let's see what happens today, what comes

---

29. *Alcàsser, enganchados al misterio,* July 27, 1997.

30. *Alcàsser, enganchados al misterio,* July 27, 1997.

31. Martí, interview.

out. Let's see if something new comes out. And that's it. It's interesting. It's an incentive. I'm very happy to come. There are some great people there. And we have good times, with the bad, of course; because, of course, you don't come out of morbidity.[32]

For the teenage girls' relatives, the fascination that the sex crimes provoked did not translate into respect. "The day I went to the trial," said Folch, "I had a lot of people behind me who kept talking and laughing. They were falling asleep and everything."[33]

The fan phenomenon revealed the extent to which the Alcàsser crimes were becoming a legend with considerable draw. Martí recalls:

There was a pregnant woman who came to the trial every day. At one point [she] said the following: "I'm having a girl, and I'm going to name my girl Míriam, Toñi, or Desireé."[34]

This example illustrates how, by this point, the sexual torture had completely dissolved into the very system that produces and protects it.

Ricart, for his part, also attracted the attention of the fans and the cameras, which latched onto the most insignificant details about him. Martí recounts, "Every day you had to do Ricart's entrance; then you went on to comment on whether he was wearing this shirt or that shirt or whether he had worn the same shirt."[35] These details did not go unnoticed by Ricart himself. Seeking notoriety and aware of the curiosity he aroused, on

---

32. *Alcàsser, enganchados al misterio,* July 27, 1997.
33. "Polémica sentencia."
34. Martí, interview.
35. Martí, interview.

one occasion he swapped his shirt with another prisoner being tried on the same day. It seems he wanted to provoke a reaction in the media and offer a new anecdote to tell. This is the real reward and punishment established by the social order: the executioner is exalted, and the victims punished through the public exposure of their bodies.

After a lengthy procedure, the trial came to an end. As was to be expected, the sentencing sparked misgivings and diverse readings. Yet, the important thing about the Alcàsser trial is not the sentence itself. Agamben reminds us:

> As jurists well know, law is not directed toward the establishment of justice. Nor is it directed toward the verification of truth. Law is solely directed toward judgment, independent of truth and justice. This is shown beyond doubt by *the force of judgment* that even an unjust sentence carries with it. The ultimate aim of law is the production of a *res judicata*, in which the sentence becomes the substitute for the true and the just, being held as true despite its falsity and injustice.[36]

What was important about the trial, therefore, was that it offered a chance to reveal the arena in which the narrative was consolidated as a simulacrum, the space in which all elements waver between the real and the fictitious.

There is no doubt that the sentence failed to close the case. The Alcàsser crimes, far from being forgotten, continued to produce truth. The discipline of sexual terror diversified, the narrative branched out, and the representations of sexual danger continued intact in a plethora of different forms. Today, the internet is the space that harbors each and every one of the meanings herein discussed. The web constitutes a virtual space in which the Alcàsser crimes are firmly installed and where the

---

36. Agamben, *Remnants of Auschwitz*, 18.

publication of photos and images of the teenage girls is infinite and indiscriminate. The repeated display of the photographs of the autopsies is a way of reinforcing women's bodies as public. "The indefinite circulability of the image," as Judith Butler observes, "allows the event to continue to happen and, indeed, thanks to these images, the event has not stopped happening."[37] This is the prolongation of punishment of women's bodies.

Regarding the end of the trial, a journalist from the newspaper *Diario 16* reflected on the effect of the dissected body: "the repetition ad nauseam, in all the country's media, of the most gruesome details of the murder of the three Valencian girls has unleashed something that could well be called *Alcàsser syndrome*, a veritable collective psychosis."[38] On the twentieth anniversary of the crimes, once again, all the details were recounted, the circumstances surrounding the events discussed, the images shown, and the psychopathy of the murderers debated. With each anniversary, the forensic details are recalled; with each news item about the perpetrators, the idea that the "bad man" is still at large is reactivated.

The Bestseller: The Novelized Vindication of Sexist Truth

I have chosen the term *bestseller* to describe the production of the books written about the Alcàsser crimes. The most interesting thing about these publications was just how effective the authors were in continuing to produce sexist truth about the case.

Through the bestseller, sexual danger narratives may convey the discipline of sexual terror in a leisurely manner, under scientific or literary guises. Although each publication was structured differently, they all ended up emphasizing the anatomical-

---

37. Judith Butler, *Frames of War: When Is Life Grievable?* (London: Verso, 2009), 86.

38. *Diario 16*, August 10, 1997.

forensic details. Even more seriously, together they produced a narrative in which they dared to describe not only the sexual torture but the feelings the girls themselves had experienced. While newspapers and TV had previously been responsible for publishing the details of the abuse suffered, the bestsellers offered an emotional recreation of the teenagers' feelings and the events that took place at La Romana house. Each book, of course, competed in the market, claiming its information had been hitherto unheard: their prologues brimmed with promises to reveal the hidden truth.

We must ask the whys and wherefores of these books in the terms proposed by philosophers Gilles Deleuze and Félix Guattari:

> We will never ask what a book means, as signified or signifier; we will not look for anything to understand in it. We will ask what it functions with, in connection with what other things it does or does not transmit intensities, in which other multiplicities its own are inserted and metamorphosed, and with what bodies without organs it makes its own converge.[39]

These books functioned in relation to the prevailing meanings of sexual violence in society at the time.

With a view to offer a closer, more in-depth analysis, I have selected two books to focus on. Although vastly different, both follow a similar structure. They are *Alcácer, punto final* by Francisco Pérez Abellán, and *Desde las tinieblas: Un descenso al caso Alcàsser* by Joan Manuel Oleaque.[40] The protagonist of

---

39. Gilles Deleuze and Félix Guattari, *A Thousand Plateaus: Capitalism and Schizophrenia* (London: Bloomsbury, 1988), 4.

40. The title of this book uses the Spanish spelling of Alcàsser. For the purposes of the translation of this book, the Valencian spelling of the name has been used in line with the original and the official name of the town at the time of publication—Trans.

Francisco Pérez Abellán's book is Miguel Ricart, one of the perpetrators of the crimes. The book offers a sexist, homophobic account in which the author pays particular attention to the sexual orientation of Anglés and Ricart. The journalist brings together Ricart's opinions on the Alcàsser case, as expressed from prison through his correspondence with a fan. At the start of the book the author states, "The privacy of the girls has been protected at all times. Particular care was taken with description of the episodes of sexual assault, so as to avoid the invocation of painful recollections for family members and friends."[41] The respect for privacy to which he refers only translated into sparing the victims' names. As far as the account of the events is concerned, it not only describes the aggressions vividly but also gives a voice to the perpetrators. He replaces the girls' names with numbers or signs, because, as he sees it, this spares individual suffering without altering what actually happened. For the author, the narration of the aggressions is crucial for his subsequent explanation of his reasoning in relation to the offenders' attitude. In this vein, Abellán's first chapter is titled "Hacérselo con una muerta" (literally, "Doing it to a dead woman"). Respecting the privacy of the girls does not seem to mean avoiding morbid language. The title, despite having nothing to do with the facts, aims to establish Anglés's sexual deficiencies. Although the journalist does not mention any names, the allusion is plain. In essence, the titles and descriptions he selects to show the reader what happened constitute the exercise of sexual violence through language.

Oleaque, in contrast, places us in the moment before the crimes. His narration brings us into the teenagers' rooms, thus purporting to offer insight into their feelings. Oleaque recounts in detail the suffering they endured and immerses us in the anguish of the girls' last moments, telling us what they felt at the end. In the author's opinion, emotional identification with

41. Abellán, *Alcácer, punto final*, 11.

the teenagers is a technique he uses to give the text more appeal, "There should be a degree of identification so that it is not simply a journalistic account. I understood that this was a way of doing it that could engage the reader."[42] The emotional aspect is dealt with using literature, the details of the autopsies using science—a science that is not as literal as it is made out to be. That is to say, when the time comes to relate the facts, both authors explain what happened by interpreting them. They do not make a literal transcription of the autopsies using forensic language: they frame the facts in a context; they stage them; they narrate them. It follows that their descriptions of anatomical-forensic details are by no means neutral.

Forensic language is technical, but neither author reproduces it verbatim; to the contrary, they situate the violence within a space, with specific protagonists and actions. They produce a detailed description of specific physical suffering. The idea of *bodily dissection* is just as present in the books as it was on TV. The difference is that on TV, the dissection is postmortem, while the bestseller recounts the teenagers' torture while they were still alive. In Oleaque's book, the reader moves from the room of one of the young women, the shy, homely girl, to *La Romana* house, where "Ricart felt her fear pulsating."[43] The autopsies are understood as evidentiary facts to be transformed into a good story. To consider these books journalistic or investigative would mean overlooking their sexist content and production. People who approach them in search of the promised truth are again confronted with the sexual danger narrative.

For his part, Abellán focuses on Ricart's and Anglés's masculinity and sexual orientation. The journalist's account becomes as much a defense of heterosexual masculinity as an ode to homophobia. For this author, sexual violence has a logical explanation, which is sexual frustration. This interpretation

---

42. Joan Manuel Oleaque, interview, December 14, 2010.

43. Oleaque, *Desde las tinieblas*, 87.

of the facts allows Abellán to move away from the official version, in which the perpetrator was Anglés. Indeed, Abellán claims that it was Ricart who was capable of carrying out such acts and attributes each and every act of sexual aggression and the three murders to him. In a less direct way, the author describes the sexual torture (using other words) as carried out under the ever-watchful eye of Anglés's homosexuality and the impossible love that he—according to Abellán—felt for Ricart.

In his opinion, only a man could commit such a crime:

> And when it came to sex, what was Antonio like? He didn't look like a powerful guy with a drill at his groin. Rather, he could have been one of those who barely gets half an erection, with anorgasmia and aspermia.[44]

Questioning Anglés's masculinity cast doubt over whether a man who was not a man could commit certain forms of sexual aggression.

Moreover, apparently, though Ricart was not gay, his sexuality had not developed "normally" either. Abellán ponders:

> Does Ricart need sex? What he had mastered of technique, he had learned on his own, by instinct, like an animal. Or with his girlfriend, the mother of his daughter. She has probably known for a long time that Miguel is a sex thief, a sex addict; another guy with more yearning than opportunity.[45]

Abellán suggests some kind of deviation in the case of Ricart, presuming the perpetrators of the triple murder must both have been either gay or sexually deviant; they could not have been "normal" men. In this way, the author manages to

---

44. Abellán, *Alcácer, punto final*, 20.

45. Abellán, *Alcácer, punto final*, 25.

exempt men as a social group from any responsibility, including himself: "According to the law that what man despises is also what he fears resembles him."[46] At the same time, he reinforces heteronormative masculinity.

For Abellán, the ability to properly perform the sex act is the backbone of masculinity. Otherwise, a man becomes a psychopath or a half man, a gay person. The text, which is mainly focused on this aspect, relates each and every aggression from this perspective, which makes the descriptions of sexual torture even more harrowing than in other books. According to Abellán's perspective, any man with a sexual dysfunction or who was incapable of giving pleasure to his partner could develop the desire to rape and torture women. The truth is that these depictions work to exonerate men of responsibility.

Another of the explanations developed by the journalist focuses on the love between the protagonists, or, rather, on the unrequited love that Anglés supposedly professes for Ricart. Thus, Anglés's incapacity puts the spotlight on Ricart, who goes from being a mere accomplice to being, in Abellán's version, the main perpetrator of the crimes. Anglés necessarily became the collaborator because he, as Abellán relates,

> needed someone else to have sexual intercourse and reserved the role of voyeur for himself. This way he would not have to go through the inevitable examination of his physical qualities: his athletic or perhaps stunted body, tiny penis, and repressed homosexual tendencies.[47]

Abellán pathologizes and ridicules homosexuality, treating it as a factor that explains violent sexual behavior toward women. However, when it comes to Ricart, he does not delve into the characteristics associated with his heterosexual condition.

---

46. Agamben, *Remnants of Auschwitz*, 52.

47. Abellán, *Alcácer, punto final*, 214.

Although this was clearly not his intention, Abellán places rape solely and exclusively within the purview of heterosexuality.

Nevertheless, the author, despite all the contradictions, homes in on a single issue that gives him doubts about Anglés: "He liked men, preferably boys, and yet he kidnaps, tortures, and rapes three young women over a few hours?"[48] Abellán's search for an answer throws up a solution that places responsibility on the girls. This prompts him to ask what kind of "girls" the murdered young women were

> It is true that they were incredibly young girls, aged fourteen to fifteen, but all three had female forms and could not be said to be androgynous. Whoever abducted them wanted to take women, not teens obsessed with looking in the mirror.[49]

When describing the assault, the author consistently uses the word *girls*, but when it comes to explaining why they were chosen, the problem lies with them: in the fact that they had womanly forms. Thus, the girls become teenagers with women's bodies, not girls dressed up as women.

This idea that the girls were already women is common to the work of both authors. Both make the point that beauty, particularly that of one of the teenagers, could have brought on the danger. Oleaque makes this point:

> Of good height, [she was about five foot five] with long, wavy light-brown hair that came down to her shoulders, light-blue eyes enlivening pale skin, shyness tempered by a faint playfulness, with all this and more, Míriam had real promise.[50]

---

48. Abellán, *Alcácer, punto final*, 137.
49. Abellán, *Alcácer, punto final*, 137.
50. Oleaque, *Desde las tinieblas*, 17–18.

Beneath all this literary rhetoric, Oleaque describes physical characteristics that, by virtue of the fact that she is beautiful, already make her a "promising" young woman. Having promise implies possession of a certain quality or aptitude that helps one succeed, in this case beauty—a beauty that she would deploy with a sweet, "shy" "playfulness."

Abellán also sees it this way:

> Before the crimes, Míriam received much affection from her grandparents, and from her uncles and cousins, for whom it meant a great deal to see her blossom, especially at that time, when she was taking the airs of a woman into her girlish heart. She had begun to be an extremely attractive girl, and in the depths of their souls, the women of the family feared lest this explosion of beauty might attract some evil.[51]

In other words, the young woman's beauty turned out to be almost synonymous with provocation, with attracting danger. This is the tipping point at which women become responsible for aggressions. The "airs" of womanhood and the "blossoming" of sexuality constitute a limit at which nonmen men lose their sanity. In absolute terms, the problem within the Alcàsser crimes is that Míriam was beautiful. Both authors, like the girls' attackers, kept their gaze fixed on the body of the teenager whom they observe, watch, and describe without her permission. They allow themselves to express an opinion about her beauty and her body; they touch it through words. And, subliminally, they hold the teenager responsible for *the(ir) gaze*, for the way they look at her. This is sexual violence.

---

51. Abellán, *Alcácer, punto final*, 35.

La Romana House and Bare Life

The following pages have the express purpose of resignifying spaces and intersections that are subtly hidden in the narrative. Their aim is to render these everyday social territories political using Giorgio Agamben's concepts of *exception, state of exception,* and *bare life.* These concepts are brought to bear on the entire Alcàsser narrative in order to decipher what I have called *the metaphor of the Alcàsser sex crimes.* I also use *no-man's-land* to designate the political space through which the heterosexist construction *the public woman* passes.

Viewing the Alcàsser case politically makes room for us to stop treating it as an isolated or exceptional event, and to start conceptualizing it as a sexual danger narrative. Once transformed into a political narrative, the text is revealed to be one of boundaries, closed spaces, sexual torture, symbolic violence, and, most importantly, invisible metaphors: a labyrinth of geometric violence is unveiled.

This idea of metaphor, of inaccessible spaces, of nameless places, of the nonexistent sites in which the symbolism of sexual danger unfurls: this is what pushed me to write this chapter as a differentiated space. In doing so, I hope to represent these symbolic spaces within the very *corpus* of the book's narrative through the ever-ambiguous metaphor: the much-overlooked symbolic violence, impossible to regularize or put into words, formidably difficult to recognize. Moreover, these are spaces that women move through on a daily basis, spaces full of violence that needs to be put into words. My goal is to politicize these spaces so as to place them at the center of our social structure. Making the metaphor of spaces visible means naming those places where women's lives and men's access to their bodies are negotiated.

Here I make the same journey as the teenagers, from the moment they hitched a ride and got into the car to the moment they reached La Romana house. I aim to rewrite the Alcàsser sex crimes, shedding light on the pathways, the political spaces that the sexist regime sets up to cover sexual violence. I aim to resituate each space, reconceptualizing the intersections, the boundaries within which the bodies and lives of women are being resignified.

Sexual danger narratives are constructed as a response to the social order experiencing a threat: the Alcàsser sexual danger narrative is a construction that safeguards the integrity of the sexual social order. This protection is inherent to the system. To put it in organic terms, the social body defends itself.

The metaphor hidden within the Alcàsser narrative is a symbolic representation: abstract figures and formulas that appear harmless at first. The many figures in which the metaphor dwells are faithful to and find their analogy in the ways in which the sexist microphysics of power was to later be transferred to the narrative. In other words, each of the small figures that I try to resignify here are those places and details that the narrative objectified and passed off as unimportant. These places have their own explanations and negotiations over rights and possibilities, and transgressions take place in each. A series of spaces, of intersections, give rise to the passage from one bodily state to another: they are not imaginary lines; they are borders that are embodied.

These metaphors could not work without the support of a political regime that makes their operation possible. They are the system's strategies to defend itself. They function in a coordinated way, never arbitrarily, and constantly produce and reproduce the social order. I associate each of these places with a form of symbolism: hitchhiking with *no-man's-land*; the forest and the city with the *state of exception*; and La Romana house with *bare life*. It is these spaces to which I turn, and which will allow me to resignify the sexual danger narrative about the Alcàsser crimes. These articulations, intersections, and areas are places pre-envisaged by the social order because they function as emergency exits. They are spaces that do not exist explicitly. They are the license the sexist system gives itself.

Three teenagers, three young women, leave the city; they cross the border. Their attitude and their freely made decision to hitchhike constitute the first boundary crossed. This is, therefore, the place in which the entire reformulation begins. The practice of hitchhiking is a transgressive act through which teenage girls put themselves in inevitable danger.

This idea of *danger*, of finding oneself hopelessly at the mercy of the threat, constitutes the empty space that opens and configures no-man's-land, a zone provisioned for and provided by the system itself. But this no-man's-land is by no means a neutral or unregulated space. No-man's-land is a demarcation of the sexist regime. It is not about being in a remote area, alone, unaccompanied, or in a dark corner with scarce passersby. These circumstances, by themselves, pose no threat. No-man's-land means, for women, belonging to no one, which implies constituting seized property. It means, above all, being a woman in the absence of male protection and, as a consequence, it means being public, being everybody's or anybody's. At first, however, no-man's-land is a space that opens as possibility and, therefore, is still governed by the rules of the city. That possibility is what mediates between the threat being real or simply one alternative. In other words, no-man's-land as such does not take shape until the threat comes to pass. Until then, it is simply a space that the system enables in anticipation of women crossing the line. It is women who put themselves in danger; no-man's-land can only be reached if one wishes to do so. Therefore, it could be said that no-man's-land is the place that the patriarchal order enables its sexist correctives to develop—or not. The social order foresees this possibility and legitimizes those spaces in which anyone can access women's bodies.

In no-man's-land, women are placed in an indeterminate space where their right to life and to their bodies is negotiated. The very possibility of danger places us directly in a different time and bodily space. The decision to hitchhike is a bodily decision and, in this sense, constitutes a transgression against the sexual regime. The young women enter an autonomous space by themselves; they are free bodies, not subject to their fathers' rule. And no-man's-land is a space that belongs to men. Because they enter and remain there with no man, the girls are watched—through a vantage point no-man's-land itself enables—by the sovereign, who may claim for themself those bodies without owners. This is a conquest that takes place not in a lawless land—for the rules of the sexist regime prevail—but in the ownerless body. No-man's-land is the place where women's bodies are both free and public; a space where men have the possibility and the opportunity to make decisions about women's lives and bodies.

This possibility of punishing teenage girls, which the sovereign has at their disposal, is exercised in no-man's-land, where these rights are acquired and reinforced. It is also the place where the sovereign power transcends, because, as theorist Rita Laura Segato notes,

> there is no sovereign power that is only physical. Without psychological and moral subordination of the other, there is only death power, and death power by itself is not sovereignty. Complete sovereignty, in its most extreme phase, implies "to make live or let die." With no control over life as such—that is, of the living—domination cannot complete itself.[1]

As the girls get into the car, no-man's-land is also the point that delimits what is socially acceptable. The figure of the sovereign is already in a position to decide on the life and death of the three teenagers. And it is at the extreme end of no-man's-land that the regime was to activate the next figure: the state of exception.

---

1. Rita Laura Segato, "Territory, Sovereignty, and Crimes of the Second State," in *Terrorizing Women*, ed. Rosa-Linda Fregoso and Cynthia Bejarano (London: Duke University Press, 2010), 74–75.

Under the state of exception, a series of specific characteristics were to be introduced, which would enable the justification of the crimes outside society. The state of exception is a dangerous instrument, for in it and from it the temporary suspension of all rights is proclaimed. The sexist regime therefore enables the state of exception by legitimizing the authority of the sovereign and the exercise of violence over women's bodies. This unwritten legitimacy, which is nevertheless socially sanctioned, is the best-guarded metaphor of the figure of the state of exception. Thus, the state of exception is enabled by the norm (that is, by the *social body*) and makes possible the momentary suspension of all rights. The state of exception is always enabled within the framework of the social norm: it is the norm that summons, permits, and shelters it. Without the regulations that configure it, it could not be implemented. In a state of exception, anything can happen under the shelter of suspension. In Agamben's words, "The state of exception is not a special kind of law (like the law of war); rather, insofar as it is a suspension of the juridical order itself, it defines law's threshold or limit concept."[2] That is to say, the established order finds in the state of exception the cover it needs to reformulate the limit of what is possible. When the situation created is activated, it has "the peculiar characteristic that it cannot be defined either as a situation of fact or as a situation of right, but instead institutes a paradoxical threshold of indistinction between the two."[3] With the state of exception, an *impasse* is reached: what is happening does not really exist for the purposes of social organization.

The moment the car does not stop at the agreed point, the state of exception is enabled, and, with it, the girls enter the threshold of indifference that the social structure condones and that the forest shelters. It must be borne in mind that the

2. Giorgio Agamben, *State of Exception*, trans. Kevin Attell (Chicago: University of Chicago Press, 2005), 4.

3. Giorgio Agamben, *Homo Sacer: Sovereign Power and Bare Life*, trans. Daniel Heller-Roazen (Stanford: Stanford University Press, 1998), 18.

state of exception serves the social group as a security system, ensuring its continuity and enabling the revalidation of the sexist structure that defines it. Thus, applying Agamben's argumentation,

> the sovereign exception is the fundamental localization (Ortung), which does not limit itself to distinguishing what is inside from what is outside but instead traces a threshold (the state of exception) between the two, on the basis of which outside and inside, the normal situation and chaos, enter into those complex topological relations that make the validity of the juridical order possible.[4]

Therefore, in a state of exception, the prevailing regulations are suspended, which makes it possible, within the norm, but at the same time outside it, for human life (in this case, the lives of the teenagers) to be regarded as bare life. As Agamben explains, activating this tool is necessary because "at once excluding bare life from and capturing it within the political order, the state of exception actually constituted, in its very separateness, the hidden foundation on which the entire political system rested."[5] The state of exception is the perfect strategy of the sexist regime: everything happens under the protection of the norm, but at the same time outside it. The difference between Alcàsser being configured as a macabre event or as a political crime lies in the role of no-man's-land, bare life, and the state of exception.

It should be noted that the potential for the teenagers' reduction to bare life is there from the moment they set foot in no-man's-land. When they hitchhike, they are already bare life, "that is, the life of homo sacer (sacred man), who may be killed and yet not sacrificed."[6] As I have explained above, *homo sacer*

---

4. Agamben, *Sovereign Power*, 18.
5. Agamben, *Sovereign Power*, 9.
6. Agamben, *Sovereign Power*, 8.

is a figure devoid of all humanity; its mortal existence depends on the decision of the sovereign. In other words, the *homo sacer* continues to live, but their life does not belong to them. In the beginning, the girls mainly fulfill the first characteristic of bare *life*: they who may be killed by anyone. As long as women are under male ownership and protection (let us say that we assign the concept *homo sacer* to *property-protection* meanings), they may have the possibility of being saved, because "life is sacred only insofar as it is taken into the sovereign exception."[7] Or, what amounts to the same thing: as long as they are under the shelter of male protection, they share with men the sacredness of life. But the controller of this category will always be the man on whom the woman depends, a legally revised metaphor for Adam's rib. Women themselves inevitably become part of bare life.

In a state of exception, the young women are taken to La Romana house. Their journey articulates the interval between the death sentence and the execution, according to Agamben's formulation:

> The interval between death sentence and execution delimits an extratemporal and extraterritorial threshold in which the human body is separated from its normal political status and abandoned, in a state of exception, to the most extreme misfortunes. In such a space of exception, subjection to experimentation can, like an expiation rite, either return the human body to life (pardon and the remission of a penalty are, it is worth remembering, manifestations of the sovereign power over life and death) or definitively consign it to the death to which it already belongs.[8]

---

7. Agamben, *Sovereign Power*, 85.

8. Agamben, *Sovereign Power*, 159.

In the journey to La Romana house, the body enters into transition: "what is at stake in the 'extreme situation' is, therefore, 'remaining a human being or not.'"[9]

In La Romana house, the consequences of the state of exception reach their peak: teenage girls are reduced to bare life, stripped of all humanity, and reduced to a life that does not deserve to be lived, that is not life. This is the biopolitical element that La Romana was to place in the bodies of a generation of women: the cautionary reminder that they are bare life.

What is important about the Alcàsser sexual danger narrative is that it has the capacity to provide and entrench new ways of securing bare life. The call for self-restraint that the story disseminates is the real danger contained in the narrative. Thus, the state of exception is not exclusively a process enabling sexual violence and torture with impunity; from that same temporary suspension of the system, it also brings new forms that guarantee bare life comes into play: "the immediately biopolitical significance of the state of exception as the original structure in which law encompasses living beings by means of its own suspension."[10] La Romana house is, then, the intersection crisscrossing our map of territories and spaces. It is precisely at that limit where bare life definitively makes its presence felt. As Agamben explains in reference to the concentration camp, in La Romana,

> precisely because they were lacking almost all the rights and expectations that we customarily attribute to human existence, and yet were still biologically alive, they came to be situated in a limit zone between life and death, inside and outside, in which they were no longer anything but bare life.[11]

---

9. Giorgio Agamben, *Remnants of Auschwitz: The Witness and the Archive*, trans. Daniel Heller-Roazen (New York: Zone Books, 1999), 55.

10. Agamben, *State of Exception*, 3.

11. Agamben, *Sovereign Power*, 159.

And if bare life is applied on the basis of the total dehumanization of the body through the infringement of all its rights, then what makes its presence felt is not only bare life in a state of exception, but the social system in its entirety. For this reason, La Romana house can be considered as "the place in which the state of exception coincides perfectly with the rule and the extreme situation becomes the very paradigm of daily life."[12]

Once the process culminated, once La Romana house was left behind, the new setup had been configured. The new biopolitical scenario consists of the incorporation of sexual danger in the bodies of a generation of young women. The issue is not only that three teenage girls suffered torture and sexual violence, but also the violence exerted on the bodies of the rest of women. A political technology is instituted on the body, which is what allows the system to perpetuate itself and constantly adapt. The Alcàsser sexual danger narrative, together with the discipline of sexual terror, are ways of transmitting bare life. In this way, the narrative consolidates the existence of new ways of ensuring bare life.

The elements introduced from the Alcàsser crimes enable forms of bodily learning that are both direct and conceptual. In Butler's words, "The epistemological capacity to apprehend a life is partially dependent on that life being produced according to norms that qualify it as a life or, indeed, as part of life."[13]

This brings me to the category of the human and the nonhuman, which are the contemporary versions of the terms *zoé* and *bios*, explored above. These dichotomies, present throughout the sexual danger narrative, are constantly delimiting the boundaries and also defining what does or does not constitute a life worth living.

---

12. Agamben, *Remnants of Auschwitz*, 49.

13. Judith Butler, *Frames of War: When Is Life Grievable?* (London: Verso, 2009), 3.

The value and meanings of a life are something women learn from the representations contained in the sexual danger narrative. In a culture that only makes women visible and sheds light on them as corpses, the discovery of the bodies was necessary. Death makes women visible on the borderline, the nontangible, nonconceptualized frontier that marks out for others the boundaries that must not be crossed. This is the limit from which there is no turning back and on which women's risk prevention is based. This is the limit that leads us into the unknown. Women's bodies, the place where torture is inflicted, are presented and made visible in death. This representation enters the collective imaginary; it enters memory and returns again to the body. In this way, the *border* that should not have been crossed is once again reconstructed and strengthened in the body of each woman. At the same time, restoring the border means restoring the right to torture and sexual violence. This is the biopolitical element that La Romana house brought to bear.

In-Corporated Narratives and the Forced Expropriation of Women's Bodies

> *To say that Auschwitz is "unsayable" or "incomprehensible" is equivalent to* euphemein, *to adoring in silence, as one does a god. Regardless of one's intentions, this contributes to its glory. We, however, "are not ashamed of staring into the unsayable."*
>
> **Giorgio Agamben,** *Remnants of Auschwitz*

To express, write, or suggest that the Alcàsser sex crimes are incomprehensible or unsayable is tantamount to euphemism and contributes to its glorification. I refuse to adore in silence any representation-discourse or narrative about sexual danger; on the contrary, I suggest fixing our gazes on it. This chapter sets out to strip away the humiliation, fear, shame, taboo, and morbidity imprinted on the Alcàsser sex crimes and, by extension, on crimes of sexual violence in general: to fix our gaze on it, to look straight at the terrifying stories. Let it be the narrative that stops in its tracks, not women.

Consequently, to say that Alcàsser is unsayable or incomprehensible to avoid acknowledging it and taking responsibility—is equivalent to euphemism, to worshipping in silence; it means (regardless of intent) contributing to its glory. We, however, are not ashamed to fix our gaze on the unsayable, and to give it a name, a voice, and a body.

The first strike against the euphemism behind the entire Alcàsser sexual danger narrative involves fragmenting the silence that surrounds it. Precisely, in this attempt to halt worship of the narrative, an individual wound, which is also collective, must be given a voice. The Alcàsser case has been told, recounted, and written about in many ways. There is no

silence about its details, but there is silence about its consequences. The brutality of the story reinforces taboo and enables
its glorification. Criminologists, police officers, forensic experts,
journalists, and writers talk about the murder, about the murderers, about the teenage girls and their bodies. And yet, there
is silence about the Alcàsser crimes. This silence is the response
of a whole generation of women who suffered the effects of the
narrative of sexual terror. In this vein, I would like to bring to
bear the words of the storied feminist writer and philosopher
Simone de Beauvoir; for, in the narrative about the Alcàsser
sex crimes, "women do not say 'We' . . . men say 'women,' and
women use the same word in referring to themselves. They do
not authentically assume a subjective attitude."[1] The narrative
about the Alcàsser crimes was one that put women in their
place. The characteristics of the crimes, together with the morbid, pernicious literature about the events, made a political
reading from the perspective of women impossible. And, in the
absence of that perspective, all that remains of Alcàsser is sexual
terror. It is precisely in women's testimonies where I situate the
(bio)political aspect of the Alcàsser case. It is for this reason,
in Giorgio Agamben's words, that "it is necessary to reflect on
the nature of that to which no one has borne witness, on this
non-language."[2]

Therefore, the aim of this chapter is twofold. First, I make
use of an idea French writer Virginie Despentes highlighted
in her book *King Kong Theory*: that "rape is the exclusive male
domain. Not war, hunting, raw desire, violence, or barbarism,
but rape, which women—until now—have never taken possession of."[3] In this vein, the objective is to remap sexual violence

---

1. Simone de Beauvoir, *The Second Sex*, trans. Howard M. Parshley
(London: Jonathan Cape, 1956), 18.

2. Giorgio Agamben, *Remnants of Auschwitz: The Witness and the
Archive*, trans. Daniel Heller-Roazen (New York: Zone Books, 1999), 38.

3. Virginie Despentes, *King Kong Theory*, trans. Stéphanie Benson
(New York: The Feminist Press, 2015), 47.

ourselves and, in this particular case, to remap the narrative of sexual danger so that Alcàsser is defined by women, not by forensic scientists, criminologists, journalists, or writers.

Second, I return to this chapter's epigraph, a quote from Agamben, to introduce another central axis that is to emerge in the subsequent discussion of women's life histories. I intentionally put Alcàsser in the place of Auschwitz for two reasons: first, as I have explained, with the clear intention of avoiding contributing to the silent adoration of the Alcàsser story. But there is a second, more definitive reason: to extract the force contained in the word *Auschwitz* and apply it also to sexual torture, femicide, and the systematic extermination of women. Women's testimonies have shown that the history of transgression is the history of aggression; they are indissoluble. As Silvia Federici illustrates, "Always, the price of resistance was extermination."[4] Representations of sexual danger are constructed and produced within the framework of feminist transgression, whether or not one is conscious of carrying it out. The prolific production of sexual danger narratives exists in response to the prolific existence of resistance on the part of women, not the other way around. That is to say, acts of sexual violence are a punishment, a cautionary reminder in response to transgression. They do not exist naturally; they exist as a consequence of a sexist regime. If the construction of docile bodies were so simple and instantaneous, the constant production of heterosexism would not be necessary.

From the life histories, we can glean the in-corporated form of the narratives, meanings, and discourses about sexual danger that women internalize throughout their lives. Sexual terror implies a certain bodily apprenticeship that begins at a very early age: the way in which sexual violence is embodied is progressive and constant. With the Alcàsser case, the repression of silence has been imposed: not talking about what happened and, in

---

4. Silvia Federici, *Caliban and the Witch: Women, the Body, and Primitive Accumulation* (New York: Autonomedia, 2004), 102.

this case, forgetting, means perpetuating it. Women's ways of expressing and experiencing the Alcàsser crimes make memory possible in political terms—that is, memory about the sexual violence of the Alcàsser crimes and the effects that this violence had on a whole generation.

The Forced Expropriation of Women's Bodies and the Political Project of Rape

To approach sexual violence through life histories is to contextualize the Alcàsser crimes through the corporal. Articulating a biography of *the public woman* is important because it grants us access to the construction of the meaning of sexual violence in women's bodies. Indeed, within each sexual danger narrative, the engine—the energy that moves the narrative—depends on the condition of *the public woman* concept. The construction of the public woman gives meaning to male protection and *the public body*; it exists to safeguard men's vested rights over women's bodies and to justify sexual violence. The sexist regime, it seems, offers one of two alternatives: you can be either a public woman or a protected woman.

Representations of sexual danger with political-sexist categories are gradually incorporated into women's lived experience. According to anthropologist Mari Luz Esteban, "Becoming a social individual implies a specific form of bodily learning."[5] In the case of women, this bodily learning entails the in-corporation of rape's political project, in which different *disciplines* distribute their bodies to the public as public. Here, the gradual construction of the public woman and, consequently, *the state of exception* and *bare life* is extremely important. Philosopher Paul B. Preciado, on the subject of gender, states that it "is first

5. Mari Luz Esteban, *Antropología del cuerpo: Género, itinerarios corporales, identidad y cambio* (Barcelona: Bellaterra, 2004), 19.

and foremost prosthetic. That is, it does not occur except in the materiality of the body. It is entirely constructed, and, at the same time, it is purely organic."[6] I associate this definition with the political project of rape. What I mean is that rape is discursively constructed—the narrative and its meanings—and, at the same time, thanks to the process of in-corporation—the knowledge of rape and the fear of aggression that intends/attempts to render bodies and behaviors docile—it is purely organic.

I draw on the concept of *matter*, as set out by Judith Butler, to define sexual violence as bodily learning:

> What I would propose in place of these conceptions of construction is a return to the notion of matter, not as site or surface, but as *a process of materialization that stabilizes over time to produce the effect of boundary, fixity, and surface we call matter.* That matter is always materialized has, I think, to be thought in relation to the productive and, indeed, materializing effects of regulatory power in the Foucaultian sense.[7]

In other words, through a repetitive, constant process—in which the sexist microphysics of power and the discipline of sexual terror partake—sexual violence is materialized in women's bodies. Butler's definition grants access to the set of regulatory norms that manifest rape and aggression in women's bodies. In turn, this enables sexual violence to be understood as an in-corporated process, rather than as isolated events or exceptions that generate fear, threat, and danger at specific points in time.

The public woman is a figure constructed throughout women's (and men's) lived experience. From an early age, women are incessantly watched. This surveillance is the first delineation

---

6. Paul B. Preciado, *Countersexual Manifesto*, trans. Kevin G. Dunn (New York: Columbia University Press, 2015), 27–28.

7. Judith Butler, *Bodies That Matter: On the Discursive Limits of "Sex"* (London: Routledge, 1993), 9–10.

of the public body: a fixed, unwavering stare locked onto their bodies and lives. In line with this idea, this chapter aims to sketch the outline of what could be called an attempt at the *forced expropriation* of women's bodies from the time they are children. Forced expropriation, in its original conception, is an institution of public, constitutional, and administrative law; it is the coercive transfer of private property from owner to state. A property may be expropriated so that it may be exploited by the state or by a third party.

There is no avoiding it: I must *forcefully expropriate* the concept of forced expropriation for the purposes of the present book. Here, forced expropriation is the public right of society as a whole—acquired by men—that attempts to transfer, in a coercive manner—through violence—ownership of women's bodies, so that they may be exploited by the sexist regime or by a third party. I consider that this term throws the continuous appropriation of women's bodies and lives by the social body into stark relief.

However, the forced expropriation of women's bodies does not mean that the objectives behind this expropriation are obtained successfully and definitively. Butler argues that the body "is not, however, a mere surface upon which social meanings are inscribed, but that which suffers, enjoys, and responds to the exteriority of the world, an exteriority that defines its disposition, its passivity and activity."[8] In other words, bodies do not yield freely to docility, but resist and transgress "precisely because prohibitions do not always 'work,' that is, do not always produce the docile body that fully conforms to the social ideal, they may delineate body surfaces that do not signify conventional heterosexual polarities."[9] This means that, within the corporal cartography, there are what anarchist writer Hakim

---

8. Judith Butler, *Frames of War: When Is Life Grievable?* (London: Verso, 2009), 33–34.

9. Butler, *Bodies That Matter*, 64.

Bey terms *temporary autonomous zones*: "The map is closed, but the autonomous zone is open. Metaphorically it unfolds within the fractal dimensions invisible to the cartography of Control."[10] These vanishing points, these zones of transgression—just like the discipline of sexual terror itself—are operative in women's bodies and in their life histories. All the aggression-transgression that occurs has to do with this resistance to bodily expropriation.

Forced expropriation entails the surveillance and punishment of women's bodies in equal parts. Surveillance and punishment are elements that I associate directly with the construction of the public body: a body with a double social imprint, watched through cautionary reminders and punished through surveillance—the patriarch and his anatomy lesson—and public exposure.

The construction of public space is the place of surveillance over women's bodies par excellence. In this political space, the sexuality and conduct of teenage girls is subject to constant scrutiny and punishment. From childhood, women's sexuality is constructed in opposition to that of men and is imbued with meanings that lay the foundations for risk and threat.

The mechanisms of transmission are manifold and diffuse: at school, at home, within groups of friends. Girls are oriented from an early age to be cautious and have a clear heterocentric orientation toward their bodies. Representations of sexual danger, in the case of women, are usually associated with their own sexuality and how they internalize and understand their own bodies. Teresa de Miguel, an activist in the Valencian feminist movement, attended public school, which she remembers as dark, dilapidated, and gray, where she suffered from the cold.[11]

---

10. Hakim Bey, TAZ: *The Temporary Autonomous Zone, Ontological Anarchy, Poetic Terrorism* (New York: Autonomedia, 1991), 97.

11. Teresa de Miguel lives in Valencia. She was forty-seven years old at the time of the interview. She began her feminist militancy at an early age, taking part in different groups. At the time of the Alcàsser crimes, she

She associates with this unpleasant space a feeling in which emerging sexuality plays a part. On one occasion, as a result of the cold, suggestions were made to the school staff that the girls could wear pants. The refusal was categorical, as was the explanation: "Girls who wear pants end up with deformed genitals."[12] This reply might appear to hark back to a distant past, but if anything can be said of myths, it is that they both persist and resist. Itsaso García, a woman from the Basque Country who is fourteen years younger than Teresa, also attended a school run by nuns.[13] She remembers her sexual education as extremely stereotyped, and feels this had quite a few repercussions:

> As a child, I didn't have a normal relationship with sexuality, because the image they portrayed was quite negative. The image of men as always out for what they can get, the whole thing about having to save your virginity for when you get married.[14]

Itsaso reports that, at school, they were shown a video about abortion featuring a late-stage pregnancy. This triggered a debate in class about abortion in cases of sexual aggression:

> Lots of people might be against abortion, but in cases of sexual aggression, it was seen as a totally legitimate option. One of the nuns went so far as to say that, in case of sexual aggression, there was no point in abortion because you only got pregnant if you got sexual pleasure from intercourse.[15]

---

was active in the anti-aggression workgroup within the Valencian feminist movement.

12. Teresa de Miguel, interview, December 18, 2010.

13. Itsaso García is from Portugalete, a town to the west of Bilbao. At the time of the interview, on July 8, 2009, she was thirty-one years old. The Alcàsser case affected her greatly, and she experienced great fear.

14. Itsaso García, interview, July 8, 2009.

15. García, interview.

Such meanings underpin the argument that it is the woman who is responsible for sexual aggression. They resolve that there is difficulty in drawing a line between a woman's consent or lack of consent when she has been assaulted. Moreover, bringing the sinfulness of women's sexual pleasure into the picture while referring to abortion is a mechanism that is still used today to impose control and to expropriate women's bodies from them. It is myth itself that endows the representation of sexual danger with its fluidity and lasting effect: it acts as an element internal to the discourse, adapting and readapting over time but maintaining a constant presence.

On other occasions, explanations about sexuality in the family environment convey derogatory content relating to women's own bodies. Teresa de Miguel recounts:

> I slept in the same bed with one of my brothers. He was the youngest at that time, six years younger than me, and one day he asked, "Why doesn't Teresa have a willy and instead has a butt that reaches all the way to the front?"
>
> My mother answered, "That's an ax-wound they gave her when she was little."[16]

Teresa's brother's uncertainty resulted, for Teresa, in a depiction of her as a mutilated body.

Warnings about men imposed a wariness in women. María Fernández, who went to a public school reports that at home,

> there was that implicit thing hovering in the air with men. You've got to be careful with men. When I was a teenager, my paternal grandmother used to tell me, "Be careful, don't get in the car with a boy, because boys can take your cherry only once. They can't take it again."[17]

---

16. de Miguel, interview.

17. María Fernández, interview, August 12, 2009.

This insecurity with respect to male intentions regarding women's bodies is not so much about precaution as it is about limiting women's free sexuality and, consequently, enabling the absolute absence of boundaries for men. If anything happens, it is the direct responsibility of women. These meanings and discourses about the body constitute the first sketches of the construction of the public body of women. This is how elements that make it possible to situate women's bodies as public are brought in from an incredibly early age.

An important moment in the transmission of sexual danger occurs with the arrival of the first menstruation. The period functions as a bodily demarcation that represents a transition in women's life experience. At this point, the whole discursive mechanism of sexual danger grinds into action. Teresa remembers:

> Once I got my period . . . from then on, the message was "beware of boys!" And if you were already afraid of boys, then from then on it was terror. So, now, what are they going to do to me? That was on an irrational level. Because on a rational level, I hit those who hit my brothers. I also dealt violence. But on an unconscious level, on an irrational level, it was: "I wonder what they're going to do to me now."[18]

I would like to make a comparison here between Teresa's testimony and a reflection from Virginie Despentes. I identify a clear link between this status of "being a woman" that the arrival of menstruation demarcates and the "being a woman" that the political project of rape imposes. In reference to experiencing sexual aggression, Despentes recalls:

> But at that precise moment I felt female, disgustingly

---

18. de Miguel, interview.

female, in a way I had never felt, and have never felt since. Defending my own body did not allow me to injure a man. I think I would have reacted in the same way if there had been only one man against me. It was rape that turned me back into a woman, into someone essentially vulnerable.[19]

Teresa's testimony clearly shows the breach the political project of rape manages to open: in her case, as she says, she used to handle violence; what's more, she defended her brothers from other boys. However, the irruption of sexual danger seems to invalidate her capacity for self-defense. In fact, as far as sexual violence is concerned, little or nothing is delimited by the first period. The period/sexuality binomial is basically based on the possibility of becoming pregnant. In this sense, the fear that is introduced is that of the father, who understands his daughter's sexuality and body as belonging to him.

In many of the testimonies of the women interviewed, the news of the first period is communicated to the father as an important event of which he should be informed. Marta Ramos recalls, "After I got my period, I came out of the bathroom, and my mother was telling my father: 'Your daughter is a woman now.'"[20] This, for the purposes of the patriarchal regime, meant the baptism of *the public woman*. For Maider Abásolo, this "being a woman" meant control and surveillance over her actions. As a girl, Maider had been the apple of her father's eye, the most sheltered child. She recalls:

My relationship with my folks changed when I got my period. I mean, even more fear, even more attention, even more concern on my father's part. A lot of pestering when it came to guy stuff. I couldn't be alone with any boy, not even a friend. The period stuff was traumatic

---

19. Despentes, *King Kong Theory*, 44.
20. Marta Ramos, interview, October 25, 2010.

because of what putting up with my old man cost at a personal level.[21]

For some of the interviewees, their first menstruation was a truly traumatic transition. This discomfort is caused precisely by the association between menstruation and female sexuality. With this type of discourse on sexual danger, an attempt is made to establish the first forms of self-restraint: the first boundary is set on sexual pleasure. Women have to be careful about what they desire, whom they desire and how they carry out this desire. In the case of Laura García, her internalization of the idea that sexual pleasure was something dirty, that its practices were wrong, led to her in-corporation of guilt and silence. She explains:

> What I remember was my best friend at a moment when I couldn't deal with this secret any longer, I said, I have to talk about something, let's meet to talk. I remember that very clearly, meeting to talk behind the fountain and saying, "I already know what I'm going to be when I'm older."
> And her saying, "What?"
> And me, "But you won't like me anymore."
> And her saying, "Tell me."
> And I say, "But, please, don't tell anyone. . . . I just have to say it."
> And she says, "Go on, say it."
> And I say, "I think I'm going to be a whore."
> And she says, "But why do you think that?"
> And I say, "I can't tell you." . . .
> I didn't tell her that I masturbated. But I knew from my mother that it was something dirty.[22]

---

21. Maider Abásolo, interview, July 1, 2009.

22. Laura García was born in a village in the north of Catalonia, but at the age of five she moved to live in a series of different towns near Valencia. At the time of the interview, on October 17, 2010, she was thirty-three

The relevance of this testimony stems from the association Laura makes with the category "whore." For her, her practices, her individual sexual freedom, and the fact that she enjoys her body meant not being a "normal woman" and, therefore, that she had to be a "whore." This line between "normal woman" and "whore" is constantly traversed by women throughout their life experience. But, in the context of this study, *normal woman* is, for the sexist regime, "public woman." On the contrary, *whore* is synonymous with women who exceed the norm: women who deviate, who transgress, who take up public space, who have fun, who enjoy their sexuality. The category "whore" has a strong symbolic meaning for the heteropatriarchy; it is a classification that aims to limit the sexual pleasure of women and their freedom. From a societal perspective, the *whore* in women's lives is the image of the woman who takes too many liberties. This concept appears constantly in identity construction and is a discursive mechanism that functions as a corrector of behavior. Marta Ramos recalls that, in her case, a wariness prevailed over her own desire:

> Me, I gave my virginity more thought than . . . I thought about it a lot. Having the chance, but holding back because, of course, what was going to happen? It was something you really wanted, on the one hand, but, on the other hand, you didn't know if you were willing to pay the price for enjoying it.[23]

This pattern, which determines that a woman has to lose her virginity in a premeditated act and with the right man, follows the scheme of *surveillance and punishment* that structures the whole sexual danger narrative: an eternal wariness of doing stuff and the price to be paid.

---

years old. Laura spent four years, which she remembers as being the best of her life, in a boarding school. She lived through the Alcàsser crimes at that school, surrounded by teenagers her own age.

23. Ramos, interview.

In a few short words, Gentzane Oyarzabal, from Bilbao, summarizes what the struggle between enjoying sexuality or being exposed to people's judgments meant for her: silencing her will in order to be respected.

> When I was a teenager, what I do remember is that I kept quiet about what I wanted and that I tried to please up to a point, because you should never be too much of a whore.[24]

This extreme, in which a woman should not appear to live her sexuality freely, has to do with the idea of female responsibility with respect to sex. The social and individual punishment suffered by women who decide to live their sexuality freely involves exhaustive surveillance from the entire social body. The public woman without male protection, who lives freely and transgresses the norm, is the standard motive for sexual violence.

In truth, the word *whore* (*puta* in the original Spanish throughout) came to synthesize all those practices that were not in accordance with what was expected of a woman. This corrective measure works effectively through social vigilance. Social punishment is added to the father's control. Maider Abásolo recalls that if a boy waited outside the school for a girl, she was the "school whore" and in the surrounding area chalk graffiti was scrawled on walls about her, calling her a "slutty whore." This is the element that puts everyone in their place. This is how a woman who transgresses the norm is punished. Maider recalls:

> I thought that it had to be a bummer to be on the radar of those guys and the occasional chick. I just thought, "Fuck, I don't want to appear on that graffiti," knowing that, well, that it could happen.[25]

---

24. Gentzane Oyarzabal, interview, December 19, 2011. At the time of the interview, Oyarzabal was thirty-two years old. She is a woman who is particularly sensitive to representations of sexual danger.

25. Abásolo, interview.

Laura García, like Maider, encountered the mechanisms of surveillance and punishment. The years she spent at the boarding school are, for her, synonymous with absolute freedom in all areas. However, she had to face criticism for wanting to enjoy and transgress the sexual norms in force:

> I made out with the people I liked. Probably I did it less than they said I did. My name was always on people's lips. Without knowing me, they started to say things about me: that I was shameless, that I was a such-and-such. . . . Well . . . that I was a skank and so on . . . they even sprayed some graffiti about me at the school.[26]

Laura remembers that she would escape from where she was staying and go up to the boys' floor. This behavior aroused all kinds of suspicion in the rest of her classmates. Laura confesses,

> It bugged me, I guess. Because I also remember that when I said I hadn't done it, that I was a virgin, nobody believed it. Of course, it was because I was so savvy, so forward, and I'd been going to clubs since I was twelve and so on.[27]

Suspicion, doubt, and blaming women's conduct are meanings that the sexist microphysics of power reproduces intermittently. The same meanings through which a news story about sexual violence is conveyed are those that can be found in the various stages of women's lives. That is why the Alcàsser sexual danger narrative managed to leave such an effective impression.

An important moment in the life experience of women occurs with the first appearance of the "bad man." For Rut Rodríguez, this first encounter, which occurred when she was

---

26. Laura García, interview, October 17, 2010.

27. García, interview.

thirteen, is very present in her life history. She was returning home with a friend, and they noticed a man following them:

> So we went the other way, and we saw him turn around and, all of a sudden, we met him again. And, in the end, I don't know what we yelled at him, and he laughed. And he didn't flinch. And he just kind of kept coming. So we ran to this friend's house . . . but then it was really scary, because, of course, as he'd kept following us so much it was like . . . even if we run, he's still going to appear around the corner.[28]

In the narrative, Rut describes a man who can appear anywhere, around any corner, and who, no matter how hard they try to avoid him, reappears with a smirk on his face. This encounter sparked the activation of a warning in Rut, the insecurity of not knowing where, how, or when he would reappear. She recalls, "From then on, there was a time . . . when we were always like: 'That's him, isn't it?' It was as if we had a half-blurred image and we always thought he was going to appear again."[29] After this aggression, Rut saw him everywhere:

> Besides, I met him again . . . and that time I was alone walking my dog. And, suddenly, the guy approached me, and I felt his presence. Maybe it wasn't the same one, but I thought it was the same one, and I was like on the alert. And the guy kind of followed me, and I started to run.[30]

Sexual aggressions consist of those situations in which

---

28. Rut Rodríguez, interview, October 25, 2010. Rut was born in Valencia in 1980. At the time of the interview, on she was thirty years old. She belongs to the generation that came immediately after that of the teenagers of the Alcàsser crimes. This event had a substantial impact on her, especially in relation to hitchhiking..

29. Rodríguez, interview.

30. Rodríguez, interview.

women experience all the discourses or meanings about sexual danger directly. In many cases, Alcàsser will be the story that unifies each and every form of aggression or dangerous situation that women have experienced up to that moment. This unification lends meaning and effectiveness to the discipline of sexual terror.

Remnants of Alcàsser: The Boundaries and the Border

> *Boundaries: we had gone out into the wild because nothing much ever happened in Mommy and Daddy's house. We had taken the risk and paid the price . . . ordinary victims of what you have to expect you may endure if you're a woman and you want to venture into the wild.*

> **Virginie Despentes, *King Kong Theory***

The remnant of Alcàsser is the place where the dissected body faces the social body and questions it. The body is a map, "a political abstract grid" crossed by a multitude of variables, axes, meridians, metaphorical parallels in which the discipline of sexual terror marks its vanishing points and its points of access.[31] This was evidenced in a remarkable way with the first consequences of the Alcàsser sexual danger narrative. Indeed, all the meanings, discourses, and representations about sexual danger I analyzed from the narrative can be found acting in the bodies of the women interviewed in one way or another.

A fundamental characteristic that appears in the life histories about the Alcàsser crimes is that largely, for the interviewees, it is configured as the first major sexual danger narrative they remember. Although their life experience may be configured by other narratives or violence, Alcàsser functions as the story that

---

31. Bey, *TAZ*, 97.

activated their sexual terror. For Itsaso García, for example, the Alcàsser case marked a turning point in her life: "I don't think that before the Alcàsser episode I have a recollection of anything that particularly marked me. I think the Alcàsser case was the reason I began to realize certain dangers existed."[32]

Everything surrounding the Alcàsser crimes produced in her a kind of enduring paranoia. It also coincided with the fact that, shortly afterward, a girl who was two years above her from her school was murdered. This event further kindled her fears:

> They came close together, two episodes in a row. It made you feel pretty bad. Right after Alcàsser I was quite paranoid. I took a knife out with me. I was fearful, thinking about it a lot, nightmares. It was bad . . . calling the elevator in the entrance hall was an ordeal.[33]

Alcàsser, for the young women of the time, meant recognizing the existence of sexual danger. Esther Hernández, from Valencia, expresses it thus:

> I remember talking about it a lot, thinking about the fact that it was something . . . it felt so real to us. It could happen to any of us, that's it, it was really rough. I don't remember having thought about a case like that with such intensity before. It had a tremendous impact.[34]

The idea that "it could happen to any of us" is directly linked to the metaphor of the cautionary tale on live TV starring Nieves Herrero in which she interviewed the teenager who

---

32. García, interview.

33. García, interview.

34. Esther Hernández, interview, December 14, 2012. Born in Valencia, Hernández was forty-three years old at the time of the interview. She attended a Catholic school and comes from a well-to-do upper-middle-class family.

did not go out that night. "How many times, Esther, have you thought that, if you hadn't been ill, you might have been one of them? How many times have you thought that?"[35] Marta recalls that the geographical proximity to the town of Alcàsser made an impression on her and her friends because it opened up the possibility that it could happen: "We experienced the whole thing close up. It was very real, very possible. Something that could have happened to you. Above all, it was the risk that'd always been there, but that was more present than ever."[36]

One of the first consequences of the story was the materialization of the "bad man." Ainize Gárate recalls:

When they told us what they had done to the girls, which was horrifying, Anglés—that was his name—had escaped into the mountains. I remember, I was ten, and we had gone to the mountains near our town, and we got lost on the way back. We got lost, and it got dark, and we were all afraid in case Anglés showed up. There would have been ten of us ten-year-old girls, but . . . it was like, "that man could show up anywhere."[37]

The "bad man" moved freely; he had the ability to be anywhere: to appear and disappear at will. Then came the first warning: a call to immobility, to a state of alert in case Anglés returned. Marta recounts:

For a long time, we were always going from house to house; the parents of so-and-so would come to pick you

35. Transcribed fragments of Nieves Herrero's *De Tú a Tú* special, broadcast live from Alcàsser on January 28, 1993, on Antena 3.

36. Ramos, interview.

37. Ainize Gárate, interview, July 6, 2009. Gárate was twenty-five at the time of the interview. She lived in a small town until she went to college. As a teenager, she experienced terror of sexual aggression and remembers the impact the Alcàsser crimes had on her.

up and take you from one place to another; never going out alone, always holding back, being afraid. That guy who'd disappeared might turn up.[38]

Anglés personified the "sack man"—a legendary figure, like the bogeyman, who can appear at any moment and "take you if you misbehave," that is, if the rule is transgressed. For Gentzane, the crimes meant taking more precautions than she was already, and the uncertainty of not knowing who she could trust:

> Then, because of that, every time you left the house, it was not only about not going home alone but also: "watch out if you come across the flats, if a car stops to talk to you. Watch out for your father's friend, watch out for someone drugging you in a bar, watch out for someone who . . ." With everything, everything, "beware, beware, watch out, watch out."[39]

Gentzane's testimony is a good example of how boundaries begin to become self-imposed.

Laura García lived through it all in a dorm, surrounded by girls:

> It was really intense. Well, just imagine watching the TV with a hundred girls! It's not like being with a couple of friends; there were a hundred of us. There were screams, "Whoa!" It was terrifying, I mean terrifying, there were screams and anxiety attacks so intense they had to be taken to the infirmary.[40]

The Alcàsser crimes sparked much fear in Laura, who

---

38. Ramos, interview.
39. Oyarzabal, interview.
40. García, interview.

remembers how she experienced the first consequences of the terror almost immediately:

> I used to love to go through the ravine . . . but after that, alone, it was like, no way, I was too scared. And if I went by bike, I didn't stop. It was like: "Ah, I'm going to wet my pants! No, no, I can't pee until I get to town. I can't stop here to pee or that Anglés will pop out by that orange tree."[41]

No-man's-land expands; spaces that were once freely traversed become potentially dangerous zones for women. This broad initial consequence made it possible to protect the essence of no-man's-land and, therefore, of *the public woman*. On top of that, through the narrative, it attempts to expropriate women's public space. Each of the interviewees had their own particular way of experiencing the first consequences of the sexual terror of the Alcàsser crimes. Hitchhiking was to be one of the root-rhizomes of the cautionary tale; behavior and ways of acting were metaphorically reformulated through the lens of hitchhiking. There is a direct relationship between the meanings published after the crimes and women's perceptions: their ways of dressing, showing themselves, being, and of identifying dangerous spaces.

I use a quote from Virginie Despentes to introduce a series of ideas about hitchhiking: the practice itself and the border that is transgressed in doing so:

> Border: I hitchhiked, I was raped, I hitchhiked again. I wrote a first novel and published it under my own, clearly female first name, not imagining for a second that when it came out, I'd be continually lectured to about all the boundaries that should never be crossed.[42]

---

41. García, interview.

42. Virginie Despentes, *King Kong Theory*, trans. Stéphane Benson (New York: The Feminist Press, 2015).

The impact of the Alcàsser crimes for Rut Rodríguez begins precisely with the guilt she felt for having hitchhiked for the first time a few months before the murder of the teenagers. As a result of the impact of the story, she thinks she was guilty of carelessness. Consequently, Rut goes through a drawn-out trial of terror and discomfort. She recalls:

> I was obsessed with it, with thinking, how could we do this? Look at what happened to those girls. The same thing could've happened to us. There were three of us, and I had that nightmare for so long.[43]

For a long time, she suffered anguish and nightmares that, in her case, materialized in guilt. Two years later, she dared to tell her mother that she had hitchhiked. Rut recounts, "One day—I remember it perfectly—the two of us [were] in the car and I said, 'Mom, I hitchhiked one day. . . . I regret it.'"[44] In Rut's testimony, a confession comes with repentance and points to a social judgment. Rut in-corporates the cautionary tale, in-corporates the biopolitical element of the Alcàsser crime: a self-judgment of her conduct and behavior. Moreover, Rut recalls with discomfort that the boys in her group constantly reminded her of the imprudence she had committed: "A friend of mine, in ethics class—I don't know what subject we were on—he started to say, 'Say it, say that you hitchhiked like the Alcàsser girls.'"[45] She remembers this reprimand, on the part of her friends, as a bad joke they made repeatedly, "You hitch-hiked, how crazy; you hitchhiked, and look what happened to the Alcàsser girls."[46] This is the trial and the penalty that are prolonged. She infers that the boys wanted to make her angry,

---

43. Rodríguez, interview.
44. Rodríguez, interview.
45. Rodríguez, interview.
46. Rodríguez, interview.

to sting her, but the truth is that this (sexist) joke functioned as a call to self-restraint. The teasing represented a punishment to correct her behavior. Rut was extremely apprehensive about her encounter with sexual danger and with the threat that was at the same time so close and so real: "I do remember I was really obsessed with it and then it was a long time before I hitchhiked again. And when I did hitchhike, it was sort of about facing that fear."[47]

The narrative about the Alcàsser crimes prompted many young women to reflect on their practices and exposed them to feelings of guilt over what could have happened. Laura recounts:

> With a friend of mine from Seville, we used to move around, we used to hitchhike. I remember, when Alcàsser happened, recalling, "All that? Damn! What could have happened in that situation, or in that other one, or that other one . . . ? I've been so crazy!" Or, "How reckless!" And some guy, I remember, in the village said, "They deserved it." And I, well, I kicked his ass, didn't I?[48]

In both cases—Rut's friends (joking about hitchhiking) and Laura's recollection of "some guy" who said the teenage girls had it coming to them—we find the representation of the correctional (male) voice that reminds women of the recklessness of their actions, of where they belong.

The experience and memories of the women directly impacted by the Alcàsser story show how the representations of sexual danger, together with the sexist microphysics of power, are tools that facilitate the materialization of threat, caution, and sexual violence in the body: Judith Butler writes, "What constitutes the fixity of the body, its contours, its movements, will be fully material, but materiality will be rethought as the effect

---

47. Rodríguez, interview.
48. García, interview.

of power, as power's most productive effect."[49] Corrections not only aim to focus on women's self-blame/self-restraint; they also serve to fortify the existence of *public women* and men's rights over their bodies and lives. Gentzane recalls a situation in which, while hitchhiking, the guy who stopped showed them what could happen to them if he had wanted it to:

> I had a really bad time with one of them once. A man stopped for us, put his briefcase in the trunk, and gave us a ride. And he was going, like, sixty miles an hour or so on a road where you are supposed to go thirty, and he said, "Now what? What happens if I don't stop now? And if you go back, how are you going to go back?" And we told him, "By bus." And, in the end, he left us at the place, but his words lingered on.[50]

"If I don't stop now," is not exclusively correctional; it is about the possibility of enabling the state of exception. It means the option of leaving no-man's-land, from whence the public woman would inevitably enter the zone of suspended rights. "If I don't stop now" means giving substance to the threat; it means endowing the state of exception with veracity. "If I don't stop now" means, moreover, acknowledging awareness of its existence and saying, as sovereign: "If I do it, it's because I know I can." Throughout the interviews, this type of situation, in which a man says, "What happens if I don't stop now?" has appeared with astonishing regularity. These threats, which supposedly materialize in simple jokes, show men's knowledge of the existence of the state of exception. This "knowledge" is in-corporated in men.

What all the testimonies agree on is that before the crimes, hitchhiking was an extremely common, safe practice in the area, and, afterward, as Marta comments, "hitchhiking stopped

---

49. Butler, *Bodies That Matter*, 2.

50. Oyarzabal, interview.

right after they [the Alcàsser victims] appeared the way they appeared; we started to go for dinner at friends' houses."[51] Andrés Domínguez lived in Alcàsser when the crimes occurred. He was young, but he remembers his parents talking to his older sister, who was also a member of the three teenagers' gang, about hitchhiking. "My parents talked about it with my sister, 'Do you do that regularly?' and my sister told them that she'd never done it, but that it was common." When Andrés started going to the nightclub, hitchhiking was no longer so commonplace. "We kept going to Coolor. That didn't stop. That thing happened, but people kept going. People didn't hitchhike anymore. In general, nobody hitchhiked from that point on. There was no fear of walking. We went as a group."[52]

Elena Díaz is also from Alcàsser, from the generation that came just after that of the three teenagers. When she started going to the nightclub, Elena was certain she would never hitchhike: "No way, never. I didn't do it, I'm telling you. When it happened, we weren't going out yet. I hadn't had the chance to do it. But, of course, after that, never."[53] However, in the testimonies I have also encountered counternarratives. Many of the women who stopped hitchhiking because of the Alcàsser crimes hitchhiked again later in their lives. A good example is Aurora López, who, although she stopped hitchhiking for a while after the crimes, later returned to the practice. She explains:

At that time, there was no fucking way I'd have thought of hitchhiking. Later, when I was older, I did. Some serious stuff has happened to me. The thing is that, for better or for worse, I'm someone who doesn't like to be afraid,

---

51. Ramos, interview.

52. Andrés Domínguez, interview, December 17, 2010.

53. Elena Díaz, interview, December 19, 2010. Elena is from Alcàsser and was thirty-four years old at the time of the interview. She experienced the crimes firsthand and, with the media broadcast of the events, suffered insomnia, terror, and generalized distress for a long time.

and I don't like to give up on something I want to do. I wouldn't like to stay at home out of fear, or not go on a trip alone out of fear something might happen to me.[54]

The great emphasis placed on the fact that teenage girls had hitchhiked materialized a warning. It was a collective and individual call for a review of the conduct and activities that women engaged in. Laura, for example, remembers reflecting on ways of dressing and being in the world. She recalls that, in order to get into the nightclubs, they used to dress up and put makeup on in order to look older. This conduct was deemed even more reprehensible after the Alcàsser crimes Laura recalls:

> When I was caught once, what a scene! "They'll rape you," and all that . . . ! And I had friends who were simply not allowed out because of Alcàsser, not allowed to go out to the nightclubs. Besides, most of the clubs were on the outskirts. . . . "They take you to the orange groves and . . . ." That was a phrase I heard several times. "They take you to the orange groves and do whatever they want with you!"[55]

Hitchhiking gave shape to a metaphor that placed on women the responsibility for what happened. Everything suggests that, in the wake of such a violent response, hitchhiking had become the most transgressive activity of the time.

Moreover, the triple crime triggered the start of a wave of terror and sexual fear that women remember in great detail to this day. The evocation of the forensic details, so abundant and descriptive in the narrative, was largely what established a

---

54. Aurora López, interview, October 21, 2010. Aurora, from a town near Valencia, was thirty-two years old at the time of the interview. After attending a school run by nuns, she set out on her own at the age of seventeen. She has an older sister and brother. As a teenager, she used to frequent the entertainment venues near Alcàsser, such as Coolor nightclub.

55. García, interview.

breach in the collective memory of the interviewees. For Elena Díaz, an Alcàsser resident, the memory that sparks most terror comes from TV. She recounts:

> The memories I have are of the things that terrified me. For example, the image of the three photographs is crystal clear. The music of the program on Canal 9 about the topic also made me shiver when I listened to it. Then, there's the memories of the program produced there live, which I think was the most disgusting thing I've ever seen. Then, the atmosphere, the general atmosphere of fear, of sadness, of unease.[56]

For the most part the interviewees remember the details of the torture: some express them explicitly; others, in contrast, broadly outline the foundations on which the collective silence about the Alcàsser crimes is based—as in the case of Teresa de Miguel, whose memories are essentially bodily. Talking about the murders causes her distress, making her uneasy, and she refuses to speak about any detail, "I think I've blocked it out. Besides, I don't think I want to remember it. I just don't want to remember."[57] Alicia, on the other hand, has a vague memory: it is not associated with any image, but she recognizes the fear she feels when she remembers and links it to an emotion. "It disgusts me," she says. "The first thing that came to me was disgust. That was more corporal, because afterward I felt such sorrow."[58]

In Rut's case, the closet in her room came to represent the suffering produced by the recounting of the anatomical-forensic

56. Díaz, interview.

57. de Miguel, interview.

58. Alicia Grau, interview, April 27, 2011. From Barcelona, Alicia was thirty-three years old at the time of the interview. As a teenager, she remembers one of her first encounters with the fear of sexual danger with the so-called rapist of the Eixample in Barcelona, who was active in the vicinity of the neighborhood where she lived.

details. A friend had told Rut the ins and outs of what had happened:

> She said, "You don't know what they did to them."
> And I said, "No . . . no."
> She said, "They did bad things to them. Well, they did such-and-such and so on."
> And I think she told me she hadn't slept well since then, thinking that she had a monster under the bed or in the closet. So, I think maybe because of that. . . . I'd lie down on the bed to sleep and, as I had the closet in front of me, I'd look at it, and that was what made me remember the fear that my friend felt and, well, also my fear of that story.[59]

The "monster in the closet" is another potent representation of sexual danger that often appears in these life histories. In the case of Elena, the "real" fear began the moment the teenage girls' bodies were found. She suffered from insomnia for months. Images of what happened came back to her over and over again:

> No, it wasn't nightmares, it was not sleeping and then having time to start thinking about it. So it was like going back to the beginning, making a compilation of everything that had been experienced, then, all the information that had appeared.[60]

Insomnia, ruminating on the representations of sexual danger, the repetition of images over and over again: all these are the ways in which the discipline of sexual terror tries to install itself and materialize. After a while, the insomnia disappears, but the

59. Rodríguez, interview.
60. Elena Díaz, interview, December 19, 2010.

discipline remains latent, to be activated over time, in the women's life experiences.

The crimes not only reinforced parental protectiveness over their daughters but also further entrenched the men's role as protectors. What is important about this figure, thus reinforced, is that the same man who protects is also the "anyone" to whom, normatively speaking, the *public woman* belongs. The fact that male protection is reinforced is a key element that attempts to produce, in turn, a learned helplessness in women. Laura recalls that the boys in her circle adopted more protective attitudes toward them:

> The guys also took center stage. "If you're with us, nothing will happen to you." It was like we needed them to be around at certain times or in certain places. It was a change. It was the hardest blow, I think. "Shit! I can no longer go as I please at anytime, anywhere, because I'm afraid."[61]

Gemma Valero, a close friend of the three teenagers, remembers experiencing intense fear and distrust of people she did not know. For a time, the boys in their circle organized protection measures. She recalls:

> When we went out or went to the arcades here, our friends always walked us home. We never went back alone. We were always escorted. I remember that. For a while, I don't remember how long. Also, at the beginning, they were more afraid at home too. Of course, of course, after they had seen everything that had happened.

Male protection contributed to restoring the space of no-man's-land. The sensation of fear after the crimes was perceived differently by girls than by boys. Thus, for example, Andrés

---

61. Gemma Valero, interview, October 25, 2011.

Domínguez does not remember having nightmares, but he does remember having a specific fear:

> I have always been afraid that it would happen again, or that it could happen to one of my sisters. And also, a little bit the role of... brother, of father, of, "Watch what you're doing!" I mean, not for me; for me I have never had that fear. For the girls most of all, for the others.[62]

For Andrés, the pervasive fear of sexual danger was not about him personally but in relation to his sister. Male protectiveness was bolstered as a result of the Alcàsser sexual danger narrative and, with it, the figure of the public woman was also reinforced.

For the most part, the Alcàsser narrative affected even those women who had a feminist background and had worked on the issue of violence against women. Teresa de Miguel was a member of a feminist group in Valencia at the time. She remembers the crimes with great anguish:

> Awful... awful. For me it was sexual aggression. Well, an aggression; I'm not sure about it being sexual, but I think it was. Yes, it was like experiencing it, I mean, reliving it. It's like, it hits you, and all the other blows you ever received multiply, or get raised to the nth degree. Not only because of what had happened to them and so many others, which is appalling, but also because of what it really meant. It was actually like every fear ever felt had resurfaced in me. I had been much more mature, felt much freer. Sometimes I was afraid, but, mostly, the fear was gone. I had been working for many years in the feminist movement so that others would not be afraid. This was a step back for all of us. That's how I felt.[63]

---

62. Andrés Domínguez, interview.

63. de Miguel, interview.

For Teresa and her peers, Alcàsser was an attack on the very heart of the feminist movement's years of work in relation to sexual aggression. Sonia Fuente was a member of the same group, along with Teresa: saying the name *Alcàsser* still makes her "hair stand on end." She recognizes, like Teresa, the panic that came over her after the crimes:

> There was much social unrest. Parents instilled a lot of fear into their daughters, a lot of terror. I remember that, like a panic . . . I don't know how to say the word. The social unrest was fear, fear of going out alone in the street. Yes, we were afraid.[64]

Sonia recounts that, at that time, her political militancy was very much focused on reclaiming the night as a space for women, handing out leaflets at train stations with the slogan, "Be back by 8 o'clock—in the morning." This slogan was itself a counter-representation of sexual danger. The work of the feminist movement continued along the lines of continuing to generate counter-representations that would reduce the scope of the narrative. Crimes like those of Alcàsser can be configured as a milestone or function as a transmitter of a threat that was already operative in the body. But, in the same way, the narrative enables and generates resistance: a counter-corporal struggle of women moving against the discipline of sexual terror and the context or normativity that produces it.

---

64. Sonia Fuente, interview, October 19, 2010. Sonia, who lives in Valencia, was forty-one years old at the time of the interview. A longtime feminist activist, she began her political activity through the pacifist movement, where she came into contact with the feminist movement. When the Alcàsser crimes were perpetrated, she was an active member of a feminist group that worked on, among other issues, violence against women and girls. This group was in charge of organizing and leading the massive demonstration that took place in Valencia to condemn the triple crime.

> *But I have also avoided telling my story, because I already knew that people would say, "well, if you carried on hitchhiking after that, if it didn't make you more sensible, then you must have liked it."*
>
> **Virginie Despentes, *King Kong Theory***

> *Silence: That which is left unsaid, which is silenced, is no mere interval in linguistic communication; it is a phenomenon full of figures laden with meaning and emotions.*
>
> **Susana Griselda Kaufman, "Lo legado y lo propio: Lazos familiares y transmisión de memorias"** [The bequeathed and the owned: Family bonds and memory transmission]

The violence involved in the construction of the Alcàsser narrative underpinned the silence around the crimes and their consequences. But in relation to the Alcàsser narrative, another variable also produces silence: silence is the only thing that society as a whole cannot judge or blame.

Taboo is the great strategy of the Alcàsser sexual danger narrative. Silence contributes to stabilizing the discipline of sexual terror and further entrenching the individual responsibility of women in situations of violence. To the extent that women do not talk about aggressions or could not discuss the Alcàsser crimes beyond the terrifying details, a taboo is established that makes it impossible to craft political mechanisms of transgression against sexual violence. In this sense, taboo protects the narrative and hides its effects and consequences.

Breaking the silence about the direct consequences of the crimes' narrative for women, along with the resituation of their past and future experiences from a feminist perspective, could engender the first paragraphs of a narrative of resistance to the Alcàsser account of sexual danger. Posing Alcàsser as a narrative of resistance generates the possibility of reworking the terms in which the narrative of sexual danger was projected. As Judith Butler observes: "If prohibitions in some sense constitute projected morphologies, then reworking the terms of those prohibitions suggests the possibility of variable projections, variable modes of delineating and theatricalizing body surfaces."[65] In this sense, (re)constructing the corporeal memory of sex crimes complements the exercise of resignifying the Alcàsser crimes. The unshared, the untold; this is the indisputable engine of the discipline of sexual terror. Transforming the untellable into the tellable resituates the story. The marks of this oblivion are bodily memories that make it possible to (re)materialize the *historical possibilities of rape* in women's bodies.

With the same logic that structures the silence about sexual aggression, the harshness of the sexual danger narrative entrenched silence and taboo. Aurora López remembers:

It was experienced in a way. It was experienced as something not to talk about; something so exaggeratedly serious that it had to be forgotten so as not to suffer; and not be talked of so as not to panic.[66]

There is a generalized lack of understanding as to why the crimes were not talked about. Sonia Fuente, who was deeply and intimately affected by the Alcàsser case, does not quite understand why she endured in silence something that caused her so much terror. She confesses:

We didn't even talk about it. We haven't even talked about it. It's like . . . a taboo. I don't know. I have no idea. I don't know why we don't talk about it. I don't even know why I don't talk about it.[67]

---

65. Butler, *Bodies That Matter*, 64.
66. López, interview.
67. Fuente, interview.

Not dealing with the pain of the violence through the collective is to aim to generate a rupture, to keep sexual violence within the "event." Taboo symbolized Alcàsser as a story without explanation or history, because "when people do not talk about their experiences, do not share their fears and longings, they cannot elaborate collective memories either."[68] In this way, the terrifying story of Alcàsser is set adrift. Therefore, to speak of Alcàsser means to elaborate a—current and past—collective memory about sexual violence. According to social scientists Norbert Lechner and Pedro Güell:

> Memory is a way of distinguishing and linking the past to the present and the future. It refers not so much to the chronology of events that have remained fixed in the past as to their significance for the present. Memory is an act of the present because the past is not a given that happens once and for all. Moreover, it is only partly given. The other part is fiction, imagination, rationalization. That is why the truth of memory does not stem so much from the accuracy of the facts as from the telling and interpretation of them.[69]

In this way, it is possible to construct a narrative that builds a genealogy of feminist transgression so as to emphatically avoid contributing to the glorification of the sexual danger narrative.

Laura García recalls something that happened at her school at a time when the details, the images, and the crime scenes became unbearable. Describing that time as extremely distressing, she charts how something that began as a prank she and her friends had played ended up becoming their collective way of

---

68. Norbert Lechner and Pedro Güell, "Construcción social de las memorias en la transición chilena," in *Memorias de la represión: Subjetividad y figuras de la memoria*, ed. Elizabeth Jelin and Susana. G. Kaufman (Buenos Aires: Siglo XXI, 2006), 39.

69. Lechner and Güell, "Construcción social," 18.

externalizing the terror they were suffering in silence. At Laura's boarding school, the rules stated that after 10:00 p.m. all residents had to be in their rooms. The girls often looked for ways to have fun, and, she remembers, "took advantage of the Alcàsser issue to stir things up." She and her friends spread the rumor that Anglés had studied at their school and knew the place inside out. Since the campus was huge and had a number of different residence halls, the idea that he might be hiding there seemed quite credible. One night, two of her friends started making noise in the bathrooms and the others did so in and around the dorm rooms. The panic that ensued was uncontainable:

> Even the staff who took care of us at night were hysterical, calling for help. The head teacher and the caretaker came up. We were all out of the rooms, but even I, who knew it was us, was shaking. All of us, all of us, holding each other, crying, it was terrible. Very, very intense. . . . We couldn't bring ourselves to confess, well, I was so ashamed. . . . I mean, we all looked at each other like, "What a mess we've made." When we got into the room . . . we couldn't talk to each other until days later, because it was so intense. Everyone was crying . . . I had been trembling, and I had known it was us.[70]

The representation that Laura and her friends provoked produced an immediate state of panic. Even those who knew it was all part of a joke needed to expel the collective tension and fear they were experiencing. Silence about the violence and about sexual terror is a tangible way of transmitting sexual danger. It also subordinates the real to the plane of the abstract, to the particular feeling of the women with regard to the violence; in other words, it keeps the sexual threat within the realm of individual fears. Sharing this silence in which sexual terror dwelled made it

---

70. García, interview.

possible for all of them to realize that the fear and terror they felt was not individual, nor imaginary, nor an exaggeration, but that it existed. In the absence of words, the body takes center stage. For this reason, I located the silence about the Alcàsser crimes in a multitude of situations reported by the women interviewed: in insomnia; in the processes of sexual terror that, like in Itsaso's case, make women go out into the street with a knife; in nightmares; in not hitchhiking; in not traversing deserted streets; in keeping an eye on the time to go home. Each and every one of these practices is composed of silences about sexual danger.

Furthermore, taboo made it impossible to construct a narrative in which Alcàsser meant the story that could change everything. On the contrary, Alcàsser was to be associated with sexual terror: it was not to be a milestone that opened the debate about men's privilege and their access to women's bodies and lives. In the case of the people of Alcàsser, they learned to hide their place of origin in order to avoid being interrogated. In addition, they feel they have a kind of stigma because they live in Alcàsser. Marta de la Fuente remembers, "When you arrive at college and say where you're from, it's the first thing people ask you. I look for a way to avoid the question and that's it and you don't talk about it."[71] Marta internalized the feeling of being from Alcàsser. She recognizes that the issue is not discussed, and she believes this is because everything is already known about it. The interference of the media is what, from Marta's point of view, caused the excessive magnification of the crimes and acted to reinforce sexual terror:

> I think it has been built up beyond what is really there.
> The shock of "Wow, how scary!"
> And, "Did you go out?"
> "Yes. I went out again and went back to Coolor."
> "Of course, you didn't hitchhike?"

---

71. Sonia Fuente, interview, October 19, 2010.

"Well, no."

No! I wasn't afraid of anything. No, I didn't notice it in the village.[72]

For so many women, the word *Alcàsser* is the gateway to horror. That is why just saying the name of the town is enough to make the association with sexual terror. Marta remembers a trip she made to Manchester with a group of work colleagues. There, she met a girl who had been affected by the story, who touched on the narrative as soon as Marta told her where she was from:

She says to me, "I got scared! I didn't want to go out in the street, and now I'm afraid to go to Alcàsser."

And I said, "Are you afraid of Alcàsser? Why? But what do you think is there?"[73]

Alcàsser is the word that channels the pain, but also the terror. In Lechner and Güell's words, "In the absence of words and symbols to account for the past, she opts for silence. And memory chooses to seize people through the gateway of fear."[74]

The Border Inscribed in Women's Bodies

Finding "the truth" or the "turning point" that the Alcàsser crimes deployed is not a matter of evidence and research, but of delving into those silent subjectivities that appear and reappear throughout the life experience of the women interviewed. Fear and the sexual danger narrative spread through discourse and the body. To ground this argument, I focus on those emotions, subjectivities, sensations, feelings of distress, behaviors, and

---

72. de la Fuente, interview.

73. de la Fuente, interview.

74. Lechner and Güell, "Construcción social," 28.

places that are triggered in the women interviewed in response to certain acts: that fear, those feelings of threat or danger that arise in given circumstances in which nothing is happening a priori but that, nevertheless, set off the alarm bell of sexual terror. Situations that, on many occasions, cannot even be explained or put into words, but that exist and affect. All this configures a certain knowledge about rape, inscribed in the memory of women's bodies, which must be made visible.

Spaces of memory are configured in the body through this "inability to put into words" or "to express." That is, it is the body's memory that comes into contact with sexual danger. There is no specific place outside the body that can be "objectively" defined as *dangerous*. On the contrary, these spaces take on importance only in the bodily memory in which given representations or accounts of sexual danger have filtered through; there are certain spaces, activities, and events that put women in touch with representations of sexual danger. They perceive it, they feel it, it has no name, but it is there. This process works through the associations women establish on the basis of sexual danger narratives, as social scientists Elizabeth Jelin and Victoria Langland articulate: "When important events occur at a site, what was once a mere physical or geographical 'space' becomes a 'place' with particular meanings, loaded with significance and feelings for the people who experienced them."[75] Regarding crimes of sexual violence, the association between the event and the space where it occurs generates both a geographical and a physical place in the corporal sphere: there is a direct association between the territory and the women's bodies. This association has to do not with the site itself but with the possibility of what could happen there. In other words, no-man's-land can be any road, any alley, any street.

The fact that particular situations cause women to feel

---

75. Elizabeth Jelin and Victoria Langland, "Las marcas territoriales como nexo entre pasado y presente," in *Monumentos, memoriales y marcas territoriales*, ed. Elizabeth Jelin and Victoria Langland (Madrid: Siglo xxi, 2003), 3.

immediately endangered is discernible in the life histories I have worked on. In each, there is a scenario in which the representation of sexual danger returns. Each of the various behaviors, attitudes, or ways of managing spaces, bodies, and activities are the direct result of the degree to which representations of sexual danger and the discipline of sexual terror have influenced and impacted their lives.

I adopt Susana Griselda's conception of the performative scenario in which the traumatic returns. The author presents the reader with the situation of children saved after World War II, in which "pain and play were again and again the performative scenario in which the traumatic returned."[76] The scenario where the traumatic returns is constituted by the physical space in which certain actions took place but also by the concrete subjectivities and emotions associated with each space. Therefore, I cannot ignore the fact that that the places to which the performative parts of representations of sexual danger return are strategies of the sexist regime to colonize silence and subjectivities.

What is traumatizing is that they are allowed to remain invisible. Specifically, in reference to the Alcàsser crimes, huts out in the fields, hitchhiking, and a stranger's car are places in which that which was traumatic in the representation returns, already in-corporated. Evidently, as we will see, the emergence of this scenario is different depending on the meanings, representations, or situations that have shaped the life experience of the interviewees.

After the Alcàsser crimes, Marta recalls her generalized fear of the street and how it also affected her friends. She extends this idea of understanding public space as something dangerous to huts out in the fields. The evocation takes us straight to La Romana house, where the teenagers were sexually tortured. Marta recalls that a few years after the crimes:

---

76. Susana Griselda Kaufman, "Lo legado y lo propio: Lazos familiares y transmisión de memorias," in Jelin and Kaufman, *Memorias de la represión* (Buenos Aires: Siglo XXI, 2006), 50.

One night I hooked up with a guy, and we went back to his parents' house, a house out in the fields. And, of course, we went into the house, and the first thing I saw was a hanger with saws, straps, and so on . . . and I made the joke, "Oh my God, what am I getting myself in to!" You know? "Have I hooked up with some kind of psychopath, is he going to tie me up and start tearing me to pieces bit by bit?" Those things stay with you like a residue. I don't know what would have happened if Alcàsser hadn't happened. I don't know if I'd have been having those kinds of thoughts, being with him at that time.[77]

Inevitably, Marta associates the house out in the country with the Alcàsser crimes. Laura García expresses a similar sentiment. She had always liked to play in the huts out in the fields, but, since the crimes, those spaces have become places of remembrance:

We loved to go into houses in ruins, to make them our own. Well, I was . . . I saw a house in ruins, and the first image that came to my mind was that I immediately imagined them there, and, ugh! I got the chills, and it was bad.[78]

Silvia Gimeno is a woman who represents "after Alcàsser" in the town of Alcàsser itself; not surprisingly, the situation that most frightens her in reference to sexual violence is "a man in a car."[79] The scenario, in which the representation returns, has a clear connection to the crimes. She recalls that once, when she was with two friends on vacation, on their way back to the place they were staying, a car stopped for them—though they were not hitchhiking—with two really nice guys inside. As the

---

77. Ramos, interview.
78. García, interview.
79. Silvia Gimeno, interview, December 14, 2011.

area where they were staying was still a few miles away, she and another friend accepted the invitation to get in the car. The third friend did not. She refused, preferring to continue on foot. Her friend's decision worried Silvia:

> I said, "Please come with me, otherwise I won't feel easy." Then she looked at me and said, "You go if you want, but I'll walk. I'd rather walk for three-quarters of an hour than get into that car." So I grabbed my other friend and said, "We'd both better get out."[80]

"Male protection" is another fundamental element for the opening of the space in which the represented scenario returns. "Male protection" is a paradox: the subject who protects is, at the same time, the one who has the social privilege—which he may or may not make use of—to attack. The fallacy that women are only safe if they are under the protection of a man is reflected in detail in Rut's life history. She considers the loss of autonomy that came with starting a relationship with a man:

> Because the fear, the fear started to come once I had a steady boyfriend. It was at a time when I had started living with my brother and another friend. I had a boyfriend, and I kind of delegated my protection to men. I used to protect myself alone or with my friends. It was like: nothing happened, nothing happened, and then all of a sudden, oh, yes, something bad could happen. Thank goodness I'm with this guy here. Though maybe he can't protect me either, you know?[81]

For Rut, delegating her personal safety to the protection afforded by her boyfriend meant consolidating sexual danger.

---

80. Gimeno, interview.
81. Rodríguez, interview.

However, after a trip she took with a friend to Mexico, in the absence of a male presence, Rut again reassigned public space as her own:

> It was like reencountering self-assurance. We were also afraid, because of course people say such bad stuff about Mexico. It was like, we started realizing nothing bad was happening, as if the world was still your domain and nothing bad happened.[82]

This is the key element on which the performative hinges: the scenario in which the representation returns can, at the same time, be the very scenario in which the trauma dissipates. The body is a map with autonomous zones where leaks, resistance, and dissidence interfere in the complex borders traced. The quotation marks I use for "male protection" signify a questioning of the concept. What is really being protected is the heterosexist system. Therefore, male protection is exactly that: they protect themselves, not women. The category of *public woman* is a representation that frequently appears in testimonies about the scenario where the performative returns. Rut recalls that, as an adult, she went camping with a group of six women friends. They settled in a mountain shelter, and she remembers being very afraid the first night but not saying as much to her companions. However, she explains:

> They were all afraid. Besides, it was a fear that was like: we're all girls here alone. We were very used to traveling alone, but suddenly it was, "Oh no, the mountains, a shelter, the road next to it: here anyone can come and fuck with us."[83]

---

82. Rodríguez, interview.

83. Rodríguez, interview..

The idea of finding themselves in the mountains, in a remote shelter, alone—even if there were seven of them, including herself—sent Rut and her companions off on a foray into the representations of sexual danger that made up their imaginary. The next morning, a group of guys rode their motorcycles along the road to the refuge and came close to where they were. For Rut's group, this meant the end of their trip and the emotional explosion of bottled-up uneasiness:

> They stood side by side. They were laughing, they were there. We were having breakfast, and I started to feel that tension I had felt all night. It was a shared tension we all felt. And there was a moment when one friend got up and, without finishing breakfast, said, "Let's go."
>
> I said, "No, no, how can we just go? Let's not run away. Let's stay a little, even if we end up leaving."
>
> But no, no, we all started to get extremely anxious. "Come on, let's go." We took all our things, loaded up our backpacks, and left for the city.[84]

Representations directly linked to women's feelings of guilt also appear in the interviews. Marta does not feel a special fear of the night; she does not think of sexual aggression as something that conditions her life. However, certain situations awaken in her, in equal parts, feelings of guilt, wariness, and fear. A couple of years ago, she went on a trip with some friends to Gran Canaria, she hooked up with a guy and spent time alone with him. His friends told her about a party in the countryside, "and I got into the car, just two big guys and me."[85] Automatically, the representation of sexual danger appeared, and she got "really tense." As a recourse, she began to ask the boys about their sisters. Without further explanation, they told

---

84. Rodríguez, interview.
85. Ramos, interview.

her to calm down and that nothing was going to happen to her. Marta explains:

> But you feel like you're exposing yourself. You've crossed the line past which it's hard to defend yourself, and to explain it, above all. They'd call me too trusting, or they'd be like, "It's on you too, what are you like," getting in a car with two guys going toward the mountains in a city I didn't know at all or have contacts in. I didn't even know them or anything. Hell, if something happened to me, I'd have walked myself right into the lion's den . . . but . . . what lion's den was that?[86]

Essentially, there was nothing to stop Marta continuing to enjoy her night; the conflict is introduced by the story that shapes her universe of meanings with respect to sexual violence. If anything had happened, Marta thinks, it would have been exceedingly difficult to explain why she was in a car in the countryside with two strangers. She knows that the resulting narrative would blame her for her conduct and, consequently, hold her responsible for whatever happened to her. Marta also uses meanings to express herself that refer directly to the structuring elements of sexual danger narratives: she speaks of "exposing herself," of "crossing a line" and going "into the lion's den," which in the context of this work personifies transgression (as with hitchhiking), no-man's-land, and the beginning of the state of exception. Moreover, in her memory, the voice of the one who knows he is sovereign, who can decide whether or not to activate the state of exception, speaks clearly, "Calm down, nothing is going to happen to you."

These ideas lead me back to the idea that representations of sexual danger are a political project that exists as a response to women's political-feminist resistance. The way toward a

86. Ramos, interview.

system of representation that we can identify with is paved by the feminist movement. In fact, the greater the production of feminist representations, the more the sexist regime tries to counteract them.

Toward a New System of Representing Sexual Danger

The narrative about the Alcàsser crimes revealed a society in transition, with social fears and concerns linked to the rights and freedoms being won by women. In this sense, the narrative is aimed squarely at foreclosing the paths to progress opened by the feminist movement. The demands of feminism, as well as its achievements, are the part of the story that has been excluded through omission. Delving into the context of the feminist movement's political activity prior to the Alcàsser crimes allowed me to identify the narrative as a strategy that pushed for immobilist elements at a time at which the sexual status quo was being destabilized. The Alcàsser sexual danger narrative aims to disarm the feminist movement insofar as it attempts to restore that which the movement had succeeded in questioning. It follows that the narrative is motivated by and constructed with a view to maintaining and sustaining sexual violence against women. This means that it is the feminist movement that endows the narrative with its political categorization.

Sexual danger narratives produce *sexist truth and knowledge* and contribute, in this way, to the maintenance of social norms. This *truth* is produced and made invisible by the metaphors that shape and coordinate the narrative. The metaphors of the Alcàsser crimes are contained in the very structure of the story, in the architecture of the words that make up the text, and in the mode by which the case is communicated or broadcast. They articulate various mechanisms, strategies, and devices that rendered sexual danger invisible as a biopolitical element of the Alcàsser crimes.

The sexual danger narrative is a technology of control over women's bodies. The narrative used the crimes' devastating impact as a means to focus the gaze on the terrifying, rather than on the causes or symbols that were already beginning to act in the configuration of the account. In the first place, the narrative scanned for blameful acts and who to blame. Practically from the outset, the focus was on the actions of the teenagers and the practices of young people as possible explanations for what happened. Youth's placement at the heart of the debate gave the system license to advance reactionary elements among the new generations. Young women and the youth became the target of the narrative.

Understanding "the youth" as a political category was the strategy that allowed society to use the discipline of sexual terror on one part of the social group: that which needed reorientation. In this study, the term *youth* was the concept that acted to channel the establishment of immobilist principles. The many debates that focused on correcting the behavior of young people were a way to promote the correct execution of the discipline of sexual terror. Youth's placement in the spotlight came to signify, metaphorically speaking, the social imperative to keep reproducing sexism in new generations and thus to undermine any potential dissidence. Therefore, *youth* delimits the first arena in which the discipline of sexual terror must be implemented. This discipline is not effective if it targets only women. In men, it also has effects that have nothing to do with sexual terror: in them, it strengthens their protective role and reinforces male power over women's bodies; that is, it familiarizes them with the privilege society grants them over women's bodies.

Moreover, the narrative constantly inverts the terms: it blames the teenage girls for what happened, shifting responsibility away from their murderers. Hitchhiking was configured as the main element of prosecution and was to be the word that would make it possible to (de)situate the sexist component of the crimes, only to replace it with social precepts and norms. This activity was used to enact a twofold punishment: on the girls for their transgression, and on the rest of young women in the form of a warning.

However, Alcàsser is not just a sexual danger narrative. At times, it has also functioned as a tale of bodily resistance. It would be inaccurate to assert that, after the crimes, the practice of hitchhiking was completely eradicated. While it is true that, for a time, young people stopped hitchhiking so assiduously, it is not true that they never hitchhiked again. Just as the system reinstated the *border*, women resisted it, reworking new maps of transgression through their bodies. Somehow, the generalized idea that the practice of hitchhiking was completely suppressed after Alcàsser has in itself constituted a dominant, seemingly irrefutable, discourse. Moreover, it encloses the "Alcàsser punishment" in an infinite loop of sexual violence, a static affirmation that reminds women, again and again, of the cautionary tale. Nevertheless, with varying degrees of fear, a good part of the women interviewed who suffered the impact of Alcàsser eventually returned to hitchhiking. This is, in itself, a counter-representation to the sexual danger narrative that I think it is important to highlight. The very act of hitchhiking again means that women resignify Alcàsser. Every time one of them enters no-man's-land, raising her thumb to stop a car, in company or alone, with or without fear, she is resignifying the sexual danger narrative of the Alcàsser crimes and indirectly weakening that restored border.

The practice of hitchhiking was to be the first boundary crossed; returning home and reinforcing the institution of the family was to be the countermeasure society proposed against sexual violence. The family would thus represent the restitution of spaces: those through which women can travel, and those through which they are automatically at the mercy of the threat. The fact that sexual danger narratives tend to reestablish the institution of the family is no coincidence. For the most part, the family is the first form of organization that distributes and classifies bodies in public and private space, the first stronghold in which sexuality is constrained by sexual danger. The Alcàsser crimes served to justify patching up the institution of the family and reinstating its power at the center of social-political organization.

The perversity of the Alcàsser narrative lies in the fact that it let the "bad man" loose to lurk around every corner, around every bend in the road. And it also showed the torture that the "bad man" could inflict on the body in minute detail. The threat is real, the danger is real, and the pain is unbearable. The idea that Anglés could be anywhere accentuated the feeling of constant threat. He who once hid under the bed, or in the closet, now roamed the mountains, had the ability to move from one city to another in the same day, had no scruples, and was, at once, everywhere.

In addition, the brutality of the Alcàsser crimes further entrenched and emphasized the construction of women's bodies as public bodies. The same meanings that allow the continuity of sexual violence, which safeguard the existence of the no-man's-land where three teenagers were reduced to *bare life*, are those that, a posteriori, were to resituate the public body—a body that was to be just as public for society as it was at the time for its attackers. This is what society protects by building the narrative: the public body of women, which anyone can access from anywhere. It is the great metaphor that restores and consolidates *the public woman*.

The media—principally TV—trivialized sexual violence and turned it into a spectacle. The treatment of the case was a way of preventing the consequences derived from such a savage act from opening a debate that would question the way society was organized and women's position within it. The force of the punishment had to be commensurate with what it was intended to curb; it had to act as a curtain, concealing the real extent of everyday sexual and sexist violence. The subjective message in-corporated the discipline of sexual terror and trivialized sexual violence. The denial of the political significance of this violence meant defining the story as an incident, an isolated occurrence. In this way, any political perspective on sexual violence was expelled from the narrative and this violence was instead included as a rarity.

The resignification of the Alcàsser crimes provides us with

a tool, a guide for understanding the sexist structure, the mechanisms, strategies, and devices that support and shape corporal indoctrination and sexual danger narratives. To resignify the Alcàsser crimes implies holding society responsible and taking stock of a *collective wound*, an act of violence that is not individual but belongs to *society as a whole*. The narrative is shaped by society; deconstructing it, therefore, entails revealing a reflection of that society. In the same way, La Romana house and the violence committed there belong to the collective, and it is in it and from it that they must be changed, relocated, and eradicated. Only by revealing society's reflection in the Alcàsser crimes can sexual violence be situated not as something individual but as something social: not as an isolated act of aggression but as a violence that exists because it enjoys the objective conditions required. That is why the Alcàsser wound will remain open until the collective closes no-man's-land and renounces the coverage of the public woman as a category and rape as a political project. This means returning to La Romana house and resituating and reappropriating the sexual violence of the Alcàsser crimes. Otherwise, in every era or generation, sexual danger narratives will inevitably continue constituting new ways of securing bare life.

Alcàsser is a political regime, in force to this day, that commits crimes against humanity. In making this assertion, I invoke the idea of the teenagers' *enforced disappearance* proposed in the introduction. This concept evokes a clear image with which I associate the description laid out above: the Alcàsser sexual danger metaphor in which we can see clearly the persistence of the sexist regime; a regime that consents to, enables, and allows three teenage girls to be forced to disappear on a road, sexually tortured, and subsequently murdered. Enforced disappearance continues to be a practice that characterizes society as a whole, and that is perpetrated under its protection. It is for this reason that Alcàsser remains entangled with the present, in a devastating embrace. Alcàsser does not stop happening.

Representations of sexual danger are systemic strategies designed to continue reproducing sexual violence. That makes the system of representation an unreliable one that does not recognize us. For this reason, any narrative has to be quarantined and questioned. These narratives are systematic terror campaigns with a specific objective: the control and surveillance of women's bodies and behaviors. This is why it is so essential to surround ourselves with a universe of counter-representations to sexual danger. It is a matter of in-corporating new representations and experiences into everyday life that counteract the "substance" and "matter" of danger and sexual terror. When I speak of "a new system of sexual danger representation," I am referring, fundamentally, to the work of the feminist movement in the elaboration of counternarratives to sexual danger. Taking the space of representation means occupying each and every one of the places the sexist regime enables for its survival and disabling them. The counternarratives to sexual danger liquidate no-man's-land, repeal the state of exception, and remove bare life from women's bodies. On this occasion, it is the public woman who colonizes the social body, dissects it, and destroys it. Counter-representations help to situate the boundaries within which the heteropatriarchal system cannot and shall not pass: the place where it is extinguished because it lacks meaning, the matter that gives it life.

The production of counter-representations of sexual danger situates sexual terror narratives in another system of meanings—a system in which no-man's-land, bare life, and the state of exception are no longer articulated by a system that constructs women as public bodies. Feminist works along these lines abound, including, of course, Virginie Despentes's *King Kong Theory*. This was probably the first book I read to offer such a powerful counter-representation of sexual violence. Despentes signifies rape as a political project, thus destabilizing the entire sexual terror narrative. Indeed, the whole text is a brilliant exercise unto itself in the reassignment of sexual violence.

The production of "counter-representations" provides a new framework, a new reading that speaks directly to the feminist empowerment of women: a strategy that meets terror and sexual violence head on. Feminist counter-representations have the capacity to modify behavior by proposing other meanings from which to understand and situate oneself when confronted with sexual violence. Representations reinforce, show, and establish behavioral systems. Thus, they are the best antidote to the victimizing, accusing, aggressive, violent universe of patriarchal rhetoric.

Using, (re)situating, and (re)signifying sexual danger narratives is, in itself, another form of counter-representation or counter-discourse to sexual violence. I believe that the Alcàsser crimes could have been the narrative to expose the power relations between men and women. Alcàsser could have marked the boundary that exposed the privilege men have over women's bodies and lives. It could have been the point at which sex crimes shined a light on the sexist regime in its entirety: a turning point that, in response, would have produced the *Alcàsser generation* as a milestone of struggle and not of sexual terror.

I use the *Alcàsser generation* to refer to the possibility of making sex crimes into a milestone of vindication, into a tool in the political-feminist struggle to turn the patriarchal terrorizing force and dynamic against itself. This could mean reappropriating sexual danger narratives as a bulwark of struggle, just as the deaths of the 146 women murdered in the Triangle Shirtwaist textile factory in New York City gave rise to March 8 as International Women's Day; and as November 25, the International Day for the Elimination of Violence against Women, commemorates the Mirabal sisters who were murdered by Rafael Trujillo's dictatorship in the Dominican Republic. In other words, it would mean making each and every one of the sexual danger narratives turn in on itself: confronting sexual terror, generating spaces of resignification and, thus, creating new symbols and representations. It is for this reason that in this work, the term *Alcàsser generation* is about producing a political-feminist analysis of the story; it is a first step toward *generating* and *proposing*—taking action for—a new system of representations about sexual danger. (Re)constructing a narrative that recognizes us and that promotes the genera(c)tion of struggle. The scope of the *Alcàsser generation* concept is not limited to those people who directly suffered the impact of the narrative. Alcàsser, I insist, is a political regime. Thus, its structure allows us to extrapolate it to any murder, femicide, or enforced disappearance of women. Therefore, Alcàsser can and must continue to produce genera(c)tion.

In (de)constructing the Alcàsser narrative, I have sought not only to analyze it but also to configure it as a turning point in the way sexual violence is represented. I refuse to allow the Alcàsser sex crimes to remain, solely and exclusively, a milestone of the sexual terror of the 1990s: a narrative that the sexist regime continues to use as a system of control over women's bodies and lives.

Most of all, I refuse to continue to hide the murder of Míriam, Toñi, and Desireé within the *exceptional*. I refuse to relegate their murders to the patriarchal margins of sexual terror. It is time to situate them in political terms and, as such, to give them—the women—a name, status, and dignity: they were sexist murders. And this changes everything: their bodies are political; their murders are political. And the response must be situated in the same terms.

From this flowing indignation, may Alcàsser and its genera(c)tion serve to contribute to the construction of a new corporal map in which women's lives are presented as free from sexual danger narratives, meanings, symbols, metaphors, and representations.

Epilogue:
Toward a Feminist Genealogy of Power

By definition, a "scar" is not just the skin that grows over a wound but also the continuity, stability, and rootedness of a corporally conjugated pain that shudders with every shift in temperature and perpetuates the persistence of memory. I like to see it as a tattoo, the eternal endurance of a memory that is immanent, that has an everyday visual existence beyond evocation. A *here and now*, but also a *here and there*.

The Sexist Microphysics of Power, first published in March 2018, was meant to be a space of reparation, a voice of outrage, a cry. In part, that objective has been fulfilled. The book's journey, the reception it received, and the doors that all of us together managed to open are gifts of incalculable political value. Initially, the lines of this epilogue aimed to assess the impact the study is having on the memories, bodies, and lives of women. To my mind, however, the release of the "documentary" series *The Alcàsser Murders* on Netflix constitutes a counterpoint that makes clarification on a number of matters necessary.

I do not want to do it; I do not want to place myself, once again, before the horror. And yet, I have to. I watch the series, and my body refuses to begin writing this text. For weeks I have been staring at a blank page; images, corporal memory, and words. I am fed up with this legitimately organized violence and its patriarchal ceremony. It makes me angry. It weighs me down. The responsibility weighs on me, it is a lead line that binds words, and this epilogue must rise to the surface on its hook.

The global release of *The Alcàsser Murders* on June 14, 2019, meant extrapolating this sexual terror and its narrative to more than two hundred countries simultaneously. What a vulgar, deceitful, disrespectful, irresponsible way to narrate the bodies of our missing women, situating them, once again, as public bodies. And with them, all of us.

The series has all the characteristics of a sexual danger narrative. Undoubtedly, in the context of my investigation, this product—just like Paco Lobatón's *¿Quién Sabe Dónde?* and Nieves Herrero's *De Tú a Tú*—would have constituted material for analysis, generating the same questions, the same issues, and the same critical imperative. Why did you broadcast these images? Why this interview? Was this testimony obtained ethically? However, the fact that the release took place a year after the publication of *The Sexist Microphysics of Power* forces us to shift perspective slightly to observe these opposing positions. The book contains everything that needed to be analyzed; it transformed sexual terror into a political site; it claimed space for change in the narrative. However, the Netflix series consciously and arbitrarily questions, challenges, and threatens everything that was (re)constructed through *The Sexist Microphysics of Power*.

Taking this idea as a starting point, I propose an exploration considering the potential of analyzing *The Sexist Microphysics of Power* and *The Alcàsser Murders* as paradigms of two opposing systems, associating a word to each that will serve as an analytical tool. Two antagonistic words (*system* and *structure*) will help define and conceptualize the differences between the construction of a sexual danger narrative and the effective political development of counter-representations to it. I associate the verb *care* (in Spanish *cuidar*, from the Latin *cogitare*: "to think") with the entire process of investigation, elaboration, and writing of *The Sexist Microphysics of Power*. I outline it as a concept, and I understand it as a synonym of *paying heed*, of causing no harm through my actions. This is feminist responsibility, methodological integrity, respect for time frames, honing terminology, allowing for the maturation and healing of memories, welcoming—giving refuge to—the words of each and every one of the women interviewed. On many occasions, *to care* has meant not publishing certain testimonies, safeguarding them in order to project a protected, almost sacred space of honesty, in which the first tentative steps could be taken toward *reparations*. The imprecise aim of putting a system of care into practice that was denied at the time (and now), not only to the Alcàsser generation but to all of us. To deny (us) care is perverse, scrupulously social, behavior, a terribly exact bodily technology in the hands of patriarchy.

Throughout my research, my guiding principle was clear: to care. And this maxim is also imprinted in the fabric of the book. In the body of *The Sexist Microphysics of Power*, I consciously introduced a metaphor, a small, silent homage that I did not share with anyone, a ritual of passage from the sacrilegious to the political. I hoped that, upon reading it, someone would notice the gesture, apprehend the meticulousness, the respect and commitment that persists to this day. Throughout the almost three hundred pages that make up the text, only twice do I allow myself to write the names of our three murdered sisters. The first time comes at the beginning of the book, when I briefly explain the context in which the enforced disappearance took place. It was a necessary introduction. In these lines, their names hung by imposition of the sexual danger narrative and, from that point on, I lacked the legitimacy to name them with dignity—no one has. We form part of a suffering social group that has trivialized their bodies and countenanced, safeguarded, and upheld their murders—a group that has produced and reproduced sexual violence through the exploitation of their bodies, of their lives, and of the testimonies of their loved ones. I would not allow myself to say their names. I did not deserve to; we do not deserve to.

Only at the end of the text, in the last four lines, do I write them again, vindicating them from a political place—a place in which the feminist collectivity shelters them and takes responsibility for caring for their memory. In that space, something noble, something worthy of respect resides, protecting their bodies—which can never be touched again—and their lives. Then, only then, did I allow myself to name them: Míriam, Toñi, and Desireé.

Secondly, and in radical opposition to *The Sexist Microphysics of Power*, I employ the word *profane* (*pro*: "before"; *farum*: "temple"), linking it to the visual narrative of *The Alcàsser Murders*. Profane is that noble space that has ceased to be so because it is outside or before the temple. All the work we collectively shared through *The Sexist Microphysics of Power*—individual reflections, emotions, and ethnographies of the body—enable a liberating feminist process of narrative reassignment. But we are also building a past, generating a landmark, a shrine for our sisters. In opposition to that, the Netflix product resituates the narrative within the patriarchal system and blocks off the place of memory from which we can break the genealogy of learned violence. In other words, by inoculating *the discipline of sexual terror* once again, they try to place us within the parameters of defenselessness, at that boundary we should not have crossed, the transgressed corporal border, the one for which our sisters were killed. Worse, it brings sexual terror to generations that had been completely unaware of the Alcàsser sex crimes; it *profanes* their bodies and, with them, our land and our memory, sweeping it all away in a devastating act, consented to, protected, and consumed by society at large. This is more than reason enough to bare our teeth, to legitimize our anger: reason enough to draw a line of fire on the ground, the border of the inviolable space we occupy.

In this vein, I intend to delve into an analysis of aspects from the five episodes of the Netflix series, which, through practical examples, can be seen to symbolize the struggle between *The Sexist Microphysics of Power* and *The Alcàsser Murders*. Although there are many aspects of the documentary that could be revised, I focus on those categories that are related to concepts previously developed in my work and that, in addition, illustrate the characteristics that the show shares with those very programs it seeks to denigrate.

More than thirty years have passed since Paco Lobatón and Nieves Herrero's "specials" shaped what I define as the "public body" of a whole generation of young women. Lobatón gave voice to this body when he played a radio recording in which Toñi, one of the murdered teenagers, has a brief conversation with a radio presenter. The young woman's voice brought her back to life for a few moments, issuing a cautionary reminder to the rest about her absence. Herrero, for her part, materialized this warning through the interview she conducted with Esther, the teenagers' friend who could not go out that night because she was ill. The figure of the young friend perfectly embodied *the metaphor of the cautionary tale*, symbolized in the question that the journalist asked her live on air: "How many times, Esther, have you thought it could have been you?"

Netflix picks up on this in two sequences. One of them comes in the first few minutes of the series, in which we hear the recording released by Lobatón, as if it were a great exclusive. The other is the testimony of Sara, a friend of Toñi's, which represents, once again, what could have happened to us all. Both shots are juxtaposed, restoring in the present day *the discipline of sexual terror* and *the metaphor of the cautionary tale*.

The documentary begins with a close-up of Luisa Gómez, Toñi's sister, and the following dialogue:

"You always said you were like a mother to Toñi. You took care of her and so on."

"I was seven years older," says Luisa.

"Was she your youngest sister?"

"Yes, the youngest."

In the wake of this response, the screen fades to black and the characteristic sound of a radio tuning in and picking up a frequency is played. Simultaneously, this sentence appears on screen: "Friday, November 13, 1992. Three girls go missing in the Spanish town of Alcàsser." Next, Toñi's greeting is heard, and the radio presenter asks her name. The text "Friday, November 13" remains, but the subtitle changes: "The day before, one of them calls into the radio." We listen closely to her voice; we relate to her; she is present, as if alive. The teenager talks about her weekend plans, claiming she will not be staying at home, and requests a song, dedicating it to all her friends. We are hurt by her words. We know what is going to happen. We would like to stop it from happening, to tell her: do not go out, *stay at home*. And, squeezed into these three little words, we can read the warning women embody, along with an entire system of control over our bodies. It is a perfect geometric violence, which allows me to establish a concentric circle in which the recording used by the series and by *¿Quién Sabe Dónde?* share the same axis; where Sara's testimony is equivalent to the interview Herrero conducted with Esther in *De Tú a Tú*.

The interview with Sara is framed in a fixed long shot. Journalist and interviewee have their backs to the camera. The first sequence shows Sara watching an interview that Esther gave in November 1992 to the TVE program *Informe Semanal* on a tablet. In it, the young woman explains how hitchhiking was a widespread practice when anyone missed the bus, while Sara nods as she listens to it. In a subsequent shot, she acknowledges (in a way that implies a pointed question) that she experienced her friend's murder as traumatic and that Esther must have felt it even more intensely. After these words, she makes a confession:

> That fateful Friday the thirteenth, around 5:00 p.m., I received a phone call from Toñi. My mother answered.
> "Is Sara home?"
> "Yes, but she's resting."
> "I just wanted to know if she wanted to hang out for a little while."
> And my mother told her, "Okay, I'll tell her when she wakes up from her nap." And of course, that call . . .

Her speech gives way to a sob she cannot contain, at which point the journalist strokes her arm; almost three decades earlier, Herrero kissed Esther from the same position. Sara literally takes over from Esther mid-scene. She ends her intervention with a jumbled thought: "At times, later, I kept thinking: What if I had . . . gone with them?" This reflection is followed by an image of an empty bench (the one that had been occupied by Sara and the journalist). The next frame shows a photograph of Toñi sitting on a bench, looking right at the camera. Little by little, the teenager's body fades away; we see her disappear; she is erased from the old photograph, and the bench on which she was sitting is left empty, intact, but without her on it. This game of visual metaphors places our bodies within the horror, the possibility. It proclaims our responsibility, and, in this way, Sara becomes Esther, and all of us become Sara.

The objectives and the treatment of testimonies discernible in this approach was evident in the invitation the producer sent me to participate. The format they had planned for my intervention did not include an interview with me: they wanted to simulate a presentation of my book with other women. According to them, my work made it possible to incorporate the impact and consequences of the crimes into the narrative. Therefore, the series' way of adopting a feminist approach was to consist in attempts to get the testimonies of the teenagers' closest friends. In other words, my research only interested them to the extent that I could open up that possibility for them.

For the production company, Míriam, Desireé, and Toñi's friends were secondary victims of the crimes and "perversely guilty for life." They conveyed this idea through a battery of questions: How did they feel about the media's actions? Were they capable—*let us pay special attention to the word "capable"*—of following the trial? What mark had the murder of their friends left on their life trajectories? How had it influenced personal aspects of their lives? What did they decide to study? What jobs had they chosen? What kind of relationships did they have with their partners? What about with their sons and daughters, and so on? At the end of the text, they referred specifically to the figure and testimony of Esther, as a way of introducing an analysis of the guilt she must undoubtedly have felt. I structured my response by analyzing each paragraph, making notes in the margins, amending each line I considered morbid, unnecessary, or abusive. I proclaimed society as a whole to be the place where responsibility resided, questioning the hidden intent of their questions: What social benefit can be derived from finding out what they have dedicated their lives to or whether or not they were capable of watching the trial? Will you also ask the men how the crimes affected their affective-sexual relationships? Perhaps it is *their* answers that we should be discussing. And I insisted that the political subject that has to answer these questions is society as a whole, not the friends of the three teenage girls. Who are the culprits, and who are we questioning? I declined to participate in the documentary and categorically refused to act as a link between them and the testimony of their close friends. My feedback and amendments received no response whatsoever.

The initial document that was sent to me began with a paragraph from the last chapter of *The Sexist Microphysics of Power*: "[It ought to be] a milestone of vindication. . . . a tool in the political-feminist struggle to turn the patriarchal terrorizing force and dynamic against itself." They were planning not to incorporate any form of protest but, rather, to objectively deactivate it; to, sophisticatedly and discreetly, (re)assemble the structure of the sexual danger narrative. When I had the chance to watch the series, it was painful to see how, despite failing to obtain the testimonies they were looking for, they had managed to replicate, using a range of resources and visual narratives, that which I had refused to participate in. But on this occasion, they will not be able to plead ignorance.

A few weeks before the release, the platform publicized the series with the assurance that "new interviews and an up-to-date analysis of evidence shed light on the 1992 murders." From a feminist perspective, the documentary certainly appears to shed light—in the sense of "shining the spotlight"—on bodies that are once again arbitrarily public. This can be seen in two characteristics of the documentary: first, in the format of the reconstruction of events; second, in the disclosure of the images of the trial, in which the defendant, the lawyers, and the prose-cutor replicate all the violence suffered by the teenagers.

The Netflix production tries to dissociate its content from those programs that broke with all the ethics of journalism at the time. The production team positions itself as the privileged narrator of an *exceptionality* that does not represent them and that, moreover, absolves them of responsibility for their own actions. They point things out and ask questions; they are the ones who judge. Above all, they position themselves as far removed from journalism. Thus, for example, the recording is coordinated by a director (who confers a certain glamour to the format), a producer, and a researcher (who, although she is a journalist, in being thus named is placed on a higher plane and distanced from the profession of journalism). They are the visible faces of the format. The testimonies of the journalists, lawyers, public prosecutors, and police officers are to be the voices that tell everything with which the producer, director, and investigator do not want to be associated.

In the first episode, in a sort of reenactment, events are reconstructed, initially, through voice messages and phone calls: "Right now I'm in front of the house where Míriam lived." . . . "I'll call you from where they hitchhiked." . . . "He tells me that he saw them for the last time here." By car, they make the journey to the club, pointing out the places through which the three girls had passed and hitchhiked. These visual techniques bring us into the emotional, vital sphere of the moments prior to the *enforced disappearance* of the three teenagers. This segment's narrative structure ends with a long shot of the entire team at a vacant plot, the former site of the club to which the teenagers had planned to go. At dusk, a technician holds up a boom microphone: the shot closes as all daylight fades. Near the end of the shot, the director can be heard saying, "All we know is that they were coming here that day, but they never arrived."

A photograph of Toñi is the image used to open the narration of the discovery of the three teenagers' lifeless bodies. In it, the young woman is leaning on a desk looking at a mirror; the watch she was wearing is clearly visible. With her image still imprinted on the screen—that is, the living body of the teenager—the voice of the journalist, Alicia Murray, describes the characteristics surrounding the discovery of the bodies and the importance of Toñi's watch for their identification. In the second episode, that same photograph precedes the testimony of a judicial police officer who recounts the removal of the bodies in situ. At the pit, using a range of descriptive resources, the officer reenacts how the discovery took place. The portrait of Toñi looking into the mirror is intermittently superimposed over this image. The next frame shows an original snapshot taken for the initial criminal investigation at the crime scene. The perverse play of images, in which photographs of the living body of the teenager are combined with those belonging to the criminal investigation, is a clear example of what it is *to profane* that which ought to be cared for. The representation of the watch has an important symbolic charge in the collective memory of women; it lays bare blatant attempts to exploit and disregard the shock, distress, and sexual terror this disclosure has the potential to provoke. Moreover, with it, the public nature of the punishment and the exhibition of women's bodies for collective consumption is also unveiled.

The producers do not abstain from narrating the sexual torture the teenage girls had to suffer. The production team outlines the context: Ana Sanmartín (the investigator) begins to read Miguel Ricart's fourth statement, in the daytime, in a built-up area, describing the events that took place from the time the three teenagers were picked up until they arrived at La Romana house. There, in the dark, illuminated by a headlamp, Elías (the director) continues reading. The entire technical team moves toward the ruined house in a line. Once inside, he describes what happened in general terms, selecting fragments in which details of the aggressions are not given—salvaging his role in the terrifying account of events. A frame gives him away: for a few seconds, the camera focuses on the criminal investigation where names and actions can be read. This distancing maneuver would have been credible if responsibility for disclosing the details of sexual torture had not been delegated to the interviewees.

Indeed, in addition, the visual content does not differ from that which turned the Alcàsser crimes into a milestone of sexual terror. It places us at night, in La Romana, reconstructing the teenagers' steps in a terrifying setting. Following the incidents from Ricart's declaration chronologically, the story continues, at dawn, with the voice of Ramón Campos (the producer) and images of the pit. Sanmartín concludes the representation in the very place where it began.

All those descriptions not read by the team were to be recounted by participants from the judicial proceedings. The series showed images of the trial, described as "new" and "exclusive." In them, Ricart can be seen testifying at the criminal court, the public prosecutor exhibiting evidence of a number of aggressions, and the lawyer Virgilio Latorre is shown describing them. The only thing the disclosure of these trial sequences shows us is pain and suffering that should not have been made public. And the fact that the account of sexual torture is *exclusive* material is precisely what divests sexual violence of its political character and the ideology sustaining it. It is turned into a mere incident— and the teenage girls into public bodies.

The problem is obvious: What unknowns have been resolved? What has been illuminated? What is apparent is that this way of conveying the events further entrenches sexual terror, trivializes violence against women, and once again propagates a high-profile murder mystery that is terrifying.

To conclude, it is fitting to expose an issue that is covertly touched on in the documentary, and that appears to redeem a number of the journalists' actions. In the first episode, Murray narrates the moments prior to the broadcast of the program *De Tú a Tú*:

> I had to get Fernando, his wife, and their eldest son in the car and take them to the concert hall [where the live broadcast took place], but the whole family wanted to get in: the grandmother, the cousin, a neighbor. . . . They all wanted to go. They wanted to be on Nieves Herrero's show,

which was a hit; you have no idea. Nieves Herrero had six chairs for the three pairs of parents. What happened? Fernando's brother showed up, another brother, his brother-in-law.... More chairs! And people kept bringing up chairs. People were totally devoted to the show.

The journalist is entitled to her own personal opinion, but the disclosure of this testimony trivializes the complex motives underlying the three teenagers' relatives' participation in the show. In addition, it holds them indirectly responsible for the logic of exclusivity, manipulation, and morbidity that the program brought with it. The journalist thus dilutes her own responsibility. In her eyes, her intervention to prevent Míriam's father from contacting other media was clearly less inappropriate than the behavior of those relatives who accompanied him to the stage. Moreover, the aforementioned situation could have been avoided if Murray had refused to take their testimonies or had decided to safeguard them from public exposure. In short, the relatives' presence on Herrero's program justifies neither the questions asked nor such emotional exploitation.

These comments evidence the expansion of a rather irksome tendency to transfer to family members and friends the responsibility for their participation in such programs. Journalist Mariola Cubells has made a similar point:

In that state of shock, you are aware that a camera is following you. But what do you do? You're dead inside, so you let yourself get dragged in. And I think at the time, we didn't realize we were intruding so much. I was a reporter in the newspaper *El Levante*, and I knew something was happening that shouldn't be, but I didn't know what. And I think my coworkers didn't know either, because we were all there for the same reason: we were seeking information. I came because we had to come, because they had just found the girls and we had to come to see what was going to happen. You know, if we could go to the parents' houses to take photos, good. We went to cover it, to be where the news was at that moment.

On the one hand, the journalist states that the relatives, despite being aware of what was happening, were not in a position to establish boundaries. However, when the time comes to evaluate her own actions and those of the media, she speaks of a semi-consciousness: a "we were all doing it." Somehow, she confers more lucidity to the families—who, although grief stricken, were aware of their actions—than to her own course of action. She thus dodges responsibility for such abuses, which were committed in a way that blames the victims who suffered them.

Here is a concrete example: at book presentations, I reproduce sequences from Herrero's program *De Tú a Tú*. From the time I started the research, I have looked at these images on numerous occasions. But recently, at a talk, I felt an anguish that reappears ever more forcefully as a result of the recent media exposure. It was very brief, just a few seconds: I observed Míriam's mother, sitting almost unconscious on set, clinging to the photograph of her daughter. This activated in me an intense pain. I identified with her. I felt the terrible sensation of losing my child while social scrutiny feeds on my broken body, collectively abusing it. And I thought: Who is going to take responsibility for this? Míriam's mother was sitting there out of gratitude to Herrero, who, as far as the relatives were concerned, was not a journalist but a person who had earned their trust. And what we ought to reflect on is the price that, as a society, we place on that gratitude. As a social group, how are we going to be able to repay the debt we owe to the families, to their friends? These questions have taken hold in me since the documentary's release.

Ultimately, this mechanism of constructing guilt is a way of collectively dodging responsibility for what we do individually and consciously. We are all to blame, but at the same time no one is to blame, because it is a collective responsibility shaped by individual decisions—a perfect metaphor for how the *discipline of sexual terror* and *the sexist microphysics of power* are propagated.

In the wake of the series's release, its content was discussed in newspapers, social networks, opinion articles, and radio programs. Though the documentary supposedly sought to question the conspiracy theory, the effect was the exact opposite. The media spread stories of people who, attracted by a narrative full of unknowns, approached La Romana house, partaking in a form of macabre tourism that Netflix was able to create and exploit. Thus begins a new phase of sexual terror in which the—once again absent—political perspective gives way to a revamped version of the 1990s milestone of sexual terror.

Numerous comments on social networks cited my work, advocating for a feminist narrative as opposed to one of sexual terror. Others saw the book as complementary to a well-structured series, situating feminism as a narrative resource rather than a paradigmatic analytical tool. And this is but one of the many tensions between the series and *The Sexist Microphysics of Power*.

I have watched the series four times. It is a document that shows photographs of the body parts of the teenagers; that relays the criminal investigation while chronologically reconstructing the crimes in the area in which the murders were committed; that broadcasts Ricart speaking at the trial and the lawyers recounting the torture as a great exclusive. And it makes me think: Is this really what you want to consume? On Twitter, you could see the comments written by young women about the fear that the series had sparked in them, reproducing testimonies almost identical to those published in 1993. The people closest to the three girls, those who had consciously decided not to be part of the documentary, have once again been exposed to a narrative that questions and harms them. Is this really what you want to consume? And, in that case, I insist: Who is going to bear the responsibility for the consequences?

It seems implausible that anyone who has read and understood my work could propose any form of compatibility with this series. You either build a sexual danger narrative or you build a counternarrative. The two formats are antagonistic. The fact that this may not be so for some people is testimony to the good health of a system that, unnoticed, entwines itself in our bodies; and to how we *organically* accept and sustain a sexist, patriarchal, misogynist structure.

The Sexist Microphysics of Power is a counternarrative of confrontation, against which stories, TV programs, or documentaries such as Netflix's, have no chance of lasting long.

This *truth* that we are building is physical, it is material, and there is no turning back. We have shared a pain that has strengthened us, claimed a narrative that belongs to us and can only be named through feminism. In each encounter, with each testimony, we complete and resignify the Alcàsser story of strategies, resistances, and feminist responses.

I envision us linked corporeally, forming the bronchial breadth of an impassable forest, stratified to the extent that no one can approach our sisters—never again. Reassigning us a story that must safeguard their (our) body in an *unprofanable* center. We lick their wounds in unison, in a conscious act of feminist *care* and truth. May this act radically transform sexual danger narratives, unfolding the rhizomes of a new *feminist genealogy of power.*

The point is that, whether or not we chose it, this wound is mine, it is yours, it is theirs, and it remains under our protection. Ours.

Acknowledgments

A great many people have supported and helped me over the years. I would like to thank them all.

To all the women who so generously participated in the interviews, I wish to extend my warmest thanks.

An affectionate thank you to Carme Miquel for her commitment to the research and her invaluable help.

I am immensely grateful to Miguel and the entire Virus publishing team for their work, their confidence in the project, and the respect they have shown the text.

For their unwavering support, I would like to extend special thanks to Dolores, Susana, Nekane, Patricia, Enar, Nerea, and Eva.

Above all, I want to thank María for her faith, for patiently reading the drafts, and for debating and sharing in each and every aspect of this book.

Index

AK PRESS is small, in terms of staff and resources, but we also manage to be one of the world's most productive anarchist publishing houses. We publish close to twenty books every year, and distribute thousands of other titles published by like-minded independent presses and projects from around the globe. We're entirely worker run and democratically managed. We operate without a corporate structure—no boss, no managers, no bullshit.

The **FRIENDS OF AK PRESS** program is a way you can directly contribute to the continued existence of AK Press, and ensure that we're able to keep publishing books like this one! Friends pay $25 a month directly into our publishing account ($30 for Canada, $35 for international), and receive a copy of every book AK Press publishes for the duration of their membership! Friends also receive a discount on anything they order from our website or buy at a table: 50% on AK titles, and 30% on everything else. We have a Friends of AK ebook program as well: $15 a month gets you an electronic copy of every book we publish for the duration of your membership. *You can even sponsor a very discounted membership for someone in prison.*

Email **friendsofak@akpress.org** for more info, or visit the website: **https://www.akpress.org/friends.html**.

There are always great book projects in the works—so sign up now to become a Friend of AK Press, and let the presses roll!

About the author

Nerea Barjola Ramos is a feminist scholar and activist whose work focuses on popular representations of sexual violence. She received her doctorate in Feminisms and Gender from the University of the Basque Country and lives in Bilbao, Basque Country (Spain).

About the contributors

Emily Mack is a translator, teacher, and amateur carpenter active in the feminist struggle and other social movements. Born near Birmingham, England, she is now based in Girona, Catalonia, where she lives, works, and agitates.

Silvia Federici is a feminist activist, teacher, and writer, who in 1972 was among the founders of the International Feminist Collective, the organization that launched the Campaign for Wages for Housework in the US and abroad. Her most important work, *Caliban and the Witch*, has been translated into fourteen languages. She is also the author of *Revolution at Point Zero* and *Re-enchanting the World*.